THE FRENCH in SINGAPORE

PLATINUM SPONSORS

GOLD SPONSORS

SILVER SPONSORS

SUPPORTED BY

Published in 2011 by
Editions Didier Millet Pte Ltd
121 Telok Ayer Street, #03-01, Singapore 068590
www.edmbooks.com

ISBN 978-981-4260-44-2

MIX
Paper from responsible sources
FSC™ C012476

Printed by Star Standard, Singapore on Olin Regular Cream 150g (from Antalis Singapore)

THE FRENCH in SINGAPORE

An Illustrated History (1819–today)

Maxime Pilon • Danièle Weiler

edm EDITIONS DIDIER MILLET

Contents

Preface

After searching for information about the French in Singapore, and having read a number of general histories of the country, we came to the realization that, unlike other local communities whose history is well known, the French presence from 1819 to the present day has never been documented. *The French in Singapore: An Illustrated History (1819–today)* retraces the history of men and women who tried their luck in a country far from home, a place which was not a French colony, or a major trading post, but just a stopover, a place of passage. We decided not to compile a complete catalogue of French settlers, but instead to construct portraits of some of these pioneers.

Stamford Raffles, who founded Singapore in 1819, spoke French and took a great interest in French culture; in fact two French naturalists were part of his expedition. Over time, French settlers, mostly clerics and traders, were drawn to this "Jewel of the East", the largest *entrepôt* in the region. Despite a difficult period in the early 20th century, the French community gradually expanded. But it is in the contemporary period, when Singapore has transformed itself from a developing to a developed country, that the French presence has intensified. At the turn of the 21st century the community is equally active in business and in the cultural scene.

During our four years of research and writing, we experienced alternating periods of euphoria (on finding a story about a Frenchman in a local newspaper, or stumbling upon some interesting correspondence) and periods of discouragement. A particularly difficult moment was when we heard from the head of the consular archives in Nantes that the folder on old Singapore was almost empty. A consular report in 1987 described the adverse impact of the war in the Pacific on the archives: they were partially destroyed before the Japanese invaded, then dispersed by Australian troops during the fighting in January 1942, and finally looted by the liberation army in September 1945. The records which did survive comprised civil documents, personnel files, pension accounts and maritime records. They were kept in the mezzanine of the consulate in very bad weather conditions, quickly falling prey to insect and rat infestations. In 1984, an official of the embassy tried to identify what was salvageable; he succumbed to leptospirosis. To avoid any risk of contamination for the rest of the staff, nearly everything remaining in the archive had to be destroyed.

Finding images to illustrate these historical events was also very difficult. There were very few French in Singapore in the early years, and photographs of them are rare indeed. Fortunately we were able to commission French artist Marion Cordonnier to illustrate several historic scenes.

Through this book we wish to pay tribute to all the French men and women who settled in Singapore, or have merely passed through. We also wish to pay tribute to a country that has given so many foreigners the opportunity to achieve their dreams.

Danièle Weiler and Maxime Pilon

ABOVE: Drawing of Chinatown and the Thian Hock Keng temple, by Marie Fauconnier, 1910. It was published in the book *Micheline à bord du Nibong*, written by Geneviève Fauconnier in 1932.

PAGE 4: *Singapore from Mount Wallich*, 1856, painted by Percy Carpenter. PAGE 5: View of St Joseph's Institution, c. 1930.

Tome II. in 4°. N°. 2

Tome 4. in 8°. Page 132

"Sincapour has undoubtedly one of the happiest positions in the world, and one of the most favourable for entrepot trading ... As a result, Sincapour, once destined to be a mere trading post, has rapidly become one of the world's most important marketplaces."

Jules Sébastien César Dumont d'Urville, 1839

Introduction

Singapore has a pre-colonial history which reaches far back to ancient times. Various sources from the 2nd century CE give the island different names, but all of them position it south of the Strait of Malacca, and describe its port functions. Located at the extreme southern tip of Eastern Asia, between India and China and between the Indian and the Pacific Oceans, Singapore was a well-known port of call on the Spice Route, which was frequently used by Chinese, Indian and Arab merchants.

The 14th century seems to correspond to a relative zenith for the island, mentions of which are found in records of the period under the name *Temasek* — "land surrounded by water" in Javanese. The *Sejarah Melayu* (Malay Annals), which blends myth with reality, records that Prince Sang Nila Utama, a distant descendant of Alexander the Great, landed on the island of Temasek around 1300 to establish a city there. He named the land *Singapura* ("lion city" in Sanskrit) after spotting a creature with a lion's head.

Towards the end of the century, a powerful warlord from Majapahit, in Java, despatched an army to take control of the island. Sri Sultan Iskandar Shah, the fifth King of Singapore, fled to the western coast of the Malay Peninsula, where he founded Malacca in 1403. The *Sejarah Melayu* goes on to say that the island subsequently fell into oblivion. It was first under the control of the sultanates of Malacca, and, from the 16th century onwards, under that of the princely families of Johor.

Taking advantage of the latest maritime technology, the Portuguese and Spanish travelled the oceans during the 15th century in search of new commercial navigational routes, establishing trading posts along the African and Indian coasts before reaching Southeast Asia. The Portuguese expeditions of Vasco de Gama, Alfonso d'Albuquerque,

OPPOSITE: A map drawn in 1752 by Jacques Nicolas Bellin (from the Richard Curtis collection). It is one of the first French maps of the region.

BELOW: A page from the *Sejarah Melayu*, 1844–1852. This is a Malay literary work covering a period of over 600 years that chronicles the history and the genealogies of rulers in the Malay archipelago.

Ferdinand Magellan and other great navigators marked the start of a new era of European expansion in Southeast Asia, slowly leading to the establishment of European colonialism in the region.

The rise of capitalism and the dynamism of Christian missionaries provided the initial impetus for this colonial expansion, while the desire to conquer new territories would only come to the fore at a later date. The Dutch, the English and later, to a limited degree, the French gradually supplanted the countries of the Iberian peninsula and formed alliances with the local princes and sultans along the Strait of Malacca, in places such as in Aceh, Malacca, Johor and Singapore.

Race to Control the Spice Trade

Control of trading posts along the Spice Route and the trading of rare and expensive commodities (such as precious stones, silk, sandalwood, nutmeg and fur) became essential for anyone seeking to increase their wealth or power. In the 16th century, the trade in pepper and spices remained primarily in the hands of the Portuguese and the Dutch. Other European merchants responded by combining their capital to finance expeditions that were supported by their respective monarchies. England, the Netherlands and France all created East India companies.

BELOW: Painting of Jean-Baptiste Colbert (1619–1683), by Claude Lefebvre. Colbert served as the French Controller-General of Finances from 1665 to 1683, and created the Compagnie des Indes Orientales françaises (French East India Company).

OPPOSITE TOP: Coat of arms of the French East India Company.

OPPOSITE BOTTOM: Painting of the port of Lorient, by Jean-François Hue, late 18th century.

In 1600, England's Queen Elizabeth I awarded a Royal Charter to the English East India Company. Founded on the basis of a limited company in which merchants participated and obtained exclusive access to the markets of the East Indies, the Company was managed from its headquarters in London by a Governor and 24 Directors—the Court of Directors—appointed by a General Assembly of the owners, to which the Company was answerable. Gradually, the Company formed a lobby to defend its interests in Parliament, as well as to obtain vital rights such as permission to acquire new autonomous territories, to print money, to raise armed troops, to engage in diplomatic activities, and to enforce law and order within its territories.

Other countries of continental Europe formed similar companies which also established trading monopolies. The Dutch East India Company was founded in 1602, followed by the Danish East India Company in 1616, and the Portuguese East India Company in 1624. Jean-Baptiste Colbert, the French Controller-General of Finances at the court of King Louis XIV, was eager to compete with these companies. In 1664, he established the Compagnie des Indes Orientales (East India Company) in the port of Port-Louis, on the southern coast of Brittany. This gave birth to the town of Lorient, which was named after the Company's first ship, *Le Soleil d'Orient*. The Company obtained an exclusive monopoly over all trading points beyond the Cape of Good Hope for 50 years, and benefited from various privileges not accorded to other French and foreign traders. It had the right to

own property in occupied lands, to print money and to engage in slavery, as well as the capacity to arm both trading and naval vessels. Although the results were generally very lucrative, assembling and carrying out an expedition required considerable effort: four years of preparation were needed and, after their departure from Lorient, the vessels took eight to ten months to reach Asia, necessitating a round trip of no less than 20 months.

The phenomenon of monsoons in Asia was also well known, and the wind patterns determined the timing of a vessel's departure and return. Monsoon, from the Arabic word *mawsim* (season), refers to the system of periodic winds which affect tropical regions. From January to April, in the region of the Malay Peninsula, these winds blow from the continent out to the sea, creating the northeast monsoon; from May to December, they blow from the sea towards the continent, creating the southwest monsoon. From Singapore, vessels heading for Siam and China would leave the Strait between December and January, and return during May. Sailors were not only at the mercy of the monsoons, but also that of pirates and cyclones. As ports of call were needed to replenish water and food supplies, carry out repairs to the vessels and allow crews to rest, the French established trading posts on Ile de France (Mauritius) and Ile Bourbon (Réunion), and like the other European powers, rest points in the Strait of Malacca.

BELOW: The Strait of Malacca, 1745, a map drawn by French cartographer Jean-Baptiste d'Après de Mannevillette (1707–1780). The map is from the Richard Curtis collection.

OPPOSITE TOP: Father Alexandre de Rhodes (1591–1660), a French Jesuit missionary and lexicographer who helped to spread Christianity in Vietnam.

OPPOSITE CENTRE: Bishop François Pallu (1626–1684).

OPPOSITE BOTTOM: Pierre Lambert de la Motte (1624–1679).

The European wars during the 18th century weakened the French East India Company. In 1763, the Treaty of Paris brought an end to the Seven Years' War between France, Great Britain and Spain, and France lost many of its trading posts. However, it managed to retain five Indian possessions: Chandernagore, Pondicherry, Mahe, Yanaon and Karaikal.

By 1785, vessels were leaving Lorient regularly, sailing under the name of Compagnie des Indes orientales et de Chine (East India and China Company), and calling at the Strait of Malacca. The onset of the French Revolution brought up the question of royal rights; the National Assembly stripped the Company of its monopoly on 3 April 1791, and the Company was dissolved two years later.

The Age of Enlightenment saw a sharp increase in round-the-world voyages. These had commercial, political and scientific purposes: the vessels carried geographers, hydrographers and naturalists. Among them was the French cartographer Jean-Baptiste Nicolas Denis d'Après de Mannevillette (1707–1780), one of the most outstanding of the Compagnie des Indes' innovative hydrographers. His British counterpart, Alexander Dalrymple, with whom he worked, paid a fulsome tribute to him: "[The maps] of the Indian seas by Monsieur d'Après de

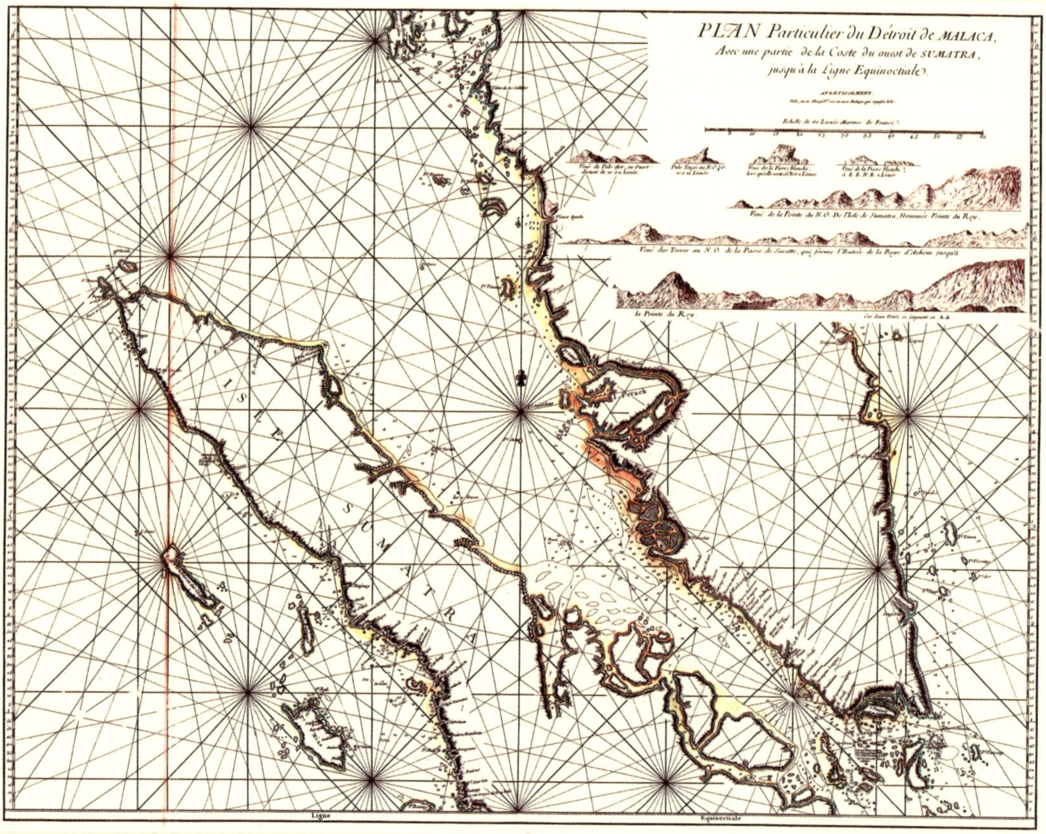

Mannevillette [...] exceed everything of the kind in Europe. It is a pity they are not translated into English for the benefit of our navigators."

Dalrymple and de Mannevillette, as well as Jacques-Nicolas Bellin (1703–1772), provided invaluable navigational charts on which variations of the name "Singapore" appeared, either as the name of the island or the strait, such as *Singa-pura* (City of the Lion), *Sinca-pura* (Gateway to China) or *Temasek*.

The 18th century's spirit of adventure and discovery also motivated trading explorers such as Pierre Poivre and his nephew Pierre Sonnerat, Jean-François de Surville and Etienne Merchant, all of whom are likely to have sighted the Singapore coastline.

The First Christian Missionaries

Apart from commerce and "scientific curiosity", religion was also a major driving force for the colonisation process. In Southeast Asia, the Catholic Church had to compete with Buddhism and Islam for the souls of the populations in the new territories. In the 16th century, Pope Julius II decided on a spiritual partition of the world—called *padroado* (patronage)—between the Portuguese and the Spanish, who were at the peak of their powers. Their sovereigns were made responsible for Catholic missions, the construction of churches and the appointment of bishops.

Missionaries often accompanied the conquistadors; one of them was the Spanish Jesuit Francis Xavier, who landed in Malacca in 1545. Franciscans and Dominicans would later become well-established in Asia. France, which was known as the "eldest daughter of the Church", of course intended to participate in the conversion of Asia. In 1615, French missionaries set out with the intention of evangelising Cochinchina (part of present-day southern Vietnam).

The French Jesuit, Alexandre de Rhodes, was active in Asia during 1620–1640, notably in Indochina. Influential and persuasive, he rallied against the Portuguese spiritual *padroado* in Southeast Asia. Later, based on his experiences in Asia, Father de Rhodes drafted the principles which were adopted by the Séminaire des Missions Etrangères de Paris (Seminary of MEP—the Paris Foreign Missions Society), founded in 1663.

This institution, headquartered in Paris, was established by François Pallu, François de Montmorency-Laval and Pierre Lambert de la Motte, in order to comply with Rome's wishes as well as to spread the universal message of Christ. Approved by King Louis XIV and Pope Urban VIII, French priests left for Asia to preach the gospel from 1664 onwards, with the aim of establishing Christian communities led by a clergy recruited wherever possible from within the local community, while respecting local customs and avoiding becoming engaged in the country's political affairs. These visiting bishops, referred to as vicars apostolic,

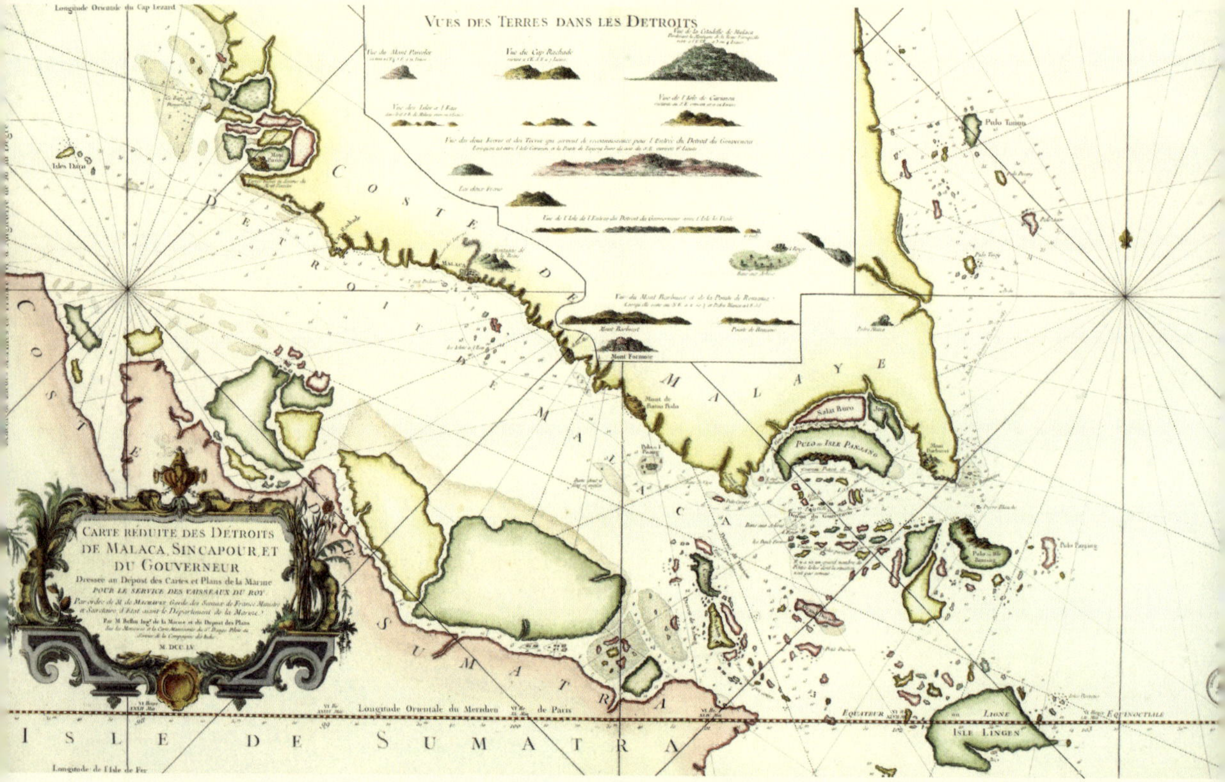

reported directly to Rome, which allowed them a freer rein as they carried out their evangelising mission.

In 1765, Pierre Pigneau de Béhaine of the MEP left for Cochinchina, where he was appointed vicar apostolic a decade later. Under a treaty signed in 1787, France undertook to support Nguyen Anh, the erstwhile emperor, in the recovery of territory he had lost during civil war. An expeditionary corps made a landing, among which were Jean-Baptiste Chaigneau and Philippe Vannier. Nguyen Anh, now emperor under the dynastic name Gia Long, remained close to Bishop Pigneau de Béhaine and Jean-Baptiste Chaigneau. The latter, having been appointed Grand Mandarin to the Imperial Court and having married a woman from a family of Catholic mandarins, became the first Consul of France to Cochinchina, and was tasked with opening up trade with France. However, in 1820, Minh Mang, the son of Gia Long, who acceded to the throne on the death of his father, declined to develop a closer relationship with France, and began to pursue a policy of isolation. During his reign, some missionaries left the country, while others were massacred. After a number of abortive attempts, France would resume its policy of conquest in Indochina several decades later.

The Foreign Missions Society of Paris was the first French Catholic institution to evangelise on the Malay Peninsula. Established in Siam since 1665, the MEP became the target of violent anti-Catholic demonstrations in November 1779, after the missionaries had refused to swear allegiance to the new king, Phya Tak. Bishop Le Bon of Siam, and priests Joseph Coudé and Arnaud Garnault, were expelled from the kingdom, and arrived in Malacca on 16 December of the same year. Subsequently, after a brief stay in Pondicherry, the priests established themselves in the kingdom of Kedah on the Malay Peninsula. Father Garnault then emigrated with the Christian community to Penang, to place themselves under the protection of Francis Light, the British founder of the colony. Garnault constructed the first Catholic church there, the Church of the Assumption of the Blessed Virgin Mary, and he became a vicar apostolic of Siam in 1787. Throughout the 18th and 19th centuries, French missionaries arrived in Penang and Malacca, and some moved on to Singapore to care for the few Christians on the island.

During the 17th and 18th centuries, the Strait of Malacca lost its commercial importance. Ports such as Malacca and Singapore became less busy. At that time, Singapore was a fishing village populated by Malays, *orang laut* ("sea people" in Malay) and a few Chinese farmers, and the Strait was infested with pirates.

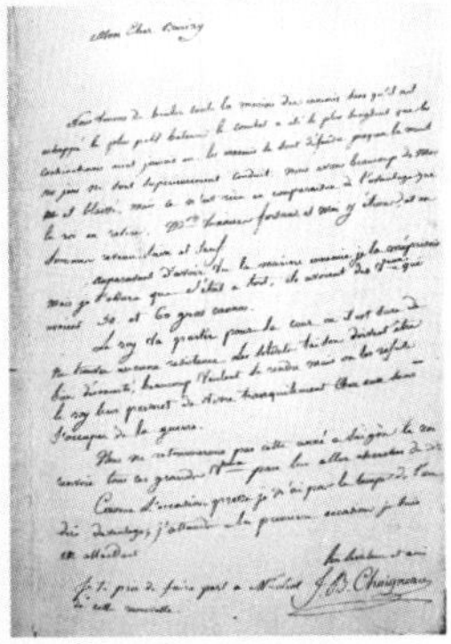

OPPOSITE TOP: Malacca, Singapore and Governor Straits, a map drawn by Jacques-Nicolas Bellin, 1755. He wrote 994 articles in the famous *Encyclopaedia of Diderot and d'Alembert.*

OPPOSITE BOTTOM: Pierre Joseph Georges Pigneau, also known as Pigneau de Behaine (1741–1799). He signed, as the representative of Nguyen Anh, the Treaty Of Versailles in 1787. That treaty marked the beginning of French influence in Indochina.

TOP: Handwritten page by Jean Baptiste Chaigneau (1769–1832).

Renewed Interest in the Region

In 1703, the British trader Alexander Hamilton was offered the island of *Sincapure* by the Sultan of Johor, Abdu'l Jalil IV. He declined, saying: "it could be of no use to a private person, tho' a proper place for a Company to settle a colony on." At the time, control of the territory was not a good investment, either for an individual or for the English East India Company. A century later, however, the situation would be different. With the growth in global commerce, the region would become a vital passageway between India and China, notably for the British East India Company (renamed from the English East India Company after the Treaty of Union in 1707) which plied the opium and tea trade. The time was ripe to convince London of the importance of controlling the Strait of Singapore, and the task would fall on a man named Stamford Raffles.

Other European colonial powers were also determined to maintain an active role in the region. Following Napoleon's conquest of the Netherlands in 1806, the Dutch East Indies colony of Java came under French control. It would remain so only briefly, for it was conquered by a British expedition led by Raffles in 1811. In 1818, Raffles, in his capacity as the Governor of Java, wrote to the directors of the British East India Company: "The Dutch possess the only passes through which ships must sail into the archipelago, the straits of Sunda and Malacca; and the British have now not an inch of ground to stand upon between the Cape of Good Hope and China, nor a single friendly port at which they can water and obtain refreshment." Raffles had read the *Sejarah Melayu*, and was aware of the natural advantages of Singapore's location as well as its strategic importance.

I

Raffles and the Founding of Singapore

Sir Thomas Stamford Bingley Raffles landed on the island of Singapore on 28 January 1819. He was accompanied by William Farquhar and a few Europeans, including two Frenchmen. As the founding father of modern Singapore, he spent only ten months on the island, spread across three different stays. Nonetheless, he stamped both colonial and contemporary Singapore with his imprint. Furthermore, this nature lover, employed by the British East India Company, would retain a life-long affinity with France.

Raffles, a Man of the Enlightenment

Born at sea on 6 July 1781 on board the *Ann*, not far from the Jamaican coast, he was the son of Benjamin Raffles, captain of a merchant vessel, and Ann Lyde. At the age of 14, and thanks to the influence of his uncle, he was recruited as an office clerk at the British East India Company in London. He possessed a keen interest in nature, spending a lot of his time between the ages of 19 and 24 gardening and observing nature.

Reaching maturity during the Age of Enlightenment, Raffles was interested in the ideas of his time. He developed his intellect and breadth of knowledge, and learned French—the *lingua franca* of the European ruling classes. He wrote: "My leisure hours, however, still continued to be devoted to favourite studies, and with the little aid my allowances afforded, I contrived to make myself Master of the French language, and to prosecute enquiries into some of the various departments of literature and science—this was, however, in stolen moments—either before the office hours in the morning, or after them in the evening." He came to master the language, according to Demetrius Boulger, his first biographer: "While he was governing Java, at a party given at the government house of

OPPOSITE: Sir Thomas Stamford Bingley Raffles (1781–1826). Raffles sat for his portrait in 1817, the year he published *A History of Java* and was knighted.

Bencoolen, a lady sang Moore's melody, *Rich and Rare Were the Gems She Wore*. Two French gentlemen at the party, the naturalists Pierre Diard and Alfred Duvaucel, regretted that they did not understand the words, but he immediately translated the song into French verses."

In March 1805, Raffles was named Assistant Secretary to the new Governor of Penang, Philip Dundas. During the six-month journey there, he learned Malay. During the years in which he was in Penang, he visited Malacca frequently. In 1807, he met William Farquhar, a Scottish officer known locally as the 'Raja Melaka', who was also employed by the British East India Company. From 1811 to 1816, Raffles controlled the island of Java, but was stripped of his position by Lord Moira, the new Governor-General of Bengal, because the Company and the British Crown concluded that Java did not generate sufficient revenue. During his stay, Raffles, a man of the Enlightenment, established social legislation, implemented agrarian reform and put an end to forced labour. He left Java for England on the *Ganges* in March 1816, and on this journey, met one of the most influential men of the century—the deposed French emperor Napoleon.

On 18 May, at approximately 3am, the vessel reached the island of Saint Helena, where Napoleon had been held prisoner since October 1815. After obtaining the necessary permissions, Raffles met Napoleon in the gardens of Longwood House. He was disappointed with the emperor's lack of courtesy: Napoleon barely looked at him, and browbeat him with quick-fire questions to which he did not wait for answers—to the point that Raffles felt that this being who "had always been a subject of his admiration" was in fact a "monster" who henceforth would rouse in him "horror, distaste and fear". Separately, Captain Travers, Raffles' travelling companion, described the meeting as "an absolutely vulgar reception". Several days later, the *Ganges* left Saint Helena and reached London in June.

During his stay in the British capital, Raffles poured his time and energy into writing *A History of Java*, and still found time to lead an active social life, mingling with British high society. He met Miss Sophia Hull at a reception and was secretly married to her two days later.

Accompanied by his young wife and some members of his family, Raffles made his way to the European continent. This seven-week journey was the subject of an account which his cousin Thomas Raffles published in 1818, entitled *During a Tour Through Some Parts of France, Savoy, Switzerland, Germany and the Netherlands in the summer 1817*. The account records that from 6 June to 25 July 1817, Raffles and his family visited Normandy before heading to Paris where they admired the Louvre, the Jardin des Plantes, the Palais du Luxembourg, the Palais-Royal, Montmartre, Versailles and other well-known sights. They dined in the most fashionable restaurants, attended a great mass at the Chapelle des Tuileries in the presence of Louis XVIII, and met world-renowned scholars at the Institut de France, such as the Baron de Sancy and the Chevalier Langles, both well-known orientalists. Raffles and his family then went to Switzerland and Belgium, after which they headed for the English seaside town of Ramsgate.

In 1818, the British East India Company sent Sir Stamford to Bencoolen (also known as Bengkulu), a southwestern province on the island of Sumatra, to take up the position of Lieutenant Governor. After assessing the problems in the region, Raffles made his way to Calcutta to convince Lord Hastings, the Indian Governor-General, to establish a new trading post to the south of the Strait of Malacca.

The Founding of Singapore

On 28 January 1819, eight British-flagged vessels anchored not far from the mouth of the Singapore River. Raffles landed, accompanied by William Farquhar. Taking advantage of dissension within the Malay Court, he obtained authorisation from the Temenggong, the territory's military commander, to establish a trading post in Singapore. In return, the Temenggong would be able to rely on British protection and be granted a pension of 3,000 Spanish dollars. The British East India Company then landed men and goods, hoisted its flag and, on 6 February 1819, signed a formal treaty. As Captain J.G.F. Crawford recounted: "The treaty was read in English by Captain Crossley, for the edification of the Europeans,

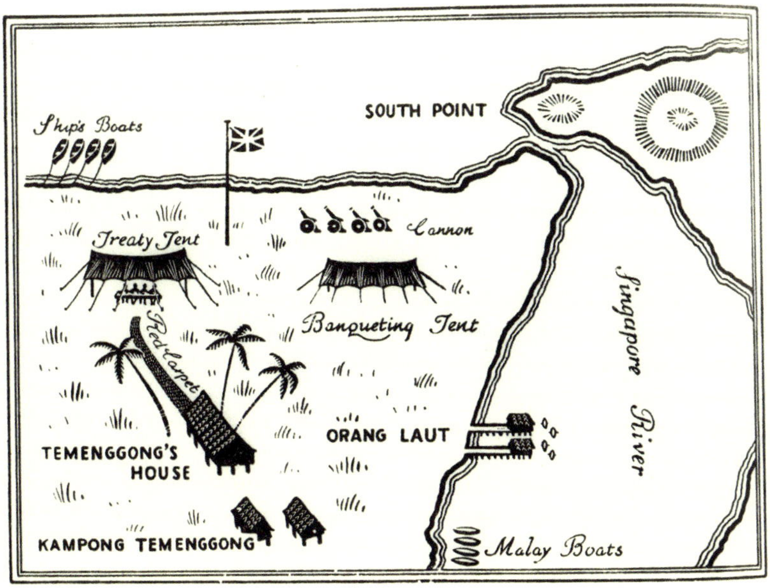

OPPOSITE TOP: Major-General William Farquhar (1874–1839), the 6th Resident of Malacca and the 1st Resident of colonial Singapore.

OPPOSITE BOTTOM: *The Emperor Napoleon in His Study at the Tuileries* by Jacques-Louis David, 1812. The painting was a private commission from the Scottish nobleman and admirer of Napoleon, Alexander Hamilton, 10th Duke of Hamilton, and was completed in 1812.

LEFT: Map showing the Treaty Tent, the house of the Temenggong and the surrounding area on 6 February 1819.

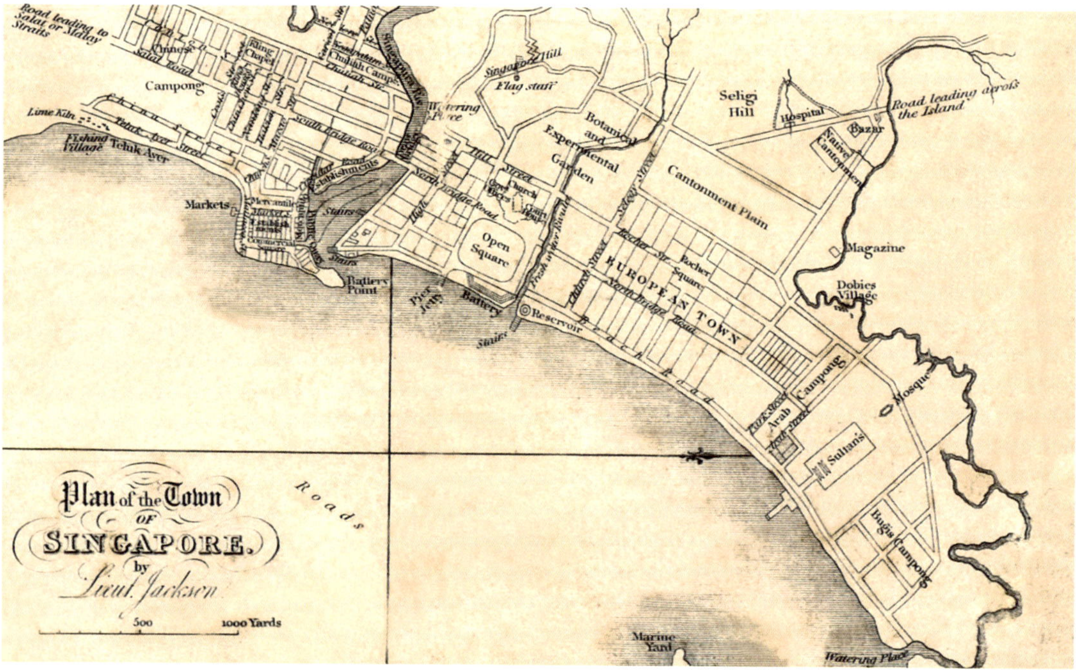

English, Dutch, French and Danes, individuals of each nationality being present. Then it was signed and sealed by Sir Stamford on the part of the East India Company, and was sealed by his Malay secretary, with the seals of state belonging to the Sultan and Temenggong (Malay princes never signing)...".

Henceforth, 6 February 1819 was considered to be the date of the founding of Singapore. On that day, Raffles also appointed Farquhar as the Resident of Singapore, and handed over a list of 23 instructions to manage the new possession of the British East India Company. Having settled these matters, Raffles left once again for Bencoolen on board the *Indiana*. The entire process of founding the port of Singapore took him only nine days.

On 31 May 1819, Raffles returned to Singapore and stayed for three weeks. He sent several letters to England to convince his recipients that Singapore really was a "good bargain" that had to be retained at all costs. He met with Farquhar frequently, giving various instructions for managing the development of the port, as well as for allocating land for settlement construction.

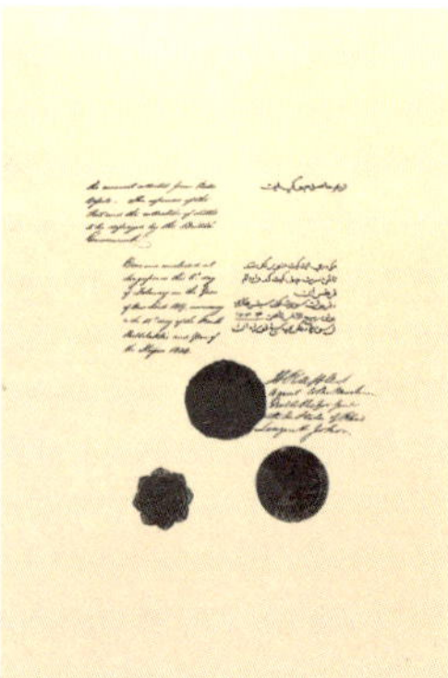

Raffles returned to Singapore for the third time on 10 October 1822, with many more projects in mind. He wanted to draft a constitution to ensure an even more prosperous future for the town, which was rapidly increasing in importance. He established town planning and founded the Singapore Institution in July 1823, which took in and educated the children of the local population.

In April 1824, Raffles suspended Farquhar from his duties as Resident, accusing him of not following instructions and of being too close to the Malays and the Chinese; he replaced him two months later with Dr John Crawfurd. Raffles also developed a body of legislation aimed at ensuring peaceful co-existence between the various ethnic communities. In order to prevent crime, he believed that the underlying causes must be eliminated, and thus prohibited gambling and cock-fighting. He permitted the use of opium on the basis that it was easy to monitor the population and to punish any abuse by means of appropriate penalties. Prostitution was also allowed, although all forms of slavery were outlawed in the colony.

With the help of Lieutenant Philip Jackson, he also implemented a settlement layout plan for the island, in which each ethnic community would have a neighbourhood. He put forward plans to develop an administrative hub, religious sites and a botanical garden. Before leaving, Raffles declared that Singapore must remain a free port, and he signed a new agreement with the local authorities. The provisions included an increased pension for the Sultan and the Temenggong in exchange for British control over their territory. After an eight-month stay, Raffles left on the *Hero of Malown*, heading once again for Bencoolen.

Family difficulties and health problems—increasingly violent headaches—led him to leave Bencoolen and return to Europe. The *Fame* set sail on 2 February 1824, carrying Raffles' valuables, collections and animals (including a tapir, pheasants and a tiger). Due to a lack of funds, the cargo was not insured and, two days later, a fire broke out at around 8:20am. In less than five minutes, the entire vessel was in flames. The cargo was destroyed, but the passengers and crew, safe and unharmed, rowed towards Bencoolen. It was thus aboard a rowing boat that Raffles watched his work disappear in smoke. The survivors managed to reach Bencoolen the next day.

OPPOSITE TOP: Singapore Town Plan, based on Raffles' instructions and drawn up by Lieutenant Philip Jackson in 1828.

OPPOSITE BOTTOM: Facsimile of the last page of the Treaty of Friendship and Alliance 1819, signed by Raffles, the Sultan and the Temenggong on 6 February 1819.

TOP: Dr John Crawfurd (1783–1868), Scottish physician, colonial administrator and author.

BELOW: Fire aboard the *Fame*, from *Stationer's Almanack for 1825*.

While preparing for a new journey, Raffles learned on 17 March that an Anglo-Dutch treaty providing for the transfer of colonies between the two countries had been signed in London. The Malay Peninsula would come under British control, including Singapore, while the Dutch sphere of influence would extend to the Dutch Indies (Indonesia). Raffles and his wife then boarded the *Mariner* and, after a five-month crossing, arrived in Plymouth. He moved to London in order to better manage his affairs, and took steps to obtain compensation from the Company for his past services and losses. In particular, he embarked on a new project: the creation of a zoological society that would surpass the Jardin des Plantes in Paris. In April 1826, he was named President of the Zoological Society, and the society was allotted a piece of land in London's Regent's Park by royal decree.

However, Raffles, weakened by numerous worries, notably financial ones, retired to High Wood, Middlesex, where he continued his correspondence. On 5 July 1826, his wife found him dead at the foot of the stairs. The doctor's report stated that he had been suffering from a brain tumour, and had had a stroke.

BELOW: Original drawing by Marion Cordonnier, Diard and Duvaucel in the jungles of Singapore.

OPPOSITE TOP: Jean Léopold Nicolas Frédéric Cuvier (1769–1832), also known as Georges Cuvier. His most famous work is *Le Règne Animal* (The Animal Kingdom), 1817.

Raffles and the two French botanists

Raffles was passionate about nature, and he evinced a kind of fascination for the animals and plants of the equatorial areas in which he lived. In 1818, he took advantage of his stay in Calcutta to get in touch with two French naturalists who were on a mission in India: Pierre-Médard Diard and Alfred Duvaucel.

Diard studied medicine, but became a naturalist under Georges Cuvier, the father of comparative anatomy and the founder of palaeontology, and Professor Emeritus at the Collège de France and at the Muséum d'histoire naturelle. Duvaucel was the stepson of Georges Cuvier; Duvaucel's mother, Anne-Marie, had married Curvier when Duvaucel was 14. The latter was interested in the natural sciences from a young age, and took up studies under his step-father. In 1817, he left for India after accepting "the honourable mission to enrich the cabinet of the Muséum d'histoire naturelle de Paris with zoological products from India, which the English have only made comparatively little use of."

J.J. Coulmann, a friend of Duvaucel's, records in his memoirs that while in Calcutta, Duvaucel met up with his colleague Diard, who had arrived there four months earlier. Lord Hastings, the Indian Governor-General at the time, welcomed the two young scientists with "... the greatest kindness. Lord Hastings owned a considerable menagerie at Barrackpore, close to Calcutta, and each time that any curious or rare animal from the depths of Bengal was sent, she (Lady Hastings) would alert Mr Duvaucel, who would eagerly bring over his illustrator, a young Malay, whose talent he had developed, and who would provide an accurate painting of the object observed and described by his master as a naturalist."

Diard and Duvaucel left Calcutta for Chandernagore, from where they regularly sent specimens back to the Jardin des Plantes. Sir Raffles heard about these Frenchmen and their museum in Chandernagore, and contacted them. According to J.J. Coulmann, "Diard and Duvaucel were preparing to make a long journey into Bengal, when, at the moment of departure, they received the proposals of Sir Stamford Raffles, the governor of Bencoolen, who had been tasked with a number of political duties in the islands of the Strait of Malacca. Raffles, impassioned by science but with scarce time to indulge in it, proposed that Messrs. Diard and Duvaucel accompany him on his journey, and continue their research while he completed the different missions with which he had been entrusted by the British government and the British East India Company. These honourable propositions were most eagerly accepted by the two young Frenchmen because they had already almost completed their explorations of Bengal and expected many more subjects for their curiosity on the islands of the Strait, which so far was little known; the governor furthermore offered to establish, at his government premises in Bencoolen, an establishment somewhat similar to that created by Lord Moira in Calcutta, and this plan, the cost of which would be borne by the governor, would provide them with every means imaginable to bring together the animals of Sumatra in Bencoolen and to observe them at close quarters; on the condition that the results of their research would be shared equally between themselves and the governor; the latter undertook to have the costs incurred reimbursed by the East India Company, while the two gentlemen promised to provide their work, time and cooperation for the scientific memoirs

which Mr Raffles wished to publish about his journey." For Raffles, this was a perfect opportunity. The two French naturalists were very close to Cuvier, they would create the botanical garden of which he dreamed, and Diard, who was a doctor, could take care of Raffles' health.

Raffles sailed on the *Indiana* on 18 January 1819, together with Diard and Duvaucel, and they accompanied him for nine months as he navigated between Penang and Indonesia. An article in the *Revue Encyclopédique* traced their journey: "they sailed for Singapore where General Sir Stamford had a number of political affairs to settle: he needed to install on his throne a Malay prince whose subjects found excessively 'anglophile'." Duvaucel described their visit at Singapore: "Upon arrival in the harbour, the governor received a visit from three of the king's aides-de-camp. These officers were not crimped, scented and richly vestured young men as we are used to; their black, shaven heads were covered with an obscurely coloured turban; a large, wide-sleeved jacket covered their oiled, burned, peeling and arched backs. At their left sides they bore a large 'kris' or dagger, and their legs were bare. These three Malays appeared delighted to see us, as though we were there for their good. The British sought to find out if there might be any advantage in seizing their island, while we, less interested, questioned them about the animals to be found there. Who do you think these poor folk listened to more eagerly? They replied with alacrity to the questions of their allies, while they shrugged their shoulders as they listened to ours."

His business concluded and the treaty signed on 6 February in the presence of the two young French naturalists, among others, Raffles continued his mission, which can be read about in the *Journal Asiatique* of 1824: "After a brief stay in Malacca, they returned a second time to Singapore and it was on this last visit that they were able to procure a Dugong (a large cetaecean), of which they sent a drawing and a description to the *Muséum*. This same description was sent by Sir Stamford to England where it was read out during a meeting of the Royal Society in London. Finally, after a few days in Singapore, the travellers left for Bencoolen and arrived there in August 1819." In a letter to Raffles, Diard stated: "You have enabled us to fruitfully explore all of the interesting countries which we have visited with you."

In order for the reports to be read in England, Raffles required them to be drafted in English, whereas the names of the plants and animals were either in Latin or in French, at the researchers' convenience. He also wanted a copy to be given to him immediately, accompanied by a dried specimen and a drawing. Even though the two Frenchmen gave him a daily report, they were also required to provide a complete description of their research each month.

TOP: Dugongs are large herbivourous marine mammals.

Diard and Duvaucel settled in Sumatra, close to Raffles' residence, in a house owned by the British East India Company. Everything appeared to be fine, except that the Company did not pay for their expenses as agreed. So they wrote to Raffles in 1820: "Sir, as we are as a result unable to rely on a fixed agreement, and on the financial means which would have allowed us to continue, over many years, a research plan for which we had every reason to expect great results, we have taken the liberty of submitting to you a few thoughts which occurred to us as soon as we were informed of the decision of the Supreme Council."

Following an exchange of letters which resolved nothing, the two young scientists proposed three solutions: to continue their research on their own, to be sponsored by Raffles himself, or to reimburse the advances provided by the Company in order to be able to maintain sole control over the research. Stamford Raffles was not in agreement with any of these options, however, replying that all of the collections belonged to the Company and that it was out of the question for them to keep anything at all, or for them to publish their research.

This earned him the following answer from Diard and Duvaucel: "However, Sir, as we wish to accede to your point of view as much as possible, we will be happy to hand over to you all of the objects which we have collected if you will agree to the following proposals: the objects sent shall be accompanied by a numerical catalogue of the species. The species in even numbers shall be shared equally, whereas with regard to those in odd numbers, the Company shall take half, plus one. In this case, Sir, we shall renounce all rights of any kind to the drawings, and you may publish them as you see fit; we even undertake, should you prefer this, to print nothing except in England, and one of the two of us shall for this purpose leave in order to accompany and care for this precious collection."

A FRENCHMAN WHO HAS TAKEN UP THE CAUSE OF WILLIAM FARQUHAR

Jean-Claude Fuchs' first stay in Singapore lasted from 1979 to 1983. Thereafter, he was a frequent visitor to the city-state, where he obtained permanent residency. In 2007, he discovered that Stamford Raffles, who had spent less than ten months in Singapore, had lent his name to 30 streets and to a considerable number of places, schools, hotels and other institutions. In contrast, William Farquhar, the city's co-founder, who was governor of the nascent city for more than four years, was not commemorated anywhere, and remained a relatively unknown figure to the Singaporean population. Mr Fuchs decided to make every effort to rehabilitate the name of the latter—especially since Farquhar's first companion, Antoinette Clément, was thought to be of French origin.

Mr Fuchs attempted to convince the authorities to name a street, a park or any other place in the historic district after Farquhar. However, the rules for naming new streets apparently would not allow this. He then held a number of conferences to present the results of his research, and participated in an exhibition at the National Library of Singapore, *William Farquhar: Singapore's First Resident and Commandant (1819–1823)*.

BELOW: *Neofelis diairdii*, or the Sunda clouded leopard. The species was named in honour of the French naturalist and explorer Pierre-Médard Diard, by Georges Cuvier in 1823, based on a drawing and skin said to be from Java.

OPPOSITE TOP: Original drawing by Marion Cordonnier of Duvaucel's gecko (*Hoplodactylus duvauceli*). The species was erroneously named after Alfred Duvaucel, a French naturalist who explored India. The museum specimens taken to Europe were credited to him, and only later were the animals found to have come from New Zealand.

Raffles also refused to accept these proposals, and, in a long letter, explained to the two scientists that they would not be reimbursed for what they had spent, or for costs on board, nor for lodging on land, which he had paid for himself. He also reminded them that they were living in a government house, adding: "You seem to forget that many of the subjects were not collected by you, but merely placed in your charge by me."

Raffles was so angry that he ordered the collections compiled by the French naturalists to be seized. He provided precise orders for packing the specimens, which the specialists Diard and Duvaucel were to supervise, and even had them watched in order to ensure that they kept nothing for themselves. Catalogued and packed in cases, the collections were to be loaded onto the *Mary*, but the two Frenchmen opposed this, saying that they had not been paid by the British East India Company for more than a year, and that, as a result, the collections belonged to them. Raffles then reminded them that they had signed a contract with the Company and that they were therefore required to surrender the collections. Then, a few days later, Duvaucel filed a police complaint, reporting the theft of certain documents. Who stole them? Why? Details on this incident are scarce. Did the Frenchmen fake a theft in order to save a few documents? Or did the English really steal them?

A portion of the collections did eventually arrived in France and an article in the *Musée des variétés littéraires* relating the journeys of Duvaucel, mentions that: "the natural history collections compiled on the island of Sumatra by Messrs. Duvaucel and Diard have been received by the Muséum d'Histoire Naturelle de Paris, and several of the most remarkable objects which form part of this are now on view in the galleries of this institution."

Subsequently, the remainder of the collections was sent to England where it had a rather mixed welcome. According to Demetrius Bolger: "When in March 1820, Raffles sent home the first half of a valuable collection illustrating the natural history of Sumatra, he received in reply a coldly worded despatch, remonstrating with him on his extravagance and forbidding him to expend any of the Company's funds in such directions. This collection was sent by the ship *Mary* to Sir Joseph Banks."

However, the two parties appeared to have reached a reconciliation. In his last letter to the two French naturalists, Raffles wrote: "Gentlemen ... No man can appreciate more highly than myself the zeal and personal exertion which you have displayed in making these collections and researches, I am sincerely desirous of securing to you the full measure of credit due to them, and I think you must be satisfied that it has always been my wish to contribute to the extension of science ... I conclude with expressing my regret at the necessary close of our public relationship, but at the same time my

satisfaction at its being about to terminate in an amicable adjustment." Diard and Duvaucel speedily replied: "Even if it has been painful to enter into a public discussion with you, it is very pleasing to receive as a reward your assurance that this opposition on our part has not altered the esteem which you have always shown to us: we are therefore desirous to also express to you how much we appreciate this further proof of your kindness."

The two French naturalists departed on new adventures: in 1820, having bade farewell to Raffles, Diard left his friend Duvaucel and joined Jean-Baptiste Chaigneau, then Consul in Hué at the court of Emperor Gia Long. He visited much of the Annam kingdom, entered Cambodia and proceeded up the Mekong as far as the Tonlé Sap—he was one of the first Europeans to admire the ruins of Angkor. He also spent much time in Malacca, and then again in Singapore, always on the search for new species. He finally settled in Batavia, where he worked for the Dutch and sent his collections to the museum of Leiden. In 1825, he was named Director of Agricultural Services for Java, where he died without leaving any written record of his travels. His name is connected to species such as the Diard's Trogon, a tree-dwelling bird with very colourful plumage, the Diard's blindsnake (*Typhlops diardii*), the heavy jumper spider (*Hyllus diardii*), the *Coilodera diardii* beetle, and a sub-species of the clouded leopard known as *Neofelis diardi*.

As for Duvaucel, he moved to Padang, and then to Chandernagore, where he put his numerous notes into order, and also looked after his menagerie. After several exploratory journeys to Sylhet, in northern India, he made plans to explore Tibet. This project never came to fruition: Duvaucel died as the result of injuries incurred during a rhinoceros hunt. His research was highly respected, and, like his friend Diard, a number of species bear his name: the barasingha (*Cervus duvauceli*), the Duvaucel's gecko (*Hoplodactylus duvaucelii*), the river lapwing (*Vanellus duvaucelii*) and the scarlet-rumped trogon (*Harpactes duvaucelii*), a bird widespread throughout Southeast Asia.

CHINESE JUNK AT SINGAPORE.

II

The Age of Adventurers (1819–1869)

Following the founding of the colony of Singapore by Sir Stamford Raffles on behalf of the British East India Company in 1819, the island became a major crossing point between China and India. As a result, French scientific, trading and diplomatic expeditions were frequent callers at this port in the Strait of Malacca, and some French citizens even decided to settle there.

Singapore, a Crossing Point

With peace finally returning following the defeat of Napoleon, Louis XVIII launched new naval expeditions in 1815. Officially, these were purely scientific in nature, but they also sought to re-establish political, diplomatic and commercial contacts, and to relaunch France's colonial endeavours.

Vessels were becoming more modern, and more importantly, their increased tonnage enabled the onboard installation of scientific equipment. Scientists eager to participate in these great expeditions formed a veritable floating academy. Cartographers, botanists, zoologists, ethnographers, astronomers and gardeners became an integral part of the vessels' crews.

The French expeditions

The Thétis

It was in this spirit of colonial and scientific development that in October 1822, the *Thétis*, commanded by Hyacinthe de Bougainville, the son of another explorer Louis Antoine de Bougainville, set out for Vietnam. At its port of call at Réunion, the ship was joined by the corvette *L'Espérance*, after which the *Thétis* set sail for Singapore. This mission to seek an audience with the Vietnamese Emperor Minh Mang was a failure, however. Bougainville did not manage to meet him, because

OPPOSITE: Chinese Junk at Singapore, 1839, by Louis Le Breton. He was the official artist of the French expedition to the South Pole and Oceania. The expedition, commanded by Dumont d'Urville, stopped at Singapore for six days.

Dr Crawfurd, the second Resident of Singapore, had warned the Emperor of the arrival of the French and spoken against them. On board the corvette was Edmond-Pierre Bigot, Viscount of Touanne, a naturalist and artist like many of the scholars of the era, who brought back several illustrated accounts of great importance and interest.

The Astrolabe

In 1826, a year after circumnavigating the globe on the *Coquille*, Dumont d'Urville, one of the great explorer-navigators of the era, left once again for a long-distance journey in the Pacific. The plan for this journey gave d'Urville his first opportunity to command an official scientific journey. At the start of 1826, as news of the ill-fated *La Pérouse* expedition reached France, d'Urville requested permission to rename his vessel the *Astrolabe*, in memory of his unfortunate predecessor.

The expedition's official artist was Louis Auguste de Sainson, while Dr Quoy, who was in charge of the zoological collections and also a skilled artist, was nominated to replace him in the event of an accident. D'Urville knew he was risking his life by undertaking such a lengthy expedition to this part of the world.

La Favorite

In hope of succeeding in Vietnam where the *Thétis* had failed, another expedition was launched on the *La Favorite*. The vessel's commander, Cyrille Pierre Théodore

OPPOSITE TOP: View of the town and Singapore River from the Governor's House, Malaya side, 1824, by Vicomte Edmond de la Touanne.

LEFT: View of Boat Quay (1834) and Malay village (1834), by Louis Auguste de Sainson, official artist of the corvette *Astrolabe*.

1. Sincapour.

2. Partie du Quartier Malais.

de Sainson del.

VOYAGE

Laplace, received orders to install Eugène Chaigneau as Royal Vice-Consul to Vietnam. However, this also ended in failure, and was once again overshadowed by the achievements of the expedition's scientists and artists. For example, Barthélemy Lauvergne, d'Urville's secretary and now artist on *La Favorite*, skilfully depicted Singapore during the vessel's call there in August 1830.

Lauvergne was not the only illustrator on board. François-Edmond Pâris, a scientist and hydrographer, was also a skilled illustrator. He had already been around the world on board the *Astrolabe* and, passionate about ships of all kinds, created beautiful prints of the junks in the port of Singapore.

La Bonite

Lauvergne returned to Singapore in 1837 on *La Bonite*, and painted more views of the island. Under the command of Commander Nicolas Vaillant, this new mission had several aims: first, to attempt to renew agreements with Cochinchina and plant the French flag in the Pacific; secondly, to collect meteorological data, and conduct studies into the Earth's magnetic field and electricity; and finally to bring back new specimens for the Paris Natural History Museum.

La Bonite was a large, comfortable vessel, but she was not very fast. She left Toulon in February 1836, crossed the Mediterranean and the Atlantic, rounded Cape Horn and then sailed up the west coast of America. After passing Hawaii and the Philippines, the ship reached Macao before anchoring in Tourane (modern-day Hué) almost a year later. Diplomatic relations this time were found to be extremely strained, as the Emperor had recently decided to put a number of Christians to death, and to exclude Europeans from Cochinchina. Vailland therefore sailed to Singapore, where he made a port call from 17 to 22 February 1837, noting in his ship's log: "Without fear of being accused of exaggeration, one can say that it is marked out for a most brilliant future." He then passed through the Strait of Malacca and set course for France's trading posts in India. Finally, *La Bonite* returned to Brest in November. Despite the Cochinchinese fiasco, the expedition was considered a scientific success. The journey had produced high-

TOP: Singapore, 1830, by François-Edmond Pâris.

OPPOSITE TOP: View of the Protestant Church, 1837, by Barthélemy Lauvergne.

OPPOSITE CENTRE: View of Singapore, 1837, by Barthélemy Lauvergne.

OPPOSITE BOTTOM: Surroundings of Singapore, 1837, by Barthélemy Lauvergne.

quality hydrographical data and magnetic studies, recorded 3,500 species, brought back 1,300 rock samples and, for the greater glory of France, *La Bonite* had flown the French Tricolour across the Pacific.

The Astrolabe *and the* Zélée

On board the *Astrolabe*, which sailed together with the *Zélée*, Dumont d'Urville left Toulon on his second journey around the world. His aim was to explore Antarctica and the Pacific Ocean, which gave him an opportunity to make a port call in Singapore in June 1839. This six-day port call enabled two crew members to create new views of Singapore: Ernest Goupil, the expedition's official illustrator, and the young naturalist, assistant surgeon and talented painter, engraver and lithographer Louis Le Breton.

Dumont d'Urville wrote: "We dropped anchor in the English port amidst 17 vessels, among which we sighted with happiness a French vessel." Later, during a visit to the President of the Commercial Court, he noted: "I had been tasked by the Minister of State for the Navy with handing over a copy of the *Maritime and Colonial Annals* to this official. He received this with great pleasure." D'Urville also recorded a meeting with the American Consul, Mr Balestier, who showed him "the engraved rock named *Batu Singapura* which is already partly destroyed through wear". He added: "We were assured that while digging during road construction, small, ancient medals had been found which indicated, as did a traced inscription close to the port battery, that before the arrival of the Malays who preceded the English on the island, a trading post had existed, established by a civilised culture. The nature of these characters allows one to suppose that this trading post was owned by the Burmese." Eventually, in a meeting with French missionaries, he discovered that relations with the Anglicans were barely amicable. After travelling across the island and visiting the plantations, he was surprised to see so few military defences on the island but admired the importance which the port had gained in a few short years.

The *Astrolabe* and the *Zélée* returned to Toulon in November 1840, enabling the French Navy to conclude their general reconnaissance of this part of the world. Even if there remained peoples to be discovered and sceneries to be described, European activities in this region would from then on be more economic and political than scientific.

The Lagrené mission

In search of new markets, France, like the other European powers, hoped to establish a presence in Asia. Its great rival, Great Britain, signed the Treaty of Nanking with China in 1842, bringing to an end the first opium war after three years of fighting, and enabling England to explore new commercial possibilities

with the opening of four ports: Amoy, Fuzhou, Ningbo and Shanghai. Eager to secure a slice of the pie, François Guizot, the Foreign Minister in King Louis-Philippe's court, despatched Théodose Lagrené to China as a minister plenipotentiary to negotiate a similar treaty in 1843.

The Lagrené mission comprised diplomats such as Charles de Montigny (the future Consul to Shanghai), a doctor, several representatives from the Ministry of Commerce and Finance, Jules Itier (a customs inspector), and Auguste Haussmann (a commercial representative who also held the title of minister plenipotentiary). Haussmann depicted their stopover in Singapore in his book *Voyage en Chine, Cochinchina, Inde et Malaisie*: "The harbour of Singapore is magnificent. In the morning in particular, when the rays of the rising sun start to penetrate the fog which often veils the town and the bankside forests, which have an enchanting air. The great ships generally anchor more than a mile from shore. To get there, one must pass before a large quantity of Chinese, Siamese, Cochinchinese junks, and Malay *proas*, whose fine, elongated form enables them to glide over the waves." Haussmann, who took an interest in the local population, adds: "It is impossible to find a greater variety of costumes anywhere else than in Singapore. The Cantonese, with their long queues, their wide-sleeved gowns and their vast trousers, [and] the Fukienese with their black turbans, mix with Malays, whose elegant form is covered by a short jacket, and who gracefully wear on the side of their heads a little cap from which escapes their beautiful black hair, floating behind them in a style reminiscent of the Middle Ages. Beside a seriously-countenanced Arab, coiffed with a large white turban and wearing a short tunic,

OPPOSITE: Painting of Louis Philippe (1773–1850), by Franz Xaver Winterhalter, 1839. Philippe was King of the French from 1830 to 1848, a period that was known as the July Monarchy.

TOP: View of Singapore River taken from the Governor's House, 1839, by Louis Le Breton.

we see a Sepoy walking with a military gait, whose red, tight-fitting clothes contrast vividly with his oriental traits, black skin, and his ancient visor-less Indian helmet in the shape of the breech bolt of a cannon, the only part of the national uniform to have survived the British conquest."

Admiral Jurien de la Gravière, who was also a member of the Lagrené mission, spoke of Singapore in his account, *Voyage en Chine*: "Singapore is neither Malaya nor China; nor is it India. It is the common centre towards which the three great peoples of the Far East, the Malay, the Chinese and the Hindu, converge in order to find out more about each other and maybe one day merge."

The oldest photograph of Singapore

Jules Itier (1802–1877) joined the Lagrené mission as a customs inspector, but he was better known as a photographer. In July 1844, he visited the Chinese quarter of Singapore. Struck by the wealth of architectural elegance of the Thian Hock Keng Temple on Telok Ayer Street, he even positioned his daguerreotype on the altar in order to obtain a view of the main door and sculpted columns. But this was not the first shot of Singapore that he took. Instead, the earliest photographic image by Itier shows a panoramic view of Boat Quay taken from Government Hill—an image which is displayed in the National Museum of Singapore today.

Itier described his arrival in Singapore in his *Journal d'un voyage en Chine en 1843, 1844, 1845, 1846*: "The frigate was soon surrounded by a crowd of little boats, in which were balanced a few half-naked Malays, who invited us to land. The smoothest of seas is needed in these parts before one dares to venture down; this thought led me to the foot of the ladder, where one of these fragile contraptions awaited, to carry me to the town, amidst Chinese and Cochinchinese junks, Malay *proas* and European vessels, which covered the large anchorage in front of the English town."

Over the course of his different stays, he got to know local dignitaries. These include Balestier, the US First Consul and sugarcane planter; d'Almeida, the Portuguese Consul, who was also a planter of crops such as pepper and gambier, coffee, and nutmeg; and Rivoire, the Chancellor of the French consulate. He also

TOP: *Boat Quay and Singapore River from Government Hill*, 1844, daguerreotype by Jules Itier.

met the Director of the Magnetic Observatory, Elliot, who invited him to dinner, and aware of his guest's passion for geology and botany, invited him to survey the island together with him and a number of important residents. Itier wrote about the picnic which accompanied this outing: "A most splendid lunch accompanied by iced champagne is served to us under an elegant Madras tent, pitched at the entrance to the jungle ...".

The Pioneers: Missionaries, Traders and Diplomats

The French not only called at the port of Singapore—records showed that a number of them settled there as well. Still, the overall European presence remained modest: 94 in 1827, and 500 in 1860, of which 271 were English, and predominantly male. In spite of their small numbers, this European minority in a predominantly Chinese city was, according to Dr Crawfurd, the Resident, "the life and the spirit of the Settlement".

Immigrants were attracted to this commercial crossroad which was almost entirely controlled by European traders. During this half-century, however, Singapore's growth stagnated, in large part due to increasing instability; the 1850s saw frequent riots.

The make-up of the French community

Although very few French citizens had settled in Singapore before 1869, France nevertheless opened a consulate. Many of the French citizens came from coastal regions (Brittany, Bordeaux and Corsica) where maritime skills and an interest in exploration were more common than in the interior regions of the country.

French travellers were surprised to meet compatriots settled on the island. One example was Dr Melchior Yvan, a member of the Lagrené mission, who, upon being invited to the home of Whampoa, a rich Chinese trader, wrote: "The Indian who had introduced me walked towards me, bowed several times and told me: 'Do you not speak English, *monsieur*?' – 'Not a word, my friend.' – 'Well! *Monsieur*, I will be your interpreter; these gentlemen should not think that they can say anything they like in your presence because you don't understand their language.' – 'But how about you, how is it that you speak French?' – 'How? Because I am French.' – 'You are French! But from which country?' – 'From Chandernagore [in India], *monsieur*, my name is Ali; Mr Whampoa has brought me to serve you, and in my capacity as a compatriot, I am entirely devoted to you.' The man who was speaking to me was tall and slender; his skin was black, his large eyes bright, his nose aquiline and his teeth white. He was wearing a huge coloured turban; two diamonds shone on his ear; a robe clung to his waist, and long trousers fell over his bare feet."

French diplomatic representation

For a French Consul to officially take up his functions at the residence in Singapore, there needed to be a ministerial decree and the consent of the British Crown. Then, with the help of a chancellor and locally recruited personnel, he could perform the various functions which were entrusted to him by the Ministry in Paris, or by the Embassy in London. The first Consul of France, Eugène Chaigneau, was posted to Singapore in 1840 to represent French political and economic interests, and to watch over the small number of French residents, who were mostly clerics, as well as French citizens passing through.

The Consul's varied functions

Chaigneau was previously posted to to (Da Nang, in Cochinchina) from 1829 to 1830, and to Cavite (the Philippines) from 1835 to 1840. In September 1840, he took up his duties in Singapore. He was tasked with collecting information on the origins of the products which passed through Singapore, and evaluating the commercial potential of the port city. He was also asked to provide intelligence of a political nature. Unfortunately, Chaigneau suffered frequent bouts of malaria and was replaced in 1844 by Aimé Rivoire. He then returned to Lorient, his hometown, where he died in 1846 at the age of 47.

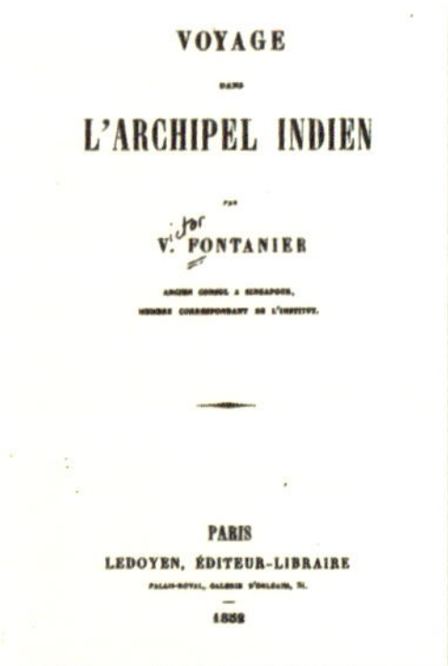
VOYAGE

L'ARCHIPEL INDIEN

V. FONTANIER

PARIS

LEDOYEN, ÉDITEUR-LIBRAIRE

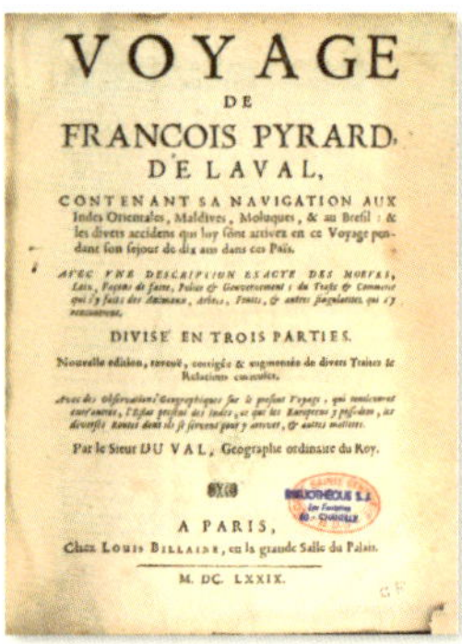
VOYAGE

DE

FRANCOIS PYRARD,

DE LAVAL,

CONTENANT SA NAVIGATION AUX Indes Orientales, Maldives, Moluques, & au Bresil : & les divers accidens qui luy sont arrivez en ce Voyage pendant son sejour de dix ans dans ces Païs.

DIVISE EN TROIS PARTIES.

Par le Sieur DU VAL, Geographe ordinaire du Roy.

A PARIS,

Chez Louis Billaine, en la grande Salle du Palais.

M. DC. LXXIX.

One of the duties of the Consul was to inform France of events in Singapore, for example, a description of the cholera outbreak which "struck the Indian town of Singapore during the equinox" (in a letter from Chaigneau dated 3 May 1841). He also reported on political and economic developments.

In the preface to his book, *Voyage dans l'archipel indien*, Consul Fontanier, who held the position from 1846, described his relationship with the English powers: "Colonel Butterworth, who governed the straits, had no doubt that I was one of the adversaries of England's policy of invasion, and that I tracked his movements with a very jealous eye."

In August 1852, Consul Gautier wrote: "If, with a small amount of entrepreneurial spirit, our manufacturers wish to follow the suggestions which have been provided to them and comply exactly with the drawings, measurements and quantities which are preferred by the populations who come to Singapore to stock up, they can hope, and with good reason, to play a wide-ranging role in the opportunities which this market can offer."

The Consulate also provided regular reports on the French community. It kept up-to-date records of registered citizens, including information on their identity, origin and profession. Once registered, they were able to enjoy the benefits of their French nationality, which guaranteed them protection in the event of trouble in Singapore. The movements of French citizens were also monitored, in case they might need to be conscripted into military service. The Consul could also

involve France in large-scale projects. Charles Buckley made two mentions in his *An Anecdotal History of Old Times in Singapore*, of France's financial contribution to the construction of lighthouses. In 1851, the Horsburgh Lighthouse on Pedra Branca, and in 1854 the Raffles Lighthouse on Coney Island, were inaugurated in the presence of the French Consul, Frédéric Gautier, who held this position from 1849 to 1856.

The Consulate's first offices faced the Padang. Victor Fontanier, Consul from 1846 to 1848, described the modest nature of the accommodation in his book, *Voyage dans l'archipel indien*: "We had only to step ashore, where we met Mr Segovia, who took us to a hotel run by a Frenchman. This was the best I had seen in India [at the time, Singapore's Governor reported to the Governor-General of India in Calcutta, so it was considered part of British India], but as his travellers came by ship, this meant that his house was packed for a single day once a month, after which solitude reigned."

Fontanier then reviewed the consulate building: a supposedly haunted house, with a relatively high rent, located close to the esplanade, and equipped with a vast garden. The Anglican reverend, Mr Maule, who had previously occupied the premises, had relocated because the Chinese owners used part of the premises as a gambling parlour and opium den. On the ground floor, there were three or

OPPOSITE TOP: Cover of the book by Victor Fontanier, *Voyage dans l'Archipel Indien*, 1852.

OPPOSITE BOTTOM: Cover of the book by François Pyrard de Laval, *Voyage ... contenant sa navigation aux Indes Orientales, Maldives, Moluques, & au Brésil ...*, 1679.

TOP: Lithograph of the Horsburgh Lighthouse, believed to be after a painting by John Turnbull Thomson. Captain Horsburgh was nicknamed "Nautical Oracle of the world", because of his knowledge of the Indian Ocean and the China Sea.

four rooms, of which one was inhabited by Mr Rey, the Chancellor, while the others were used as stores. On the first floor, there was a small lounge and two bedrooms, as well as a large, relatively airy balcony where receptions were held. The kitchen, bathroom and the stable were housed in separate structures, as was usual at the time. Finally, a small Chinese-style house was used as the Chancellery, in front of which stood the mast flying the French Tricolour.

The staff

The staff of the Consulate consisted of not only the French, but also some local staff. Consul Fontanier described them as follows: "We had to have a cook, a groom, a sepoy, a labourer or *coolie*, and a maid-servant or *ayah* [*amah*]; and in this area we restricted ourselves to the strictly necessary: our neighbour, a seamstress, had no fewer than us. The number did not matter, and we could manage not to be served; there was sometimes nothing to eat, so inedible were the dishes that were prepared for us. We were accustomed to none of the vegetables, greens or fruit. Meat was rare [to come by], and as this was only sold by the quarter, the majority of what we bought had to be thrown out because of the heat. Rice, local chicken and bad fish comprised our normal fare.... Without Whampoa, a rich Chinese trader, we would have had no meat, butter or even bread. For us, he fulfilled the duties of a steward."

The Consulate also recruited secretaries and translators from among the French-speaking Indian and Indochinese communities. There was no lack of work, because the French Consul would step in to provide representation for an allied country which had no official representative in Singapore. For instance, Fontanier was concurrently the Consul of France, Belgium and Spain.

The Consul, assisted by a chancellor and clerks, also fulfilled the duties of a civil service official. Records were kept, including documents relating to French sailors dead or missing at sea, and children born during the journeys, which seemed to be a fairly frequent event.

The official representative of France also served as a notary. He provided the reading of wills, recording financial settlements, and issuing "informal powers" to the sailors and officers passing through. All of these documents were issued in the presence of witnesses, who were usually French traders, consular personnel and sometimes members of the clergy.

Catholic missionaries meet the peoples of Asia

At the start of the 19th century, Singapore's population comprised *orang laut* Muslims and a few planters whose religions were Chinese in origin. Archaeological artefacts dating from the 14th century indicate that Buddhism, Islam and a variety of Asian religions were practised by the island's first inhabitants. With the arrival of the Europeans, Christianity began to take root, thanks to the work of the Christian missions. Catholic missionaries such as the Franciscans and Jesuits made their appearance in the region from 1819 onwards. According to a census taken in 1849, 52% of the population were Buddhist, Taoist or Confucian, while 41% were Muslim, 3.5% Christian and 2.8% Hindu.

HOO AH KAY (WHAMPOA) (1816–1880)

Hoo Ah Kay was a well-known Chinese businessman and community leader. Born in Whampoa (present-day Huangpu), China, he came to Singapore in 1830 and worked for his father's company, Whampoa and Co, which supplied meat, bread and vegetables. His nickname, 'Whampoa', was derived from his birthplace as well as the name of his family's business. Hoo took over the business when his father died, and he became the exclusive ship chandler to the British Royal Navy. His fluency in English gave him an edge in business and social interaction. In 1869, he became the first Asian to be appointed a member of the Legislative Council (1869). Hoo was also well known for hosting lavish dinners at his home. Henri de Ponchalon recalled the inevitable visit to Whampoa, who received all foreign travellers: "We went to Whampoa to have tea, the necessary start and conclusion of all Chinese visits."

Watercolour painting by Edward Cree (1814–1901), inscribed "*Mr Whampoa's entertainment, 21st September 1844*". Cree was an Englishman who studied medicine and served as a surgeon in the Royal Navy for 30 years. He kept a journal which he illustrated with watercolours.

The Protestant presence

Even prior to the founding of Singapore by Sir Stamford Raffles in 1819, Christian missions based in Malacca had visited Singapore. A few months after the signing of the treaty between Raffles and Sultan Hussein, the London Mission Society's (LMS) Ultra Ganges Mission established itself on the island.

This Protestant mission aimed to educate Malay and Chinese children with the view to gradually convert them and their families. With an insufficient mastery of Malay or Chinese dialects, however, the missionaries were largely unable to preach. On the other hand, the British Protestants formed sizeable congregations. After the signing of the Treaty of Nanking in 1842 and the establishment of European concessions in China, many missionaries left Singapore for the Middle Kingdom, a more fertile land for evangelisation. Despite this, the Anglican mission continued its work thanks to the personal intervention of Reverend Benjamin Peach Keasberry and his wife Charlotte, who stayed on.

Two new missions landed on the island, however: in 1834, the American Board of Commissioners for Foreign Missionaries arrived, with Reverend Ira Tracey; and in 1837, the Church Missionary Society of the British and Foreign Bible Society established a presence with the Squires, a husband and wife team. In addition, men and women such as the Reverend Keasberry, Miss Grant and Miss Sophia Cooke were deeply involved in their religion, and built churches, chapels, schools and dispensaries.

The Missions Étrangères de Paris (MEP)

In October 1821, on his way to Penang to take up his duties there, Father Mathurin-Pierre Pécot of the MEP called at Singapore. In a letter sent to his superior, he described the handful of Catholics, adding that "I do not think this would be any place to sow a mustard seed."

Two months later, at the request of Bishop Florens (MEP), vicar apostolic of Siam resident in Bangkok, Father Laurent Marie Joseph Imbert made a brief stopover in Singapore on his way to China. He noted that the Catholic community comprised a dozen people, leading a miserable life—probably Chinese fishermen or descendants of the Portuguese who had previously settled in Malacca. He recommended that given the lack of a permanent presence, a missionary should visit this tiny community from time to time. He concluded his report by suggesting that the diocese of Bangkok extend its jurisdiction to cover the island. In 1824, a few of the Catholics in Singapore sent a petition to Bishop Florens to request a priest on a permanent basis.

The "quarrel of the jurisdictions"

The bishop's reply was negative: he did not have enough staff, and in his view, Singapore fell under the Portuguese jurisdiction of Malacca, according to the

padroado. This was a 15th-century treaty which divided the world between the Spanish and Portuguese, who were at that time at the height of their powers. However, in 1827, Bishop Florens (MEP), as vicar apostolic of Siam, received jurisdiction over Singapore from Rome.

This presented Catholic Christians in Singapore with a variety of options when attending services, namely those held by the Portuguese Padre Maia in the house of Dr d'Almeida, those of the French missionary in the house of Mr Denis McSwiney, or mass with the Spanish Padre Yegros. At the height of their rivalry, these clergymen would try to resolve their differences by means of excommunications and PR campaigns. Finally, in 1832, Father Jean-Baptiste Boucho, a Penang-based missionary, succeeded in convincing Padre Yegros to leave this quarrel over jurisdictions in the hands of the relevant religious authorities. In 1841, by decision of Pope Gregory XVI, the Singapore community was placed under the jurisdiction of the vicar apostolic of the Malacca peninsula, under the control of the Missions Etrangères de Paris.

In the meantime, tensions arose once again between the French and Portuguese communities, and these would continue until June 1886, when a concordat was signed between Pope Leo XIII and King Dom Luis of Portugal. Even though jurisdiction remained firmly in the hands of the Parisian missionaries, the Portuguese congregations of Singapore would come under the Bishop of Macao. Further agreements were signed in 1926 and in 1950, but the issue was only finally resolved in 1981, according to W. Ann Trindade of the University of Melbourne.

The construction of Singapore's first Catholic chapel

Bishop Courvezy of Siam, and Father Etienne Albrand, both MEP missionaries, embarked on a project to erect Singapore's first Catholic chapel. On 11 December 1832, a local newspaper announced: "After a lapse of many years, the Catholics

OPPOSITE TOP: Bishop Laurent Marie Joseph Imbert (1796–1839).

OPPOSITE BOTTOM: Bishop Esprit Marie Joseph Florens.

TOP: View of the Singapore River from the Esplanade, 1845. This was published in Charles Bethune's *Views of the Eastern Archipelago*.

BELOW: Father Jean-Marie Beurel's passport-visa for his trip to the Philippines. It was signed by the Spanish Consul Segovia in Singapore in 1846.

OPPOSITE: Father Jean-Marie Beurel.

in Singapore have become desirous of possessing a Church for the celebration of Divine service, and have been grieved for the want of such. Divine providence has, at length, come to their aid. Through the medium of an open subscription towards this object, the greatest part of the obstacle has been surmounted."

The British Resident in Singapore, Samuel George Bonham, provided a piece of land along Bras Basah Road (the present site of the Singapore Art Museum). On 9 June 1833, the completed chapel was blessed by Father Albrand, who had supervised its financing (made up of gifts from the Christians of Singapore, and from the MEP in Paris) and even donated his own money, and who had also overseen the completion of the works and built a rectory. The chapel formed a starting point for the expansion of Catholicism, which by the end of the 1830s would have almost 400 followers in the colony.

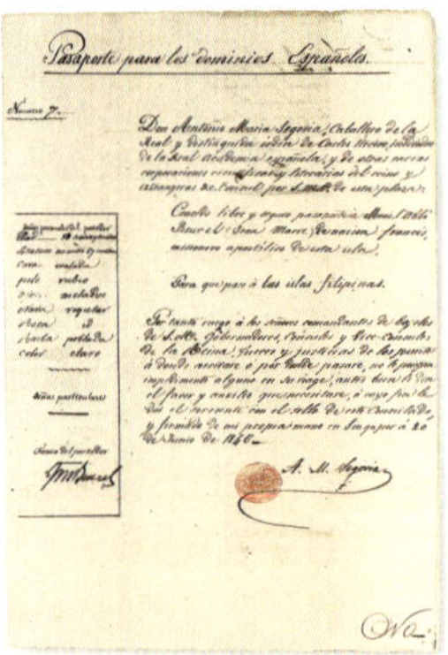

A leading figure in the MEP: Father Beurel

MEP missionaries played a vital role in the development of Catholic faith and education, and also in social initiatives. A number of French organisations such as the Ladies of Saint Maur and the Brothers of the Christian Schools eventually joined them. One of these missionaries, Father Jean-Marie Beurel, left a very special mark on the history of Catholicism in Singapore, because of his personality, his work and his devotion to the different ethnic communities.

The difficult construction of the Church of the Good Shepherd

Father Beurel held his office in high esteem, and wanted the Catholic religion to expand across the entire island at any cost; it was this tenacity that would lead

FATHER JEAN-MARIE BEUREL (1813–1872)

Jean-Marie Beurel was born on 5 February 1813 in Plouguenast, in northern Brittany. In August 1838, he became a deacon at the Séminaire des Missions Étrangères, and was ordained a priest in March 1839. Despatched to Singapore, he arrived on the island on 27 October. He was 26. The following April, Bishop Courvezy (1792–1857) named him head of the Catholic community of Singapore. A tireless, intelligent worker, full of initiative, he spoke English, Portuguese and Malay fluently, but did not master the Chinese dialects. From the information given in his "passport-visa", we know that he was 1.67 m tall, had fair skin, red hair and light brown eyes.

In 1857, he was stricken by a severe bout of gout and, in 1859, in a letter addressed to Bishop Boucho, he gave his two-year notice for health reasons, hoping to make way for a younger missionary. He left the island nine years later, on 3 December 1868, weakened by a series of strokes. According to the anonymous author of *Journal d'un futur missionaire 1865–1872*, the MEP seminary in Paris housed "three renowned invalids, including Father Beurel, pro-vicar of Malacca, who suffered from ankylosis, but was frequently shaken by tireless laughter." He passed away on 3 October 1872, and is buried in the cemetery in Montparnasse.

to the success of numerous projects, including the building of the Cathedral of the Good Shepherd, which still stands in Singapore today.

The Catholic community had been using the French chapel built in 1833, but it was soon too small to accommodate the new converts and the colonial population. So Father Beurel decided to embark on the construction of a new place of worship. His superior, Bishop Courvezy, resident in Bangkok, disagreed, believing that a simple extension to the chapel would be sufficient.

Despite this, Father Beurel's project made progress. Governor Samuel Bonham and the religious authorities eventually agreed on a plot of land at the corner of Victoria Street and Bras Basah Street on which to build the church, as well as on another piece of land at Fort Canning to house a Christian cemetery. Father Beurel then began to raise funds for the construction work. He appealed to all Christians, even promising prayers to Protestants in exchange for donations! He also received assistance from Queen Marie-Amélie of France, who sent 4,000 francs.

In October 1842, Father Beurel held a meeting with the Catholic community to discuss plans for the church. It was a tense meeting which ended in failure, with Bishop Courvezy imposing his plans and rejecting those of the well-known architect J.T. Thomson, even though they had been approved by the British authorities. This made the bishop even more unpopular in Singapore, especially as he had used 3,000 Spanish dollars of the church construction funds to invest in a venture with the Seth Brothers, Armenian traders who went bankrupt three weeks later.

Parish support for Father Beurel

On 21 November 1842, Father Beurel was sent away from Singapore to Moulmein, in Burma, to the great annoyance of the Catholic community. During his absence, Father Freycenon took care of the parishioners. On 9 December, without asking for the advice of the Bishop of Siam, with whom he did not get along either, Father Freycenon revived the stalled project to construct a church. The new plans, by the architect Denis McSwiney, were for a building which was cheaper and easier to maintain, and were then approved. However, the missionary's initiative incurred the anger of his superior, who decided to send him home. Father Freycenon then left the MEP for good.

The Singapore parishioners wrote a letter to the Bishop of Siam as well as to the directors of the MEP to demand Beurel's return of the Breton missionary. Father Beurel returned to the island on 11 April and, on Sunday 18 June 1843, organised a ceremony to lay the foundation stone. A document—translated into five languages (Latin, French, Portuguese, Chinese and Malay) and signed by Bishop Courvezy, Father Beurel and other officials—some English, French and Spanish coinage and a few newspapers such as the *Singapore Free Press* and the *Straits Messenger* were placed in time capsules laid in the foundations of the church.

Because of his unaccommodating personality and the financial problems which his ill-advised investments had caused, Bishop Courvezy left Singapore in December 1843. According to Father Beurel's diary, no one regretted the bishop's departure. A year later, he was replaced by Bishop Boucho, who left Father Beurel in charge of Singapore.

The church remained unfinished due to a lack of funds. Father Beurel launched a new appeal to raise funds for the construction of the steeple. In his letter dated 9 October 1845, he wrote: "Our Church has a roof at last but the steeple is not completed yet. I am sending letters of appeal far and wide. I will soon be considered a real nuisance. But I don't care as long as I succeed in this project." He wanted a majestic church, worthy of the glory of God, and between 1844 and 1846, he headed for China and the Philippines to seek funds there, leaving Father Anatole Mauduit to take care of his island flock.

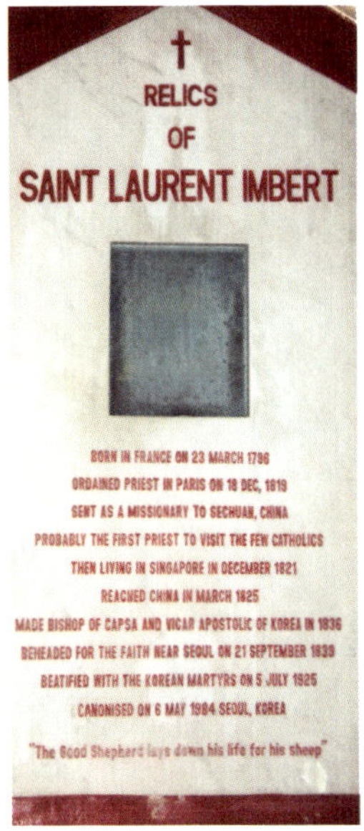

Mission accomplished: Singapore's first Catholic church

Four years after the first stone was laid, on 6 June 1847, and in the presence of almost 1,500 people, Father Beurel blessed the Church of the Good Shepherd, so named in honour of Father Laurent, martyred in Korea in 1839.

In September 1859, Father Beurel ordered the construction of a rectory and started to furnish the church with statues and paintings purchased in France. The missionary was by then one of the leading personalities in Singapore, and often received French citizens passing through. In 1866, during his voyage through Asia, the Count of Beauvoir attended a service: "On Sunday, we found the church full of Chinese and men of colour. They all sing the litanies in Chinese, in a series of *tsing-tching-tsang-hong-king-sing*, in a spritely tune which would make you laugh out loud, were it not for the holiness of the place. In view of the diversity of the congregation, the wise priest must preach in five different languages in succession: Chinese, Malay, Malabar, Pidgin-English and English."

A visionary akin to Raffles

Like Stamford Raffles, Father Beurel understood that Singapore's dominant population would be Chinese. He therefore encouraged the construction of churches to serve the different Asian communities. In June 1839, he also welcomed a Chinese priest: Father John Tschu, ordained in Bangkok and sent to Singapore to care for his compatriots.

Nor did Father Beurel forget the Chinese on the plantations and, in 1846, he despatched Father Anatole Mauduit to Kranji to build a chapel dedicated to Saint Joseph. In 1853, another MEP priest, Ambroise Maistre, erected a chapel and rectory in Serangoon, in the northeast of the island, on a 40-hectare plot donated by the government. Before long, a veritable "Catholic farmers' colony" had been established, with its own school. Later, in 1857, to meet the growing needs of the

OPPOSITE TOP: Bishop Jean Baptiste Boucho.

OPPOSITE BOTTOM: Bishop Jean Paul Hilaire Courvezy.

TOP: Relics of Saint-Laurent Imbert at the Cathedral of the Good Shepherd.

THE ARCHITECTURE AND INTERIOR DECOR OF THE CATHEDRAL OF THE GOOD SHEPHERD

The overall plan is inspired by St Paul's Church in Covent Garden, London. In the shape of a Latin cross, the architecture follows the Palladian style developed in Singapore by George Coleman, a former colleague of Raffles who in 1833 became the island's first Superintendent of Public Works. Inspired by classical antiquity, this style focuses on geometric shapes and seeks to create a harmony of volumes. It borrows elements from Roman architecture (porticos, cupolas, galleries of columns) and adapts these to the tropical climate by adding numerous porches and large windows. The construction of the steeple was only completed in 1847, to plans by Charles Dyce, High Sheriff for the Straits settlements.

Father Beurel chose the church's furnishings and, with the support of patrons, imported paintings from France representing the Stations of the Cross as well as the martyrdom of St Sebastian, statues of the saints, and even Antwerp marble, which was laid in 1860. The church was enlarged several times, notably in 1887, enabling it to accommodate 600 worshippers, a record at the time. The building was solemnly consecrated as a cathedral on 14 February 1897. The Cathedral of the Good Shepherd was gazetted as a national monument by the Preservation of Monuments Board in 1973.

TOP: Painting sent by Father Beurel to Paris on the completion of the Church of the Good Shepherd.

Chinese community, Father Beurel bought 30 acres of land from the British East India Company to build a church in Bukit Timah. Father Adolphe Issaly, the General Hospital's chaplain, joined him on his mission in the jungle.

The Church of the Good Shepherd eventually could not accommodate all the settlers, Eurasians and the several hundred Chinese and Tamil Indians. Also, communication problems were increasing, with each community having its own language. Father Pierre Paris then decided to build a new place of worship which would welcome Chinese and Indians and offer religious services in their own languages. This was the Church of Sts Peter and Paul on Queen Street, built between 1868 and 1869, which Father Paris adorned with three bells.

A man of many resources

Father Beurel is also to thank for establishing the first Catholic schools. Despite a difficult start, these became very popular due to their accessibility to all students, regardless of their race or belief. To finance these schools as well as many other projects, Father Beurel had no qualms about going into business. Together with a Chinese friend, he bought a 17,000-tree nutmeg plantation—a rather unfortunate investment because, in 1857, a terrible epidemic struck the plantations. He also used his own money to bring his projects to life, or to ensure that projects underway stayed alive. Between 1852 and 1863, for example, he donated $4,877 to enable the school for boys to continue operating.

In 1845, with Bishop Boucho and Fathers Albrand and Bigandet, he embarked on the drafting of the *Litteræ apostolicæ* and the *Avis particuliers aux missionaries*, advice for aspiring missionaries. Father Beurel also bequeathed a collection of notes on his daily life in Singapore from 1829 to 1849, which he compiled under the title: *Les Annales de la Mission catholique de Singapore.*

Nor did Father Beurel neglect Singapore's sick, often visiting the island's hospitals. With the help of Tan Tock Seng's widow, he opened an annex for women at the Tan Tock Seng Hospital. He also worked with the Sisters of the Congregation of Saint Maur to open an orphanage and a shelter (the Refuge) for widows and destitute girls, to prevent them falling into prostitution.

The religious imprint on education in Singapore

From the mid-19th century onwards, several French congregations developed the education system in Singapore, providing it with a degree of quality, modernity

FATHER PIERRE PARIS (1822–1883)

Born on 19 January 1822 to a peasant family, Pierre Paris joined the MEP in 1851. In 1855, he arrived in Penang, and then lived in Malacca where he learned Tamil, Malay and Chinese. He landed in Singapore in 1856 and, two years later, took charge of the Chinese and Tamil communities. A colourful, well-known and well-regarded character island-wide, he could be seen on Serangoon Road every Sunday morning, a Chinese umbrella in one hand and a walking cane in the other. He criss-crossed Singapore to perform his duties: giving mass in Serangoon, walking more than ten kilometres to give another in Tamil at 11am, then heading to the prison to hold a religious service, teaching catechism to Asian children at 2pm, and finally, at 3pm, singing Vespers in Chinese at the Church of Sts Peter and Paul.

His weekly schedule was equally well established. On Mondays, he would receive members of the Chinese community who required his advice; on Tuesdays, he devoted himself to the Chinese living in the jungle; Wednesdays were reserved for the Chinese living in town; on Thursdays, at home in Serangoon, he would teach catechism; on the remaining two days of the week, he would take confessions and participate in more down-to-earth activities.

In 1874, he became pro-vicar of the mission. However his increasing age made it difficult for him to walk such long distances. He asked Bishop Boucho for funds to buy a horse and carriage—the bishop sent him 70 dollars. The following year, he once again picked up his quill to ask how, given his finances, he was supposed to feed his horse! This little anecdote hints at the poverty in which many missionaries lived at the time. Father Paris died in Singapore in 1883 and is buried in the Church of Sts Peter and Paul.

Father Pierre Paris

and continuity. Previously, the peninsula had been home to schools in which the children (boys only) learned Arabic in order to be able to read the Quran, as well as where the Chinese taught their language and culture.

The British authorities were relatively reticent about investing in education, and Raffles believed that children should study in their mother tongue. However, he decided to establish an school to provide education for all, using private funds, and furthermore encouraged missionaries to settle on the island. On 5 June 1823, he laid the foundation stone for the Singapore Institution. By December, however, the assembled funds had been squandered, and the Institution's building would be remembered as Jackson's ruins, after the name of the architect.

For its part, the Anglican Church opened a school for Malay boys in Kampong Glam. In 1835, the Reverend Samuel Wilson founded another school for Malay and Chinese children. Due to a lack of resources, however, these schools soon closed their doors. In 1844, an attempt was made to restart Raffles' Institution by opening a school for girls, but with very low numbers: six boarders and five day students; meanwhile, the Protestants established a school near Hill Street. The education system really took off due to the French Catholic missionaries, and in particular thanks to the tenacity of Father Jean-Marie Beurel.

The founding of the first Catholic school: St Joseph's Institution

After blessing the foundation stone of the Church of the Good Shepherd in 1843, Father Beurel concentrated on the task of establishing schools.

In 1847, he called upon Philippe Bransiet, Brother Superior of the Congregation of the La Salle Brothers (also called the Congregation of the Brothers of the Christian Schools) whose educational principles were revolutionary for their time: teaching was in the vernacular rather than Latin, and was free for the poor.

Father Beurel also wrote to Queen Marie-Amélie of France and to his superior at the MEP, and then embarked on collecting funds. To the Queen he wrote: "I

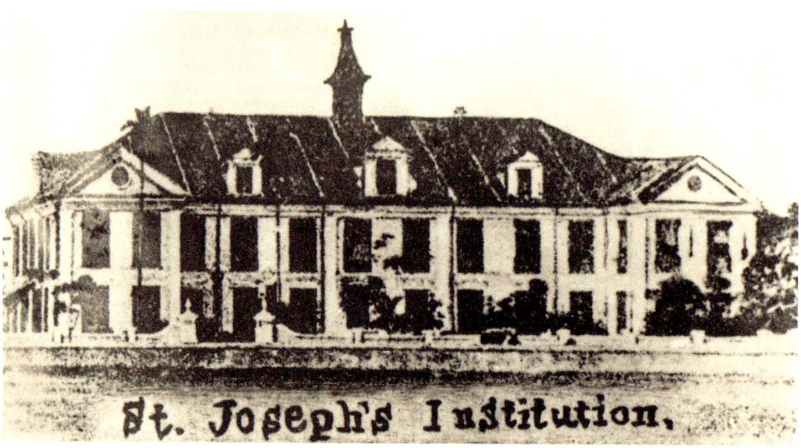

do not wish to rest until I have a good school. It is absolutely necessary to implant in the hearts of children a truly Catholic faith...".

Two years later, his calls remained unheard, but he refused to be disheartened. Nevertheless, by May 1849, the prospect of opening a school looked remote: there was no reply from the La Salle Brothers, nor any sign of encouragement from the Archbishop of Paris. And so he continued his battle alone, in July informing his superior, Bishop Boucho, of his decision to open a school for girls on a plot of land which he had just acquired close to the church: "So I am not yet at the end of my worries, I want to unite in the same establishment a school for young girls and an asylum for orphans and for the destitute."

OPPOSITE: View of St Joseph's Institution, 1867.

BELOW: *La Julie*, the vessel which carried the French missionaries in 1851.

A battle won: the school opens its doors

Finally, in July 1849, Bishop Boucho, vicar apostolic of the Malay Peninsula, authorised Father Beurel to establish a school in Singapore. In 1850, he left for France to meet Brother Bransiet, who promised him the assistance of the English-speaking La Salle Brothers. He also met the Mother Superior of the Ladies of Saint Maur, to urge her to consider opening a school for girls and an orphanage.

In December 1851, Father Beurel boarded *La Julie* with six Brothers from the Congregation of the Christian Schools and four Sisters from the Ladies of Saint Maur. Three of the brothers left for Penang in order to start up a school there, but the other three remained in Singapore with him. However, Irish Brother Gregory Connolly did not see eye to eye with Father Beurel, and Brother Swidbert Doyle often fell ill, so it was therefore Brother Liéfroy Bajon, the only Frenchman in the group, who managed the school which opened on 1 May 1852, named St John. Seventy-five boys of all races and religions followed the courses given in the old St Joseph's chapel on Bras Basah Road.

The three Brothers initially lived with Father Beurel, but complained of the lack of privacy and did not like the meals, which invariably consisted of cheese, bananas and pineapple, and with only water to drink. Furthermore, wearing their heavy black cassocks and woollen socks which were so sweat-drenched they could not remove them in the evenings, they were unable to take their customary daily walk because of the heat. The fact that their salaries were paltry also increased their discontent. Four months after their arrival, they decided to move to a house on Mount Sophia. Despite those inconveniences, the school doubled its enrolment in less than a year, taking in a total of 145 students.

Father Beurel continued to look for money to build a second school, as the first was too small, and, on 19 March 1855, the foundation stone of St Joseph's Institution was laid.

His problems were far from over, however: there was never enough money, and the misunderstandings and difficulties increased. The extremely popular Brother Swidbert would soon die; he was so beloved by his students, and held in

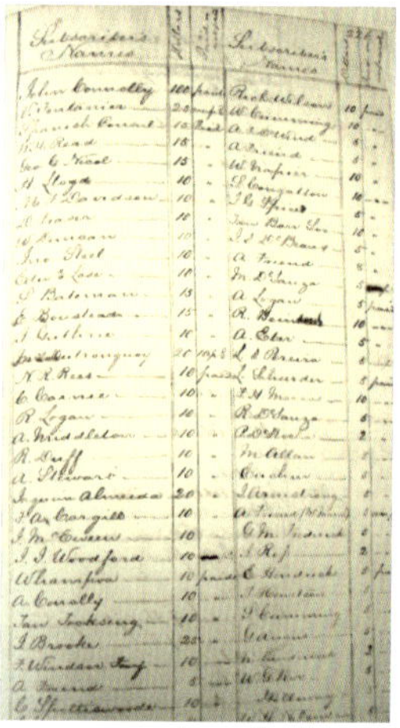

such high esteem by their parents that he was interred in the Cathedral of the Good Shepherd; in 1907, a plaque was placed there to honour him.

Misunderstandings and difficulties

Brother Modeste arrived from France to replace Brother Swidbert, but the parents were unhappy with his teaching, and removed their children from the school. The Brothers, seeking to enlarge the school, acquired a one-hectare plot of land on Mount Sophia, beside the house in which they lived, but as Father Beurel had to pay practically every expense from his own pocket, relations became tense between the clergymen. As Father Beurel was at the time also raising funds to establish a girls' school, the Brothers were further enraged: they disapproved of the construction of this new building while they were still awaiting the construction of their own. When they opened a parallel tuition-charging school, the Academy of the Sacred Heart, to improve their standard of living, Father Beurel was furious. He complained to his superior and stopped paying the Brothers who taught at the new school. The final straw came when the missionary was no longer able to pay his debts, and the school was at risk of closure.

Calm returns

In 1863, Brother Lothaire, arriving from Penang, took charge of the tuition, a task he would retain until 1871. Young and dynamic, he was determined to complete construction of the school whose only stone had been laid eight years earlier. To do so, he sold the house on Mount Sophia for $3,500, launched a subscription and borrowed money from the Sisters. For its part, the Singapore government decided to offer bricks at cost, but, as the Istana was under construction at the time, there were no bricks available for the St Joseph's Institution. The building was finally completed in 1867. This provided the brothers with lodgings, and the conflicts finally abated.

The Ladies of Saint Maur and education for girls: The Convent of the Holy Infant Jesus (CHIJ)

Father Beurel also wished to open an educational institution for young girls. After 12 years of toil, the missionary once again made his way to France. He visited the Ladies of Saint Maur who made up a lay community, took no religious vows, and worked to provide popular education. Father Beurel hoped that they would come to take care of his new school.

A first attempt

The first mission from the congregation of the Ladies of Saint Maur left Antwerp in December 1851 on board *La Julie*. The voyage was so long and difficult that the Mother Superior died en route. Sister Pulcherie, another member of the

TOP: Father Beurel's accounts ledger.

mission and the only one to speak English, spent a lot of time with the Captain during the endless journey and, on arrival in Singapore, decided to leave the Ladies of Saint Maur. However, Father Beurel, in need of staff for his girls' school, persuaded her to head to Penang to help the Sisters there. She was however not welcomed by her former Sisters, and returned to Singapore where she married a resident of the island. A third Sister also fell gravely ill and died a few years later. The two remaining Sisters, both 22, were unable to manage the mission by themselves and were sent to Penang.

Mother Mathilde, a headstrong woman

In Paris, Mother Superior de Faudoas chose Mother Mathilde to lead the second mission to Singapore. Mother Mathilde told the Sisters who would accompany her (French Sisters Appolinaire and Damien, and an Irish Sister Gregory): "Sisters, you are going to Singapore … you will need double the strength and triple the vocation. Here you have to change your way of life if you hope to live and work effectively in the tropics. No European woman could possibly wear the same heavy cloth, work so intensively and devote so many hours to prayer in such an enervating climate as she did in Europe—unless she wanted to commit suicide."

The four Sisters left Southampton in September 1852 on the *Bentinck*, arrived in Egypt, descended the Nile from Cairo, and joined a caravan which crossed the desert to reach the town of Suez. From there, they boarded the *Indostan*, and after a trying journey, landed in Penang in October. There they opened a school where they taught for a year, waiting for Paris to send more Sisters.

Sister Gaëtan Gervais, Sister Patrice and Sister Léonard formed part of a third journey. In addition, in 1854, Sister Mathilde, Sister Appolinaire, Sister Gregory and Sister Gaëtan left for Singapore, leaving Sister Damien in Penang.

A precarious existence

Partly with his own funds, Father Beurel bought Caldwell House, built by the architect G.D. Coleman in 1840 at the corner of Victoria Street and Bras Basah Road. Before the arrival of the Sisters, he wrote: "I am doing repair work on the house, so that it will adapt perfectly to our Sisters and their classes. Nothing will be forgotten! All has been organised for the settlement of your dear Sisters and we are impatient to welcome them."

Upon their arrival, however, Mother Mathilde noted in her diary: "The house itself was correct, but all the rooms were very untidy with many things broken: not any door anywhere, even at the place it is most convenient to have one. To use this humble room, we needed to hide ourselves with an umbrella."

After an enthusiastic welcome, Father Beurel took them to the Church amid a crowd of well-wishers and a multitude of flowers, and then, after mass, led them to the house. Almost everything would have gone well, despite the pitiful state of

MOTHER MATHILDE: A WOMAN OF CHARACTER (1814–1911)

Born in 1814, Marie-Justine Raclot spent her childhood on a Lorraine farm. At the age of 12, she was sent to a boarding school run by the Sisters of the Holy Infant Jesus at Langres, where she quickly adapted to a spartan lifestyle. She decided to become a nun and become a missionary in Asia, preferably in Japan.

In March 1835, she took her first vows in the monastic community of the Sisters of Saint Maur, and took the name Sister Mathilde. For the next 17 years, she taught in Bagnoles, in Languedoc, where her superiors recognised her great patience and sense of justice. However, during all of these years, she never forgot her desire to become a missionary and, when she learned that the Congregation wanted to establish itself in Malaya, she prayed fervently that she would be selected. Disappointed not to be part of the first mission, she nevertheless persevered, and trained herself to tolerate the equatorial climate by sleeping with all of the windows closed, and covered under thick woollen blankets. When Mother Superior de Faudoas began to organise the second departure for Malaya, she chose Sister Mathilde to lead the mission. And thus she landed in Singapore in February 1854.

She worked to develop the Convent of the Holy Infant Jesus for 18 years before finally realising her childhood dream of being sent to Japan. In 1872, she became the first female member of the clergy to enter the country, where she remained until her death in Yokohama, in January 1911, at the age of 97. Her enterprising and determined nature left a strong impression in Japan, and some Japanese still travel to Suriauville in Lorraine to visit her childhood haunts.

the house, if only someone had thought to offer them something to drink and eat, but no refreshments were provided until a merciful parishioner brought them dinner. Mother Mathilde recorded the occasion: "Hymns, flowers and complimentary speeches are all very fine, no doubt, but not very filling."

Ten days later, the girls' school, which eventually became known as the French Convent or the Convent of the Holy Infant Jesus (CHIJ), opened its doors to 14 European and Eurasian students under the disapproving eye of the Protestant community. Thanks to the personality of Mother Mathilde, the school acquired a reputation for charity and generosity. As for the Sisters, they lived in such penury that they occasionally had no money for rice or bread.

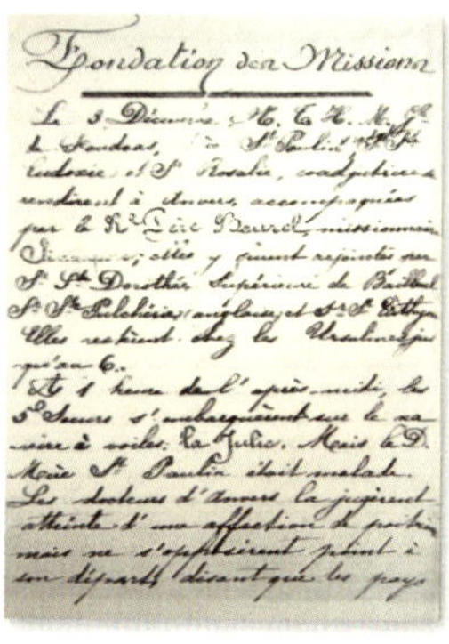
Fondation des Missions

Efforts rewarded

One year after the opening of the CHIJ, in 1855, Mother Mathilde described the school as "a very spacious, calm and meditative place, without any ornament, even our big brown altar has no candlestick, the tabernacle with a cross which comes from somewhere else and yet no holy water basin."

The school grew slowly. The European and Eurasian population remained relatively small, whereas the Asian communities began to appreciate the presence of the Sisters. In 1862, some 145 students enrolled, of which only 63 were able to pay for their studies. The school was divided into two departments: wealthy

students on the upper floor, the poor ones on the ground floor, and each class received an education appropriate to their social status. Despite donations and the young girls' needlework which the sisters would sell, lack of money remained a problem.

The legacy of Father Beurel

The development of Catholicism and of the Catholic schools in Singapore was, to a great extent, the work of Father Beurel, whose perserverance, visionary spirit and strong character provided the foundations for this success. His influence can still be felt, as his buildings remain standing in the heart of Singapore.

The adventurers

In 1819, when Sir Stamford Raffles made Singapore a British colony, the interior of the island (which was a dense jungle which the settlers would only gradually tame) was already home to a couple of dozen gambier plantations operated by the Chinese on the hills of Bukit Selegie, which later became Mount Emily. These planters had their homes on the banks of the river, and each year when junks from China would berth, they would sell their gambier and buy products that these ships brought in.

OPPOSITE TOP: Mother Mathilde.

OPPOSITE BOTTOM: Page from Mother Mathilde's diary, recounting the founding of the mission, 1851.

TOP: View of the Sisters' lounge in Caldwell's House. The Sisters would gather around the octagonal table to write, sew or knit.

BELOW: Interrupted Road Surveying in Singapore, 1835. A tiger lunged at G.D. Coleman and a group on Indian convict labourers while they were building a new road through the jungle.

An island covered with hills and jungle

Many 19th-century French adventurers provided fascinating accounts of their arrival in Singapore and, very often, described a paradise: "The harbour of Singapore is magnificent. In the morning in particular, when the rays of the rising sun start to penetrate the fog which often veils the town and the bankside forests, which have an enchanting air," wrote Auguste Haussmann, a member of the Lagrené mission, in 1847.

The island was hilly and covered with trees (there were already timber operations on Pulau Ubin). The climate was hot but healthy, and there was plenty

TIGER ATTACKS

In 1850, at least one coolie was killed every day by tigers, attracted by the increasing number of workers in the Singaporean jungle. French Consul Eugène Chaigneau noted: "The Chinese grow pepper and gambier, log wood and clear the jungle in spite of the tigers which often come to interrupt their work. Five of these ferocious beasts have been killed by the Chinese in the first nine months of 1841, after taking more than 50 people. We have found out with certitude that these tigers swim across the strait which separates Singapore from the Peninsula." Auguste Haussmann also mentioned the tigers: "They appear noiselessly, often entering the farms, and sometimes even the suburbs of the town, it is said. A trustworthy person, one of our missionaries, assured me that the Bishop of Singapore one day found himself face to face with one of these terrible animals, which had come to pay him a visit in his living room. The beast was polite enough to retire without causing any harm to the master of the house."

of fresh water. Even though the hill of Bukit Timah was visible from all around, the jungle which surrounded it was so dense that no European and only very few Malays had penetrated it.

The town was growing rapidly and reached 10,683 inhabitants in 1824, including 148 Europeans. The island's resources were however limited: a few spice, pepper, gambier and fruit plantations. John Crawfurd, who succeeded William Farquhar, declared: "The soil of the region, with very few exceptions is infertile. For such plants as rice, the sugar-cane, the indigo-plant, pulses, maize, tobacco, the soil must be considered as ill-suited," before adding that there were too few hills for growing coffee, much fertiliser was required for nutmeg, and that it was impossible to grow cloves. Nevertheless, the plantations gradually expanded and roads were built to reach into the centre of the island. French Consul to Singapore Eugène Chaigneau in 1841 described the construction of these communication routes: "Singapore is a deportation destination for Indian criminals from Bombay and Madras who are condemned to forced labour, who are placed together with those on the island itself who are condemned to the same sentence, most of whom are Chinese. They form a chain of approximately 1,500 prisoners of which the local government takes every advantage, especially for road construction; the daily improvement in the roads and communications facilities are proof of this."

Missionaries in the heart of the jungle

By moving to the plantations, the Catholic missionaries hoped to convert the Chinese who lived in poverty. Father Mauduit's Saint Joseph chapel at Kranji was moved to Bukit Timah (it would later be rebuilt, in 1905 and 1965).

Life on the plantations was harsh: the workers were poor, and the dangers constant. An MEP report states: "At Singapore, the Chinese Church is within the forest. The zeal of Father Mauduit had overcome all the obstacles and his little flock is increasing everyday. His catechumen are admirable, full of simplicity and fervour. They are poor, and their priest even poorer than them all; he considers himself lucky when he gets enough rice and plantains for his meals."

In August 1860, Father Augustin Périé of the MEP joined the Bukit Timah parish, and his *Souvenirs de Malaisie* provides us with very graphic accounts of his many adventures with the jungle animals. Father Périé recalled: "One Saturday evening, on a very dark night, a Christian rushed into my home utterly scared, screaming: 'Father, Father, an enormous snake!'" Father Périé snatched up his rifle "to go on the hunt for the monster snake … In the corner of the house, I spotted a magnificent boa, coiled up and occupying an area of at least two square metres. The monster had seized hold of a little dog and the poor animal's entire head was inside the snake's mouth." The tale of the fight with the boa was truly epic, and the snake was no easy opponent. "It weighed 60 kilos and measured

five metres in length, with a circumference of 33 centimetres," said Périé at the end of his description. The boa was butchered, cut up and cooked. "I kept the skin, which has been most useful in repairing my trunk as I prepared for my departure for France," he concluded.

Tigers, snakes, monkeys and insects all found their homes in the thick jungle. "My dilapidated rectory", wrote Father Périé, "was literally invaded by a very peculiar species of small coffee-coloured scorpion, whose song was somewhat akin to that of a cricket. It reproduced in and lived in the joints of woodwork. Its sting resembled a touch of fire, and produced unbearable pain throughout the body. There was also a larger scorpion, which was blue-black in colour."

Pioneer planters

Nutmeg

For John Crawfurd, the second Resident of Singapore, the craze for the profitable crop of the nutmeg tree was a real "mania". Between 1841 and 1848, nutmeg plantations doubled and, for the first time, the Europeans moved out to settle closer to their plantations. Victor Fontanier, French Consul to Singapore in 1846, had a poetic view of the nutmeg trees: "Other elegantly undulating hills surrounded this one (the government hill) and were planted with nutmeg trees, delicate trees which required as much care as orange trees at home, and whose fresh greenery gave the countryside the appearance of a vast garden." In 1848, there were 58 plantations, the majority of which were owned by Europeans, with a total of 60,000 trees. However, from 1849 onwards, prices dropped and a disease spread rapidly, devastating many of the trees: plantations which had previously provided 20,000 nuts per day now only produced 2,500. By 1860, not a single

THE MISSIONARIES AND THE SECRET SOCIETIES

If jungle animals and illnesses did not make life on the plantations difficult enough, bandits and thieves who had fled the authorities in China and members of the secret societies (*hoey*) further menaced the lives of the population. In 1851, the *Singapore Free Press* reported that a secret society, known as the *Tan Tae Hoey*, had put the interior of the island to the sword in order to drive out Christians from these rural territories, which they wished to control. Numerous plantations were thus destroyed, but the British authorities refused to intervene, as it appeared that Chinese temples as well as plantations belonging to the *Hoey* had also been destroyed. The violence seriously affected the work of the planters as well as the business of the traders in town, and a small police detachment was finally sent out. Father Augustin Périé filed a complaint with the police commissioner against the *Hoey*, who had put a price on his head: "He welcomed me with kindness," he wrote, "took note of my deposition against the Kenlok sect and smiled as he told me: 'your head is expensive, at $1,000! I only have a price of $500 on mine'."

OPPOSITE: Father Augustin Périé.

LEFT: Nutmeg, in a drawing from the William Farquhar collection.

,nutmeg tree was left on the island. Father Jean-Marie Beurel thus lost part of his investments. Many planters also found themselves ruined.

Pepper and gambier

Singapore developed primarily as a port, *entrepôt*, and as a place of exchange and trade. As the population increased, so did unemployment, which provided a workforce for the return of agriculture. The land and climate were very suited to the growth of coconut, mango, mangosteen, durian, pineapple and, in particular, pepper and gambier. Pepper and gambier were the most profitable as crops but, over the longer term, left the land exhausted. The market for gambier flourished in the 19th century: locally, gambier was chewed with betel nut, and it was exported to the West for use in the skin tanning and dye industries. The cultivation of these two complementary plants was monopolised by the Chinese, but after several years of cultivation, the ground was no longer fertile enough for continued production. While there were numerous coconut and wicker (for rattan) plantations on the island operated by the Chinese and Malays, the Europeans themselves embarked on the cultivation of new crops.

Sugar cane and coffee

In 1835, a French planter by the name of Beauregard embarked on the cultivation of sugar cane, settling in Paya Lebar, an isolated area at the time. Unfortunately, he was attacked by a gang of 30 Chinese, led by two Malays. He escaped alive, but lost his plantation. In 1839, a Mr Le Dieu, a Frenchman, established the Singapore Joint Stock Coffee Company. In order to launch the project, he published an enticing prospectus: the plantation would be located eight kilometres from the centre, on Serangoon Road, and coffee cultivation was sure to be supported by the island's government. Shares were expensive: $100 each, but the company expected revenue of $12 million annually over the short term. The prospectus concluded with the following: "To what a pitch of agricultural and commercial prosperity would not then Singapore attain if we saw half of the Island covered with plantations of coffee." However, the plantation would never see the light of day. Two years later, when the shareholders demanded accountability and wanted to know where their money had gone, no traces of Mr Le Dieu could be found.

Sago

Sago is a starch extracted from the flesh of different palms, including the sago tree, native to Southeast Asia. The flour gives off a pleasant vanilla fragrance.

Jules Itier, on the Lagrené scientific mission, described the preparation of sago: "Eight to ten Chinese were busy working on the raw flesh of the sago palm tree (*metrouglum-sagu*), which Malays from the interior of Borneo and Sumatra bring to Singapore, using the following preparations: the raw flesh is washed in a vat, on a taut fabric which allows the starch to pass through, while capturing the woody fibres; the starch precipitate is decanted, and the residue is poured into long boxes whose bottom, pierced with holes, is covered with a very tight-fitting cloth, allowing water to filter through. The starch is then dried in the sun, and then sieved. The substance thus obtained is in the form of a perfectly white flour which squeaks in your fingers. In this state, it is shipped in great quantities to England to be converted into a gum and used for priming fabrics."

Over the decades, the plantations continued to grow and to attract Europeans, including Frenchmen who achieved varying degrees of success.

Gaston Dutronquoy and the London Hotel

In the mid-19th century, travellers passing through Singapore and pioneers who wanted to put down roots all required lodgings. However, the choice was somewhat limited. In 1839, Gaston Dutronquoy established the London Hotel on High Street, an establishment which was often called Dutronquoy's Hotel. Dutronquoy may have been French or Belgian. His hotel was the most famous in Singapore, and where the majority of travellers stayed. He ran the hotel with his wife, and in 1841 moved to a new location close to the Esplanade, a two-floor bungalow which belonged to the architect G.D. Coleman.

Dutronquoy was also the island's first photographer. He opened a photographic studio in his hotel, where he made use of the new daguerreotype technique. He offered portraits at a cost of $10 for a single person, or $15 for a couple. Unfortunately, no photographic print from that time has been found. On the ground floor of his hotel, he installed a theatre which he named the Royal Theatre, and which operated until 1845.

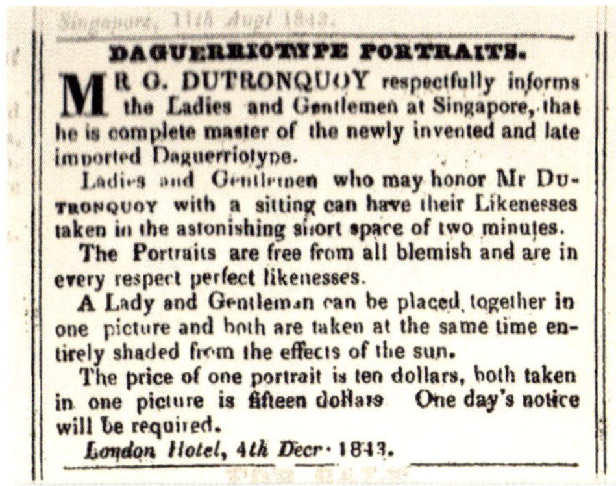

DAGUERRIOTYPE PORTRAITS.

MR G. DUTRONQUOY respectfully informs the Ladies and Gentlemen at Singapore, that he is complete master of the newly invented and late imported Daguerriotype.

Ladies and Gentlemen who may honor Mr DUTRONQUOY with a sitting can have their Likenesses taken in the astonishing short space of two minutes.

The Portraits are free from all blemish and are in every respect perfect likenesses.

A Lady and Gentleman can be placed together in one picture and both are taken at the same time entirely shaded from the effects of the sun.

The price of one portrait is ten dollars, both taken in one picture is fifteen dollars One day's notice will be required.

London Hotel, 4th Decr. 1843.

In 1844, Dutronquoy moved his hotel a second time, this time to the elegant home of Edward Boustead, at the corner of High Street and the Esplanade. The new London Hotel was able to welcome families. Most members of the Lagrené mission stayed at the London Hotel. Melchior Yvan, enrolled in the mission as a doctor, described the premises: "Mr Dutroncoy's hotel is built in the middle of a vast garden where great tropical trees grow freely. The walls have large windows which are very close to one another, and decorated with bamboo blinds, which give the house the appearance of a birdcage." He also described his room, with its whitewashed walls, an immense China porcelain bowl, a table and a bed. The beds were "great rush frames hidden under a mosquito net, lined with a palm mat and two bolsters. One lies on the bed dressed in a pair of vast Moorish Bengal canvas trousers, and falls asleep perfectly cooled by the night-time air, which flows freely all around."

In 1851, with the help of qualified doctors from India, Dutronquoy opened another hotel to house the invalid and convalescent. This establishment was located in the New Harbour, enabling travellers arriving from Europe to be housed close to the quays. Trying his best to help the sick, Dutronquoy even recommended a kind of "ice-cap or rather wig", which was intended to assuage high fevers.

Then, 16 years after his arrival in Singapore, he disappeared mysteriously, probably accompanied by his wife. According to a rumour then, he was murdered close to the Muar river south of Malacca, during an expedition in search of gold. The following year, the hotel was acquired by a French woman, Madame Esperanza. She kept the family's private lodging house, which she called the Family Hotel, and offered *prix fixe* meals. The hotel had an excellent reputation, confirmed by Auguste Benoit de la Grandière in *Souvenirs de Campagne 1858–1860*: "The Hôtel de l'Espérance is the best in town. It has fine rooms, good food, spacious bathrooms, billiards and bowls, but everything is very expensive there."

Mr Poiron, Singapore's first dentist

In the 19th century, France was known for its accomplishments in the field of medicine, and dentistry in particular. There was no dental practice in Singapore between 1819 and 1869, merely itinerant dentists. Yet, in June 1835, a formally trained dentist worked in Singapore for the first time. This was Dr Poiron, who placed the following advertisement in the *Singapore Chronicle* newspaper: "Mr Poiron, surgeon and dentist from Paris, has the honour to inform the inhabitants of Singapore that during his stay at this port he intends to exercise his profession. The knowledge which Mr Poiron has acquired in his profession and the care he exercises, as well in the surgical as in the artificial branch of his profession, has

OPPOSITE: Sago, in a drawing from the William Farquhar collection.

TOP: Advertisement placed by Gaston Dutronquoy in the *Singapore Free Press*, 7 December 1843.

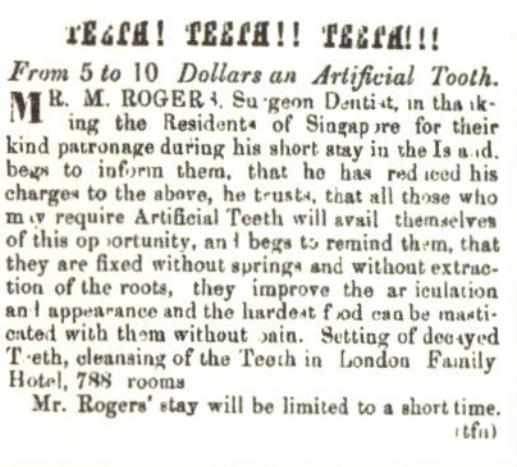

TEETH! TEETH!! TEETH!!!

From 5 to 10 Dollars an Artificial Tooth.

MR. M. ROGERS, Surgeon Dentist, in thanking the Residents of Singapore for their kind patronage during his short stay in the Island, begs to inform them, that he has reduced his charges to the above, he trusts, that all those who may require Artificial Teeth will avail themselves of this opportunity, and begs to remind them, that they are fixed without springs and without extraction of the roots, they improve the articulation and appearance and the hardest food can be masticated with them without pain. Setting of decayed Teeth, cleansing of the Teeth in London Family Hotel, 788 rooms

Mr. Rogers' stay will be limited to a short time. (tfn)

gained for him the confidence of the first Physicians and the most distinguished families in Calcutta during a residence of more than three years, which he hopes to continue to merit at the hands of those ladies and Gentlemen, who may do him the honour to employ him."

As an itinerant physician, the doctor would visit the patient or operate on a public bench. Professor Lee Yong Kiat, in his 1978 book, *The Medical History of Early Singapore*, stated that pulling a tooth in the 1840s cost $5, a filling with gutta-percha (a gum-like resin from the sap of the gutta percha tree) would cost $6, and inserting a gold tooth $17.

In 1855, Dr Poiron was joined by one of his Parisian colleagues, Dr M. Rogers. The latter also placed an advertisement in the local press, in September 1856: "Mr Rogers, Surgeon dentist, from Rue Saint Honoré, 270, Paris, begs to announce that he fixes artificial teeth after a new system, without springs or wire, and without extractions of the roots, from one to a complete set. Decayed teeth restored by a paste which hardens in five minutes, especially recommended for the front, which it renders and restores their former colour and strength."

Singapore as seen by travellers between 1845 and 1867

Frenchmen passing through Singapore included diplomats, scientists, writers and the very first "tourists". They often left behind written accounts of their port call.

Arrival in Singapore

For travellers arriving from Europe, Singapore was the gateway to China. Dr Auguste Benoist de la Grandière, in his *Souvenirs de Campagne 1858–1860*, wrote: "Its picturesque location and the diversity of the races which trade has brought together there created a very special character, and created one of the most curious towns of the Far East."

In 1857, in *Souvenir d'une ambassade en Chine et au Japon*, the Marquis of Moges described Singapore as a city throbbing with activity. "Barely anchored, the frigate was surrounded by a swarm of canoes loaded with eggs, vegetables, fruit and birds … Soon, all of these Malays, Hindus and Chinese were climbing the sides of the ship on all sides, claiming to be laundrymen or merchants … This was a microcosm of Asia, local colour to the hundredth power."

OPPOSITE: Dentist's advertisement in *The Straits Times*, 21 October 1856.

BELOW: *Singapore from Mount Wallich*, 1856, painted by Percy Carpenter. This panaroma stretches from Pearl's Hill on the left to beyong Tanjong Rhu on the right. In 1885, Mount Wallich was levelled so that the earth could be used to reclaim Telok Ayer Bay.

Various impressions

For some, the discovery of the Eastern world lacked charm: "Two bridges have been thrown over the river. The quays on the left bank present a series of quite nice houses, which form the European quarter. On the right bank, there is a long row of stores and arcades of shops, which are horribly dirty and filthy. The bazaar is located close by. This entire part of the town is almost entirely populated by the Chinese exiled from their homeland by poverty, who have come to exercise their industry and activity here, in this young, flourishing colony in which they multiply with astonishing rapidity … They look miserable and sickly, and live constantly in an atmosphere tainted by the filth which they allow to accumulate around their homes. This foretaste of China was entirely unattractive to us," wrote Auguste Haussmann in 1847.

For his part, the Count of Rochechouart, a diplomat despatched to Beijing in 1867 who spent a dozen years in the Far East, took a rather unfriendly view of Singapore: "We landed on the quay and fell into the hands of a swarm of cab drivers who quarrelled over us; the majority of these individuals, of Indo-Malay mixed race, wore nothing more than a loincloth. One of our persecutors won the day, and brought us in triumph to our numbered cart."

A very colourful population

The diversity of the population was particularly striking to travellers. After weeks at sea, they would land in the middle of a coloured, lively multitude, which generated an extremely wide range of reactions.

In 1858, Henri de Ponchalon wrote: "Apart from the Europeans, it is possible to meet specimens of every Asian nation … The *Saône* is surrounded by canoes filled with pineapples, bananas, mangosteens … The Malays rowing them shout

OPPOSITE: Original drawing by Marion Cordonnier, A Journey from the Cairo desert to Suez.

to us: '*Dis donc, dis donc* [Do tell!]'. For this is how they call the French: they only remember these few words of our language, which we use often."

Auguste Haussmann evoked the unenviable plight of the Europeans: "European society in Singapore is very small, and lives here rather unhappily. The oppressive daytime heat makes it impossile to go out except in a carriage; we normally use long, low old carts, a type of square box called a palanquin drawn by a single horse which a black coachman accompanies on the road as he holds him by the reins, exciting him with gestures and his voice ...".

In the 19th century, these adventurers had to endure a long, painful journey to reach Asia. The Suez Canal had not yet been dug, but even without this, the route through the Mediterranean was faster than via South Africa.

Passengers arriving from Marseille disembarked in Alexandria and then travelled to Cairo, either on boats along the Mahmoudieh canal, or in feluccas on the Nile. From Cairo, they headed overland to Suez before boarding a ship to travel out of the Red Sea.

Travellers have left us with beautiful descriptions of this part of the journey. They first spent a night in Cairo, then faced 150 kilometres of desert on camel-back—ladies were entitled to a palanquin, but gentlemen had to make do with their saddle. Later, with the advent of roads, this desert crossing could be completed in less than 48 hours, in horse-drawn trailers.

Victor Fontanier, Consul to Singapore, recalls: "Camels were hastily assembled to carry our luggage, and we were put in cars very similar to an omnibus, drawn by excellent Arabian horses ... We made a stop at the height of the heat to take our lunch, which had been sent in advance from Cairo; we then saw two horsemen riding flat out to announce the arrival of the ship from India. This was very pleasant news, as we were thus sure not to have to wait long in Suez. At the station in time for dinner, we witnessed the interesting spectacle of a caravan in the desert. The camels which had left before us, but which we had overtaken, now rejoined us, and they were made to kneel in order to rest. Come evening, their drivers performed their ablutions and their prayers, and then busied themselves with their meal; with the approach of night, they lit torches, and all of this produced a very picturesque effect."

This was followed by their arrival in blistering heat in Suez, on the coast of the Red Sea. The passengers then boarded a steamer which would call at Port Saïd, Bombay, Colombo and Singapore before continuing to Saigon, Hong Kong, and finally China or Japan.

In 1857, the opening of a railway between Alexandria and Cairo made the journey more pleasant. The completion of the Suez Canal in 1869 marked a complete change. The crossing from Marseille to Singapore was reduced from three months to one month. Henceforth, the transport of goods and the journey of Europeans to Asia would be a much more pleasant experience.

By permission of Messrs Fraser & Neave Ltd Singapore.

III.

Life in the Jewel of the East (1869–1914)

The years 1860–1870 constituted a decade of major changes for Singapore. The disappearance of the British East India Company enabled the merchants in Singapore to manage the city's commerce more effectively. Singapore also saw its trade develop in a spectacular fashion following the completion of the Suez Canal. In the meantime, France increased its presence in the region following the successful conquest of Indochina, while in Singapore, the small French community continued to grow.

The opening of the Suez Canal and its consequences

The revolt by Sepoy Indian soldiers in India in 1857 led to the disappearance of the British East India Company and the implementation of an administration which reported directly to London via the India Office based in Calcutta.

Ten years later, irritated by the slow speed with which the administration took decisions, the Straits Settlements business community put pressure on London to obtain a change of status. In 1867, the new Governor, Sir Harry Saint George Ord, implemented a more effective administration manned by better trained staff. The Straits Settlements became a Crown Colony, and the territory came under London's direct control. The Straits Settlements were henceforth to be managed by a Governor, assisted by executive and legislative advisors, and supported by a competent administration. Singapore's merchant community welcomed the appointment in 1873 of the new Governor, Sir Andrew Clarke. London requested him to visit the neighbouring Malay States, the site of recurrent disturbances. In 1874, Clarke signed the Treaty of Pangkor, obtaining control over the State of Perak. In order to improve the tin and rubber trade, the British then took control

OPPOSITE: Map of the Straits Settlements and Federated Malay States, 1907. The Straits Settlements shown in red, were created in 1826. On July 1896, the states of Perak, Selangor, Negeri Sembilan and Pahang became the Federated Malay States, a British protectorate. Johor was independent until 1910.

BELOW: Flag of the Crown Colony of Singapore, Straits Settlements (1874–1942).

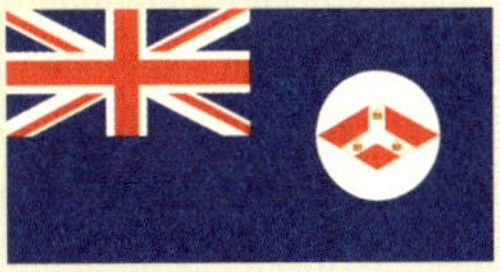

of Negri Sembilan, Selangor and Pahang, forming the Federated Malay States in 1895. The port of Singapore thus strengthened its position as the region's hub.

The Suez Canal and its impact on Singapore

At the same time, between 1859 and 1869, work on the Suez Canal was proceeding under the direction of the French diplomat and engineer Ferdinand de Lesseps. The new canal would enable ships to sail between Europe and Asia without having to go around Africa. De Lesseps received little help from Napoleon III, despite the two men being cousins by marriage. Queen Victoria also took a dim view of the canal, which threatened British dominance of the routes to India.

In 1875, however, the English bought up the shares of the Compagnie Universelle du Canal Maritime de Suez from the Egyptians, and thus became one of its shareholders. The French initiative to build the canal would therefore have major repercussions on the development of the port of Singapore.

For thousands of ocean-going vessels, Singapore gradually became a port of vital importance thanks to the coal it imported, notably from Borneo and Sumatra. The first major shipping lines to use steam established themselves in Singapore in 1845. Port traffic on the island increased considerably—the port infrastructure was modernised with the development of the New Harbour and the Tanjong Pagar Dock Company, and new means of communication were installed thanks to the Cable and Wire Company. With the opening of the Suez Canal in 1868, the number of vessels transiting through Singapore surged dramatically. Trade volume in Singapore reached a total of $58 million, and five years later, $90 million. Between

THE CONQUEST OF INDOCHINA

Begun in 1858, France's conquest of Indochina was a progressive affair, only being completed in 1897. From 1865 onwards, the Chamber of Commerce of Marseille aimed to "make Saigon into a French Singapore". The presence of the Chinese, the tensions between the different Indochinese provinces and France's haphazard imperialist aims however made the country's enforcement of its dominance a long, laborious process.

In 1883, France made plans to take control of Tonkin. On 26 May 1883, Jules Ferry obtained the necessary funds from the Chamber of Deputies for the Tonkin expedition, which was tasked with taking control of the Red River delta and installing a protectorate. However, the British did not welcome France's arrival in the region, and the British Colonial Secretary decided that no French ship should be allowed to refuel in Singapore, and that an embargo be imposed on any product which might be of assistance to the French army. Nevertheless, there were ways around the embargo.

The French cavalry needed 400 horses for its conquest of Tonkin, and it made a call for tenders. A British trader, John Dill Ross, made an offer, knowing that he could buy a horse for $15 in Singapore and sell it to the French army for $40. He had to obtain 400 horses at short notice, and smuggle them to the French army. In his memoirs, Ross wrote: "The steamer *Paklat* would go alongside Jardine's wharf at 2pm, when the horses were to be run on board. Directly after this operation was over, the *Paklat* was to steam outside the harbour limits to avoid any attempt at arrest by the Chinese Consul or the Colonial Secretary. The *Paklat* was not a big ship and the voyage from Singapore to Hanoi in bad weather would have been unpleasant enough in any event. It was a strange sight! Fore and aft of the bridge was a dense mass of horses swaying from side to side with the heavy motion of the labouring ship. During the storm, all the horses were kicking, squealing and savaging one another, most mercilessly. Yet the result seems to have been surprisingly moderate. Four horses with broken legs were shot and six more were cut and bruised. But that was all."

1873 and 1913, traffic increased eight-fold. Eventually, trade in tin, rubber, copper, sugar and fuel oil would establish the *entrepôt* functions of the port on a local, regional and global scale. The increase in colonial conquests in the region (France in Indochina, Spain in the Philippines) and the opening up of Siam, China and Japan to the world led to a general expansion of trade.

The transformation of the city

The opening of the Suez Canal also enabled Singapore to become the "Jewel of the East". The city's population grew, which led to multiple changes to its countryside and organisation. The town, laid out around the Padang, expanded westward with the construction of the New Harbour (since renamed Keppel Harbour), eastward with the development of Geylang, Katong and East Coast Road, northeastward with River Valley Road and Orchard Road extending towards Tanglin, and northward with the extension of Serangoon Road. The population's poorest often concentrated in the respective ethnic quarters established by Raffles, whereas the European population, including some French,

OPPOSITE TOP: Sir Andrew Clarke (1824–1902), second Governor of the Straits Settlements to have been appointed under Colonial Office rule in 1873. Clarke Quay and Clarke Street are named after him.

OPPOSITE BOTTOM: *Opening of a new dock at Singapore*, 1869, wood engraving. The Victoria Dock in New Harbour was opened in October 1868, by Governor Ord.

and rich Asian traders (the Chinese tycoons, the Peranakan *babas*, etc.), settled not far from the town centre in houses surrounded by greenery. This was the period in which the first "black-and-white" colonial homes appeared with the development of the bungalow by the architect George Bidwell.

As part of this same movement, the physical appearance of the town underwent a change. Cavenagh Bridge opened in 1869, connecting the business district of Commercial Square with the administrative district built by convicts sent from India. The year 1882 saw the completion of the General Hospital and the Central Police Station. Five years later, in 1887, the Raffles Museum and Library were inaugurated and the Esplanade was expanded thanks to the reclamation of Connaught Drive. The construction of the Thomson Reservoir was completed in 1868. The municipal engineer, James MacRitchie, saw to its expansion and the reservoir was subsequently named after him. Victoria Memorial Hall was inaugurated in 1905, and Victoria Theatre in 1909. Electric streetlights illuminated the town centre from 1906 onwards. Rickshaws, imported from Shanghai in 1880, came under competition from the tramway, which started service in 1882 (this was initially steam-powered before being electrified in 1906) and, from 1906 onwards, the first automobiles. In 1891, Léon Caubert, a visiting Frenchman, noted that as he crossed the town, he followed "a route served by a steam tramway; this travelled along the extremely well-built quays which were lined with the offices and stores of the main trading houses."

Commercial and *entrepôt* activities gradually replaced those of the plantations and the jungle. These transformations were made possible due to cheap labour. Between 1825 and 1873, construction work (clearing, and the construction of roads and bridges, in Raffles Place and other locations) was essentially undertaken by forced labour brought from India to serve their sentences. They also worked in the brickworks, and as assistants to carpenters and building contractors.

Communications became modernised. Singapore was connected to Europe by telegraph in 1870. The first private telephone company opened for business in 1879. At the start of the century, a letter had taken six months to arrive, but now only took a few weeks; the same applied to newspapers, which enabled the population to keep abreast of world news.

Photographic studios also opened their doors at this time. More than 20 such businesses circulated images of the new city, notably in the form of postcards. Among these was a German, G.R. Lambert, who was active from the beginning of the 1880s, providing panoramic views of the island, images of colonial edifices and portraits, both of Europeans and locals: his 3,000 snapshots would make him and Singapore famous as the "Liverpool of the Orient".

Tourism also started to develop. New hotels were built, such as the Hôtel de l'Europe, the Adelphi Hotel and the Raffles Hotel (1899). At the start of the new century, Raffles Hotel became a gathering point for colonial high society, and a

OPPOSITE TOP: G.R. Lambert photo of Orchard Road Police station, c. 1894. The auxiliary police station was located at the junction of Scotts Road and Paterson Road.

OPPOSITE CENTRE: G.R. Lambert photo of the original 1887 front block of the Raffles Library and Museum, 1890s. The architecture was guided by the Renaissance principles of balance and symmetry. It stands in stately fashion at the junction of Stamford Road and Orchard Road. It was renamed the National Museum of Singapore in 1965.

OPPOSITE BOTTOM: G.R. Lambert photo of the south end of Cavenagh Bridge, 1880s. Cavenagh Bridge was used for all manner of traffic, from carriages to rickshaws to pedestrians. Later it was converted into a pedestrian bridge. It is the oldest bridge in Singapore that exists in its original form. Initially known as the Edinburgh Bridge to commemorate the visit of the Duke of Edinburgh, its name was changed to Cavenagh Bridge in honour of Major General William Orfeur Cavenagh, the last India-appointed Governor of the Straits Settlements, who governed from 1859 to 1867.

Museum. S'pore

hotel with a global reputation. Bugis Street also achieved renown, or rather infamy, due to its many prostitutes.

The comforts of colonial life

The daily lives of the colonial population also improved. In 1905, the opening of the Singapore Cold Storage Company increased the availability of products imported from Australia (meat, butter and fresh fruit). The electrification of the town centre and certain private residences in 1906 enabled the use of fans. Leisure opportunities varied from cricket matches for the young and energetic, musical concerts on the Padang and hours spent drinking and eating.

The end of the 19th century was marked by the appearance of clubs (the Yacht Club in 1881, the Golf Club in 1891, the Polo Club in 1899, and the Teutonia Club in 1900), theatres, libraries, reading rooms, museums, and fine restaurants. Tennis was all the rage, and the first film was shown at City Hall in 1901. Colonial life became more sophisticated, with a growing number of household staff to make the daily life of the Europeans more comfortable. The new Asian bourgeoisie, who spoke English and sometimes French, adopted a western lifestyle and held eminent positions in fields such as law and medicine.

The Botanic Gardens, created in 1859 merely as a pleasant place to visit, rapidly became a subject of study by botanists and researchers. Henry Nicholas Ridley, its first director, worked there for 23 years on the cultivation of rubber—he was nicknamed Mad Ridley or Rubber Ridley. The garden was also a popular destination for travellers, as the Count of Rochechouart wrote in 1878: "Coming out of the Protestant church, we took a car to visit the Botanical Garden. One of the governors of Singapore had the happy idea of establishing a park on a hill a few miles from the town, in which he assembled all of the species of plant life

TOP: *Excés de vitesse* (Travelling at an excessive speed), c. 1910. Postcard produced by the Messageries Maritimes, showing a Sikh policeman stopping a speeding rickshaw puller.

RIGHT: Chinese *ayahs* in Singapore, 1890s.

OPPOSITE TOP: The Botanic Gardens, c. 1900. The gardens were built in 1859, after the Agri Horticultural Society was granted 32 hectares of land in Tanglin by the colonial government. The land had been obtained from the merchant Whampoa Hoo Ah Kay, in exchange for some land at Boat Quay.

OPPOSITE BELOW: Advertisement by the bookshop Kelly and Walsh Limited, promoting French books. *The Straits Times*, 15 September 1894.

from the neighbouring forests, all interspersed with sandy pathways and great green lawns with gracious contours and learned curves; this was the most beautiful park that one could imagine. One could spend many happy hours there studying all of the botanical treasures that it contains."

The effervescence of the British port and the conquest of Indochina also attracted the interest of French traders. The French community would gradually develop as part of Singapore's perpetually changing landscape. The British census of 1871 counted a French community of 51 people, and in 1911, 128—tiny proportions of the total populations of 96,087 and 303,321 respectively.

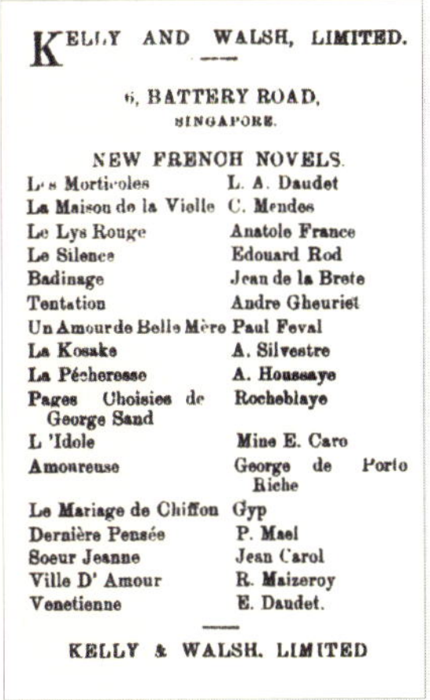
KELLY AND WALSH, LIMITED.

6, BATTERY ROAD,
SINGAPORE.

NEW FRENCH NOVELS.

Les Morticoles	L. A. Daudet
La Maison de la Vielle	C. Mendes
Le Lys Rouge	Anatole France
Le Silence	Edouard Rod
Badinage	Jean de la Brete
Tentation	Andre Gheuriet
Un Amour de Belle Mère	Paul Feval
La Kosake	A. Silvestre
La Pécheresse	A. Houssaye
Pages Choisies de George Sand	Rocheblaye
L 'Idole	Mine E. Caro
Amoureuse	George de Porto Riche
Le Mariage de Chiffon	Gyp
Dernière Pensée	P. Mael
Soeur Jeanne	Jean Carol
Ville D' Amour	R. Maizeroy
Venetienne	E. Daudet.

KELLY & WALSH, LIMITED

The French community: identity and activities

Portraits

The geographic origins of Singapore's French community gradually changed from the early decades of the 19th century onwards. Frenchmen from France had originally formed the core of the community, mainly comprising clergy, traders who came to try their luck, and diplomatic personnel posted to the colony. At the end of the

BELOW: Original drawing by Marion Cordonnier, of some Indian "renouncers" who became French.

century, they were joined by people from France's trading posts in India or Indochina seeking a better future; categorised as "French subjects", these new arrivals found employment with French companies, or in the French Consulate.

The Indian "renouncers"

In 1881, local staff working for the French administration in the Indian trading posts of Chandernagore, Pondicherry, Mahe, Yanaon and Karikal saw a change in their status. Essentially, the French Third Republic offered anyone who renounced their personal status (in other words, their caste) the right to become French: these were the so-called "renouncers". This Renunciation bestowed electoral and financial advantages when the staff moved to other overseas territories, where they were categorised as "French subjects".

In addition, when France embarked on the conquest of Indochina in the second half of the 19th century, Tamil soldiers were among those boarding the warships leaving from India as well as farmers with their herds who provided food and transport to the French troops. Settled in Cochinchina, in Saigon, they were joined in 1860–1870 by Indians from Pondicherry who worked as minor officials first in the Cochinchinese, and later the Indochinese, administrations. They held positions such as tax collectors, interpreters, lighthouse keepers and policemen, and the majority converted to Catholicism.

Often, Indians at the end of their military service would also decide not to return to India, but to stay and work for French companies. Sometimes they stopped in Singapore on their way to Indochina, and decided to stay. They took up staff positions at the Consulate of France, and at French companies such as the Banque de l'Indochine, which opened for business in Singapore in 1905.

They included for example Ramasamy Douressamy, 38 years of age in 1916, a clerk at the Chancellery in Singapore. The birth certificate of his son, dated 2 July 1916, was issued in the presence of Pavadé Radjagobalou, a clerk at the Banque de l'Indochine, and Mariappen Douressamy, also a clerk, both of whom were living in Singapore.

Some, such as Mona Kader-Soultane, were the recipients of honours from the Republic. In 1924 the lifestock importer received the rank of Knight in the National Order of the Legion of Honour: "Mr Kader Sultan is the first French Indian subject, and one of the most important members, of the Muslim group of Singapore. He is a member of the Muslim Advisory Board of Singapore, where he serves as a Justice of the Peace. Originally from Karikal, he owns the Straits Cattle Trading Company." In 1954, when Pondicherry was returned to Indian control, almost 4,000 Pondicherry natives living in Singapore had to choose either French or Indian nationality.

The Indochinese

French rule abroad was based on a principle of assimilation, and colonial France bestowed a special status on its most loyal servants in Indochina. The colonial master also aimed to disseminate the French language and "enlightenment". Consular edicts contained information identifying Annam or Saigon-born "French subjects" in Singapore, where they were able to find work with government bodies or French companies. For example, young Trinh Chung Tiet, the daughter of Trinh Thi Hung, an employee with the Banque de l'Indochine, born on 5 January 1919 in Singapore was issued her birth certificate in the presence of Mr Le Dinh Quang, secretary and interpreter at the Consulate in Singapore, as well as of Liew Van Hu, an employee with the Banque de l'Indochine.

The French Eurasians

In Southeast Asia, from the 16th century onwards, European colonisers sometimes married Asians. Their descendants would form the Eurasian community. Officially recognised in British censuses from 1849, Eurasians, according to a definition of the time, "have 'Asian' blood from their mother (Malay, Chinese, Indian, Indonesian, etc.) while from the father they inherit a European family name and culture, as well as their Christian faith." Although the Eurasian community grew in size, it never exceeded 2.2% of the total population of Singapore.

The Eurasians, who were able to draw from the experience of two cultures, often worked for the colonial administration. They were also represented in commerce, education, office work, medicine and the law. Christian by faith, their children went to missionary-run schools, in contrast to the colonial settlers, who often preferred to send their children to Europe to complete their education. The Eurasian community living in Waterloo Street, Queen Street, Selegie Road and Katong was generally Portuguese in origin. British and French Eurasians, fewer in number, had no area of their own; it was officially forbidden for the British and French to mix with the local population.

But very few French lived in Singapore, and the fact that most of the French were married couples or clergy explains the low number of mixed marriages. The local population was regarded as lowly by the whites, and marrying an Asian was not viewed in a favourable light by colonial society at the time, and by the French in particular. Having an Asian mistress was fine, but marrying her was not: one risked being ostracised by polite society. The French generally married other

French, or other Europeans. However, some Frenchmen do appear to have braved the ban, as some Eurasian family names are rather French-sounding: Cherbonnier, L'Angellier, La Fabre, La Porte, Le Mercier, Lombard, Longue and Poulier.

The Eurasians also had strong connections with members of the French community, and particularly with the priests of the MEP, as they were often fervent Catholics. Life in Singapore was by no means ascetic, however. Opium dens and brothels were frequented by both residents and French visitors.

French writers calling in Singapore

In 1883, Lieutenant Julien Viaud left Brest for Tonkin. This soldier was none other than the writer who wrote under the pseudonym "Pierre Loti" and he made two stops in Singapore. "Very quick shopping, in a cab, to the Chinese or Hindu

INSIDE THE OPIUM DENS OF CHINATOWN

Visitors were intrigued by opium dens. The Count of Beauvoir, in 1870, recorded: "Two police constables ensured that we were able to walk safely (something which would have been impossible without them) in the Chinese area to which this vice is restricted. We entered a bamboo shed: 30 or so Chinese were laid out on fetid mats; beside each burned a small coconut oil lamp ... For four coins, they buy ... a little packet of juicy, greenish opium, the size of a mint pastille, spread out on a tin sheet; they arrive every evening at around seven or eight o'clock, and don't leave (if they are able to wake from their torpor) until the first glimmer of daylight ... heating until red hot a needle which they roll over with delight; they coat this with opium which cakes onto the needle, and then place a bubble there of which resembles a pea on the capillary hole on the base of the pipe. They then lie down and toast the opium by lighting the lamp; three or four nervously coloured puffs, which are then released in opaque clouds by their quivering nostrils, and the ecstasy begins. Their eyes die and half-open time and again; their lips hang loose; their chest rises and swells with pleasure, only to fall again with a sigh! They swoon and collapse, almost lifeless; then they no longer even cast inert looks; their white, horrible, convulsing eyes remain fixed upon the dim lamp. The bamboo pipe falls to the ground, and the man, delighted by his hallucinations, lies there like a sordid cadaver in this one-night cemetery, beneath the thick, funereal fog of the poison."

Chinese opium smokers inhaling opium on a raised bed, 1870s.

AH KU, *KARAYUKI-SAN* AND FRENCH PROSTITUTES

As colonial Singapore gradually transformed itself into a hub of global commerce, it witnessed an inflow of mostly male immigrants. From 1860 until after the First World War, there was approximately one woman to every 14 men. It is therefore scarcely surprising that prostitution developed rapidly, with the *Ah Ku* arriving from China, and the *Karayuki-san* from Japan.

For Westerners, the situation was even worse: there was only one woman to every 20 bachelor males. No settler living in Singapore would dare be seen with a lady of the night, however, and they visited the Japanese or European prostitutes in secret.

The latter came from France, Central Europe or Russia. They often landed in Singapore with their pimp. In 1905, the Secretary for Chinese Affairs listed 30 European ladies of the night working in eight brothels. These girls often embarked upon their profession in Europe, and came to Asia in search of a better future. The pimp would send the brothel a file containing the physical characteristics of the girl, her real age as well as the conditions which the establishment would need to satisfy. Sometimes, the procurer would promise work or a rich husband to the girls to persuade them to get on the boat. Upon arrival, they would be sent from brothel to brothel across the region. This letter, written by a matchmaker in Singapore to a brothel keeper in Madras, is quite illuminating: "I have a friend who would like to become inmate if it can be arranged. She is a young French girl of twenty-three years old, a pretty little blonde with black eyes. She would like first to know your terms and the net profit she might expect daily."

Until the 1920s, the European brothels were mostly located in the Bugis area, on Malay Street. Some were managed by matrons who sometimes had a French-sounding name, such as Madame Blanche, Madame Laurence or Mademoiselle Yvonne to distinguish themselves from the *Ah Ku* or *Karayuki-San* establishments.

In 1913, the British authorities prohibited European women from registering in a brothel, and their pimps were arrested and expelled.

Karayuki-san, photo by G.R. Lambert and Co, 1890s.

pagodas, to the bazaars. But my mind was elsewhere. An Indian girl, whom I spoke to last July, at sunset ... Upright, curved, with superb and deliciously gentle eyes, her waist in a tight red loincloth; an ideal beauty; the beauty of a dancer, the beauty of a pagoda, as mystical and sensual as both." This short port call would produce a novel, *Une relâche de trois heures*, in which Loti tells of his nocturnal encounter with this beautiful Indian.

In his novel *Pécheur d'Islande*, Loti kills off the character Sylvestre in Singapore, and writes: "We crossed this Babel as the sun rose. And what emotions we felt there to find, a couple of steps away from the foul Chinese swarm, the calm of a French church. In this high white nave, where I was alone with my crewmates, the *Dies irae* was sung by a missionary priest echoing like a gentle magical incantation. Through the open doors, we saw things which resembled enchanted gardens, admirable greenery, immense palms; the wind shook the great trees in bloom, and a rain of crimson red petals fell partly into the church."

In the tradition of the explorer-adventurers, Victor Segalen, a Navy doctor, archaeologist, novelist, visionary poet and orientalist, also sojourned in Singapore after being in China. Unlike Loti, he wrote harshly: "Singapore does not interest me. I criticize it for merely being a busy transitorium with no depth or indigenous attraction ... It unloads and re-loads. It weighs and gauges. Singapore is an easy museum for travellers."

Although Jules Verne never visited Singapore, he described it in 1872 in *Around the World in Eighty Days* as if he had: "It is a park intersected by beautiful roads. A nice rig, drawn by these elegant horses ... transported Mrs Aouda and Phileas Fogg through the clumps of palm trees with their vivid foliage, and clove trees, whose cloves are formed from the button of the half-opened flower itself. There, the pepper bushes replaced the spiny hedges of the European countryside, the sago palms, great ferns with their superb branches, varied the aspect of this tropical region, nutmeg trees with their varnished leaves saturated the air with a penetrating perfume. There was no lack of alert and grimacing bands of monkeys in the woods, nor maybe of tigers in the jungles ...".

Sixty-four years later, Jean Cocteau set off on a trip around the world in 80 days, like the Jules Verne hero. His account was published in the *Paris-Soir* newspaper from 1 August to 3 September 1936, and in book form, *Mon premier voyage*, in 1937. Cocteau, an opium smoker, remembered: "Last night, in an attic into which 20 or so friends were piled around the lamps, my neighbour on the next mat woke with a start and plunged in surprise directly from his dream onto our pale figures. Behind the partitions, pipes sang. I thought I could see us from afar in a mirror suspended on the wall, and I realised that the frame of the mirror was a window opening to other windows, to other lamps, to other smokers … Singapore has its own Luna Park. It even has two. Some French friends, the Coupeaus, took us to dinner at the oldest, the New World. No whites. Here, the intermingled races separate to sit at the theatre. Chinese theatre, Malay theatre, Muslim theatre, Japanese theatre, so close is one to the other that the music and the dialogues become confused … during the preparations for the meal, we ate little skewers of meat with spices, at an Arab open air kitchen. The skewers were cooked over coals, dipped in a half-peppery, half-sugary reddish gold sauce. The dish was the best that I have tasted in the Orient."

The planters

At the end of the 19th century, Singapore remained a land of plantations. While some crops such as nutmeg failed, others were cultivated with great success.

Léopold Chasseriau, one of Singapore's great planters

In the mid-19th century, a Frenchman named Donnadieu settled in Penang and grew sugar cane on his plantation in the Val d'Or. In 1850, Léopold Chasseriau, a 25-year-old Bordeaux native, came to the Malay Peninsula to try his luck. He arrived from Mauritius, where he had some experience in agriculture, and he joined forces with Donnadieu.

Five years later, Chasseriau set up his own plantation, the Ara Rendang Sugar Estate, which he renamed Malakoff to commemorate the French victory in the Crimean War. He also built a factory to refine the sugar, with machinery brought from France. At the beginning of the 1870s, he sold Malakoff to a European, and moved to Singapore with his family.

Donnadieu, meanwhile, came to a tragic end. "Murdered by pirates" was the headline of *The Straits Times*. The French Consul, Gautier, wrote: "Donnadieu was assassinated on his boat on his way to his plantation, and his manservant was in league with the assassins."

In his diary, Henry Keppel also reported the return of Donnadieu's body to Europe: "To preserve it, the body was sealed in a large cask and filled with rum. Sailors were notoriously superstitious in those days, and so the contents of the cask were withheld from the crew. Nevertheless, it didn't take them long to find out that the cask in the hold contained rum. Blissfully unaware of what

OPPOSITE TOP: Pierre Loti (1850–1923). French Navy officer and writer, and also a member of the Académie Française in 1892.

OPPOSITE TOP RIGHT: Tanjong Katong, seaside villa, 1916. The Eurasian enclaves in Singapore were originally in the Waterloo Street and Selegie Road areas. Later the community bought houses in the Katong and Upper Serangoon areas.

OPPOSITE CENTRE: Victor Segalen (1878–1919), a French naval doctor, ethnographer, archaeologist, writer, poet, explorer, art-theorist, linguist and literary critic.

OPPOSITE BOTTOM: Jules Verne (1828–1905), the French author who pioneered the science fiction genre.

TOP: Drawing of Singapore, in Jules Verne's *Around the World in Eighty Days*, first edition, 1873.

the cask contained, every drop of the rum was tapped off by the time the ship reached port."

Léopold Chasseriau very soon headed the largest tapioca plantation on the island, which covered 1,200 hectares of land in Bukit Timah. His plantation rapidly became a model for the entire southern Malay Peninsula. It included three processing factories with steam-powered machinery. Chasseriau became known for his strictness with his workforce. The team leaders, *mandur*, urged the coolies on by shouting *Jalan! Jalan!*, and another *mandur* watched these team leaders. The seats of the coolies' trousers were regularly inspected to see if they were dusty from sitting on the ground to rest.

Chasseriau also embarked on the cultivation of coffee, and was the first to import a more resistant African strain from Liberia. When he retired, he left the property to one of his brothers. In 1885, the business became a public company with a capital of $250,000, of which only 120,000 was paid in. In 1889, only 800 acres of land remained under cultivation. Léopold Chasseriau died in an accident in Aden in 1891—he was around 66 years old.

The company very quickly went into liquidation. In 1898, the land and the property were reclaimed by the Singapore Municipality, to become part of the reservoir system. The "Chasseriau planters and manufacturers" brothers still

retained two profitable plantations on Mount Pleasant, which were known as Tasek and Champedah, as well as a gutta-percha factory. They worked with Alsagoff and Co, producing mainly coffee, pepper, tapioca and sugar cane. They also became involved with Clément Favre, a Frenchman who had pineapple plantations in Malaya.

In 1901, the house on the Chasseriau Estate plantation was sold. On 18 August 1902, the Swiss Rifle Club opened on Bukit Tinggi, where it is still known by residents as the Chasseriau Estate.

Original drawing by Marion Cordonnier, *Plantation*.

Gutta-percha fascinates the French

The name gutta-percha (*Palaquium percha*) comes from the Malay words *getah* (rubber), and *perca* (cloth strip). It is a tropical evergreen tree which can reach 30 metres in height. It produces a yellowish-brown, leathery-looking latex. To harvest the substance, the tree is cut down and rings are cut in its bark. When heated, gutta-percha takes on a plastic-like appearance and is highly water resistant.

The first samples, sent in 1843 to the Royal Society of Arts in London, were of particular interest to Michael Faraday, a physician and chemist known for his work in the field of electromagnetism and electrochemistry.

Several varieties of tree provide latex of this kind, notably *Isonandra gutta*, from the Sapotaceae family, which was grown in Singapore but has largely disappeared due to over-exploitation. The plantations which had been established in 1847 were decimated in 1857 due to the high demand for gutta-percha following the discovery of its insulating properties and resistance to seawater. In 1851, for example, during the laying of the telegraphic cable between Great Britain and France, gutta-percha was used to protect the underwater electrical cables.

To avoid destroying the trees, new extraction processes were tried out. When the trees were grown on plantations, their fresh leaves were chopped off, crushed and boiled in water. The rubber was then separated and compressed into blocks. In 1892, a French chemist, Dieudonné Rigole, established the Gutta-percha Manufacturing Company Limited, to extract latex, and he established his operations on Pulau Ubin. Perhaps this is why the island has a waterway named *Sungei Perancis*, literally "the French river".

Rigole became partners with two other Frenchmen, Arnaud and Sérullas, and the trio tested a new extraction process, using the leaves and buds, which contain higher amounts of gutta-percha. The partners began to feud with each other, and exchanged impolite letters which were published in *The Straits Times*. Sérullas began to doubt the efficacy of the new extraction process, and accused Rigole of fraud. The company did not survive.

Gutta-percha continued to pre-occupy the French in Singapore, both planters and traders. The Chasseriau brothers, in partnership with Favre and Co, bought dried gutta-percha leaves to process and trade.

In 1902, some 14,000 gutta-percha trees were planted on Bukit Timah, but their fruit was unfortunately attacked by hordes of small bats, which were impossible to kill with a rifle. The seeds did not reach maturity, and the plants were unable to reproduce.

For some, such as Adolphe Combanaire, who spent 20 years of his life in or around Singapore, gutta-percha was a veritable passion. In his book, *In the Land of the Headhunters: Across Borneo*, published in 1902, he recounted how he crossed the entire island of Borneo in search of these trees.

However, the exploitation of gutta-percha would soon be replaced by the intensive cultivation of rubber.

Henri Fauconnier: A rubber pioneer

At the start of the 20th century, the young Henri Fauconnier left his native Charente, where his family owned a cognac business. With the death of his father and the lacklustre state of the business, he left for England where he taught in a school on the south coast—and learned English. One morning, a classified advertisement in a newspaper caught his attention: planting sago in Sabah (a Malay enclave in Borneo) was an opportunity not to be missed. Fauconnier seized the idea and, thanks to a childhood friend, Franck Posth, who provided some capital, set off in March 1905 from Marseille together with Jean Audoin, another young man from the Charente area.

Once in Singapore, however, they discovered that there was no future in sago, and, on the advice of local British rubber planters, changed their plans. One of the planters, a Mr Bailey, took them on as trainees. The two young adventurers then found a plot of land and settled in the middle of the jungle in Rantau Panjang, beyond the Selangor river.

In 1906, Fauconnier met Adrien Hallet, a Belgian agronomist and banker, who during his port call in Singapore had heard of these Frenchmen who had settled in Malaya. Three years later, with the help of his mother, Fauconnier bought some land, built the Maison des Palmes there, and established the Société des Plantations Fauconnier et Posth with Hallet's help. The plantation operated well and rapidly became a benchmark for other planters.

During a trip to Sumatra with Hallet, Fauconnier discovered the oil palm, and brought a few plants back to Malaya. From 1910 onwards, the Fauconnier clan rebuilt itself in Malaya with the arrival of his family and friends from Charente. However, the First World War shattered Fauconnier's momentum. He returned to his lands in 1919 to address the overproduction crisis, and established

OPPOSITE TOP: Inscribed "Packing gutta-percha at Ross's godown", 1870's. A godown in East Asia refers to a warehouse, or a storehouse for goods at a port.

OPPOSITE BOTTOM: Adolphe Combanaire (1859–1939).

TOP: Henri Fauconnier (1879–1973). He was a French writer, known mainly for his novel, *Malaysia*, which won the Prix Goncourt in 1930. He was part of the Groupe de Barbezieux, which comprised the writers of three Charentais families: Fauconnier, Boutelleau and Delamain, who were childhood friends in the town of Barbezieux, in the Charente *département*, France.

LEFT: Henri Fauconnier at a rubber plantation in Malaya.

BELOW: Fruit sellers, postcard.

OPPOSITE TOP: Advertisement for Bastiani 's shop on High Street, *The Straits Times*, 29 December 1894.

OPPOSITE BELOW: Original drawing by Marion Cordonnier, *The Bastianis*.

SOCFIN (Société financière des caoutehoues). In 1925, he left for Tunisia and settled in Radès.

In 1910, Bishop Barillon of the MEP traced the history of the plantations in Singapore: "25 years ago, spices and sugar cane still reigned. Beautiful gardens of nutmeg and clove trees sprawled over the flanks of the mountains, while immense sugar cane plantations spread their luxuriant vegetation over the plains. Gradually, however, the prices of these goods dropped until their cultivation was no longer profitable. Coffee cultivation suffered the same fate as that of spices, and then it was the era of the Rubber Boom. The country is now covered with rubber plantations, and we are at the height of the rubber era. This transformation is no doubt due to the progress which the industry has made in the manufacture of automobiles, aeroplanes and other similar products."

As Singapore was not large enough for their cultivation, rubber trees, palm trees, coconut trees and spices gradually disappeared from the island's countryside to make space for the city and its port activities.

The traders

There were three main reasons why French traders were keen to set up shop in Singapore: in keeping with British tradition, it was open to all communities, the opening of the Suez Canal brought more shipping companies, and the population was increasing. The majority of French traders imported wine, perfumes, construction materials and foodstuffs, and they all gained first-hand knowledge of the local market.

Joseph Bastiani and the pineapple trade

Joseph Bastiani was born in Corsica, the youngest in a family of ten children. His father died while Joseph was still young. He and his elder brother established a modest fruit and vegetable business, using the new process of canning. At the age of 16, Bastiani left Corsica to seek his fortune on the continent. He worked for several years in the vineyards of Bordeaux, Burgundy and the Loire Valley. Decorated during the war of 1870 and suffering from a broken heart, he signed up as a sailor on a Messageries Maritimes vessel at the end of the conflict. During one journey, he met the writer Joseph Conrad, who recommended that he settle in Singapore. Shortly thereafter, in 1874, Bastiani moved to Singapore.

Bastiani discovered that millions of good quality pineapples were being wasted due to spoilage. With his brother, Bastiani established a pineapple cannery at No. 5, High Street, as well as a boarding and lodging house in their home at Tanglin. Their lodgers were often French, Swiss or people passing through who preferred to avoid colonial society in the major hotels. At Bastiani's, the atmosphere was fun, and this attracted a certain kind of traveller. Georges Cassel,

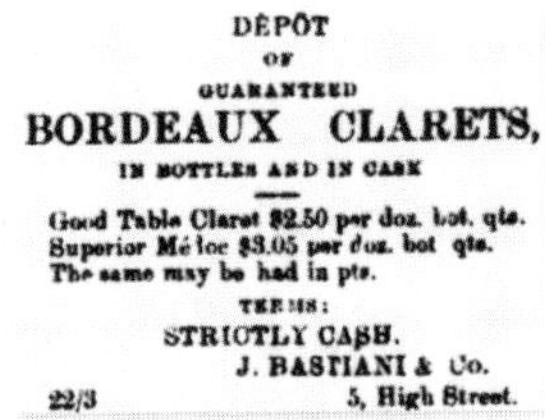
DÉPÔT
OF
GUARANTEED
BORDEAUX CLARETS,
IN BOTTLES AND IN CASK
Good Table Claret $2.50 per doz. bot. qts.
Superior Médoc $3.05 per doz. bot qts.
The same may be had in pts.
TERMS:
STRICTLY CASH.
J. BASTIANI & Co.
22/3 5, High Street.

a Frenchman who worked for the trader Delahaye, described Joseph Bastiani in his diary as "a little round man, with an excessively plump, badly shaven face with little black eyes and a very loud laugh, like those folks from the South who work on the French steamships, and who tell you tall stories while shouting very loudly". Cassel also wrote about Bastiani's wife: "… she wasn't aware that she was in Singapore. She was a large, honest woman, who had been brought up to run a shop in Marseille. In Singapore, she withdrew herself; she was dull, and no longer had any character. She needed her country around her."

Bastiani quickly expanded his business. The two brothers brought in French machinery for the manufacture of canned fruit. In 1882, they announced that new imported products were now on sale in the shops at Nos. 6, 7, 8 and 9, High Street, including thoroughly European delights which the settlers missed: Roquefort and Camembert, mustard, stuffed pork knuckle, chocolate, Lyon sausage, liver pâté with truffles, galantine, ortolans, black pudding, sausages, fresh butter, nougat, liqueurs, red and white wine and perfumes.

The Bastiani brothers then branched out into confectionery and cakes which were in high demand for receptions, all the while producing approximately 5,000 cases of pineapple daily, and experimenting with canning other tropical fruit such as mangosteen in syrup, which won first prize at the Paris International Exhibition of 1889.

J. Bastiani and Co, which can still be found on High Street, also installed machinery for the manufacture of soft drinks, and imported the first bottles of Badoit mineral water. The company developed a trade in wine, which it distributed across Asia. The Bastiani brothers further expanded their business by importing construction materials. In 1892, after almost 20 years in Singapore, Bastiani decided it was time to retire, and handed the business over to Joseph Cardella, his brother-in-law. Bastiani, then 51 years old, settled in Nice where he built a new canned fruit factory.

Meanwhile, Cardella failed to manage the business in Singapore properly and in April 1896 established a separate wine business at No. 15, Raffles Place. Bastiani, unwilling to watch his business falter, returned to the island to take the business back in hand. He discovered that Cardella had sold some of the canning machinery to a Mr Gaggino, and that the stickers on the boxes manufactured by Gaggino were identical to his own—and that he was being sued for plagiarism. In the summer of 1900, however, Bastiani sold his pineapple cannery, and then, in spring 1902, the entire business.

At 60, Bastiani finally retired for good in Nice, where he died 21 years later. *The Straits Times* dated 5 January 1925 paid homage to him: "Of a rough exterior, Mr Bastiani nevertheless possessed a generous heart and an appeal to him for charity was never turned down."

Clouët—a forgotten name, but an enduring business

Alfred Clouët was one of the first French pioneers to establish himself in Singapore with a flourishing company. His story is one of both legend and economic success. The story goes that Clouët, a young Breton enlisted in the colonial troops on their way to Indochina, landed during a port call in Singapore in 1892, and, unable to resist the charms of the island, did not return to his ship. To earn a living, he opened a cannery for sardines in oil, packed into flat, rectangular "Portuguese" boxes. But how much of this is true? There is a certain degree of doubt, as Clouët and his wife Gabrielle are listed as passengers arriving in Singapore in 1893 on a Messageries Maritimes ship from Marseille. Did he return to fetch his wife after a few months of investigation in Singapore? The historical record is unclear.

The French emblem in Singapore

If the story of his arrival in Singapore remains somewhat hazy, that of his business is not. As a symbol for his brand of sardines, Clouët chose the rooster, the French emblem for *par excellence*. The branding took on an indigenous flavour when Chinese traders started referring to the *Cock Brand* of sardines as "*Ayam Brand*" (*ayam* being the Malay word for chicken, or rooster).

Clouët rapidly integrated into the island's colonial society. Initially at No. 79, Waterloo Street, he then moved his offices to No. 3, Malacca Street. His business prospered and gained recognition: at the Paris Universal Exhibition of 1900, he won two gold medals for his products. Clouët became a notable member of the community, and even acted as the Belgian Consul during the absence of M.L. Groetaers. He also attempted to convince his countrymen to settle in Singapore, writing in a local newspaper "that French capitalists will easily find investment opportunities on the Malay Peninsula".

On 23 March 1901, however, his warehouses on Malacca Street burned down. Undeterred by the setback, Clouët set up temporary trading premises at No. 8, Battery Road, and later at No. 7, Raffles Quay. Another property that he once owned was a cottage located at No. 105 Orchard Road, which had the distinction of being one of the first homes in Singapore to be supplied with gas.

In addition to his sardine and fish cannery, he also traded in perfumes, under the name *Chop satu ayam* (One Rooster Brand). Like Joseph Bastiani, Clouët's business was threatened by counterfeits: he discovered that a Mr A. Gaffoor was selling similar perfumed products under the name *Chop dua ayam* (Two Roosters Brand). He took Gaffoor to court, and won.

A beautiful partnership

Victor Clumeck, born in Jaffa, was brought up in the French-speaking Jewish community of Cairo. He was still young when he first arrived in Singapore with his mother. At the age of ten, he started working as an apprentice in a shop; at 14, he found work in the offices of Maison Clouët and Co. In 1903, he formed a "good match" with Marie, one of the daughters of a rich trader, Frankel, in a ceremony attended by the Consul of France and his wife.

Four years later, Messrs. Clumeck and Clouët entered into a partnership under the name A. Frankel and Co, and imported construction materials. But the company became known as A. Clouët and Co.

During the First World War, Clouët's sons, Clarence and Francis, left for the front. Their mother, who also returned to Paris, died in 1914. The Clumeck and Clouët business continued to prosper, however, and Alfred Clouët retired to Nice many years later, passing away in 1965 just short of his 100th birthday.

OPPOSITE TOP: Alfred Clouët.

OPPOSITE BOTTOM: Logo of A.Clouët and Co Ltd, which was founded in 1892.

BELOW: Advertisement for the car "De Dion-Bouton", *The Straits Times*, 7 September 1904. De Dion-Bouton was a French carmaker and railcar manufacturer operating from 1883 to 1932. The company was founded by the Marquis Jules-Albert de Dion, Georges Bouton and his brother-in-law Charles Trépardoux.

The Dupire brothers

Louis, Jules and Paul Dupire arrived in Singapore in 1897. They initially imported Mumm champagne, Dubonnet tonic wine and Contrexeville mineral water, and from 1903, dairy products such as Isigny butter. In December 1904, the Dupire Brothers business issued a calendar for the new year, which came with a sample of sterilised Brittany milk.

From their premises at No. 8, Raffles Quay, the Dupire brothers also imported De Dion-Bouton cars—at the time the world's leading car brand—fitted with extra strong Michelin tyres. In 1906, their ads proclaimed that the prices they charged were lower than in London. In February 1908, the Public Works Department purchased a De Dion-Bouton in Singapore for the Superintendent of Works and Surveys (this un-British purchase was sharply criticised in the *Penang Gazette*).

Another article in 1906 reported the following mishap: "A week ago Paul Dupire was driving a motor car along Collyer Quay. His brother who holds a licence to drive was with him. Mr D'Arcy Symonds, assistant Superintendant of Police obtained a summon against P. Dupire and, yesterday he responded pleading that he was learning to drive and had his brother with him. He was charged $5 and it was said that learners must take their lessons in districts where there was less traffic than at Collyer Quay."

The Dupire brothers later acquired a franchise for Michelin tyres, and the reins of the brand. They also imported a six-cylinder Bayard-Clément sports car, which could reach speeds of 103 miles per hour. In 1909, the Dupire brothers passed their business to M.W. Lambert.

The Dupire family was by now well-established in Singapore. In 1911, little Marie-Thérèse Dupire (the daughter of one of the brothers) was one of the ladies of honour at a grand wedding held at the Cathedral of the Good Shepherd.

Like many entrepreneurs at the beginning of the century, the Dupire brothers expanded their commercial activities. In 1920, Louis and Paul entered into a partnership with the Johnstons, who were gambier, pepper and copra planters. In the end, however, like many French traders upon retirement, the Dupires sold their business and returned to France. Louis Dupire settled in Hyères, close to Toulon, where he died at the age of 73.

Confectionery, pastries and bakeries

Clément Favre was the first confectioner to settle in Singapore. He arrived in 1882 from Marlioz, in Haute-Savoie, and provided home deliveries. Orders were taken by Mrs Zimmermann, whose husband Charles ran a shop at No. 32, Killiney Road. For Christmas, Favre advertised: "… cream chocolate, biscuits from Paris, nougat from Montélimar, quince paste, European and Singapore crystallised fruit …"

In August 1883, he opened a shop at No. 113, Hill Street with M.L. Duc. His advertisements featured enticing sweets: "… glazed chestnuts, a large assortment of candied fruit: strawberries, raspberries, lemons, ginger, pineapple, mangosteens, jams and marmalades made from local fruit such as guava, pineapple ...". In October 1884, he opened a candied fruit-and-pineapple packing factory and teamed up with Léon Goupille five years later. In Paris, he won two gold medals for his products.

Clément Favre died in Singapore in 1889. His business continued, however, thanks to Goupille, who hired a pastry confectioner from Paris in 1891. In 1896, Goupille moved to Parsee Lodge on Robinson Road and worked with the Chasseriau brothers in the gutta-percha and pineapple business, leaving his pastry business to a Chinese company, Tan Lian Swee and Co.

In January 1895, Lucien Beaulieu opened the *French Bakery* at Nos. 206–209 Orchard Road. The new bakery was spacious, modern and well-aired with a cement floor and tiled walls. Its ovens produced 1,000 loaves daily, deliveries of which started as early as 4am. He also produced pastries, including wedding cakes, and *crèmes au chocolat*. Later, besides bread and cakes, he sold perfumes, soaps, wines, cheeses (Port-Salut and Brie), Lyon sausage, and "freshly picked" cherries and prunes.

In 1896, his wife passed away. A religious service was organised at the Cathedral of the Good Shepherd in the presence of the entire French community and the Russian and Italian Consuls. Beaulieu's trade collapsed six months after his wife's death, and the business went into liquidation.

In March the following year, Beaulieu teamed up with M.A. Launay, but their business was unsuccessful and he was sued for his debts in 1902. He was unable to pay for his stock of liqueurs purchased in France. To make ends meet, he rented out four of his houses, but was forced to sell his shop in the end. Finally, Beaulieu sold everything he owned and, as he was ill, was quarantined on St John's Island in September 1903.

Some members of the French community were involved in illegal trading. *The Straits Times* of 12 March 1906 reported that a French woman, Madame Guyot, had appeared at court for the illegal transport of spirits. Her cargo contained 15 cases of Clairet, as well as a case of gin. Through an interpreter, she told her story: she had arrived from Hong Kong and, so she claimed, the wine was spoiled and she hoped to turn it into vinegar. She added that she was unaware that a permit was required for the transport of such items, and she offered to pay what was due to the court. The shipment was confiscated.

French-run hotels

In 1858, Mr and Mrs Casteleyns opened the Hotel de l'Europe at No. 36, Hill Street. A classified advertisement in *The Straits Times*, written in French and English, recommended it for its cleanliness, comfort, service and in particular its "excellent French cuisine, overseen by Mrs Casteleyns herself". In 1865, the couple bought up the Hotel de l'Espérance. They renamed it after their first establishment, the Hôtel de l'Europe. In 1869, Casteleyns handed over the business to Mrs Hjelmstrom and Mrs Becker. Later, the Hôtel de l'Europe was transformed into a rival of the Raffles Hotel, under the name Grand Hotel de l'Europe. In 1910, it changed hands once again, and became the Adis Building Hotel.

French standards of excellence in the hospitality and restaurant industries were widely recognised in Singapore. In December 1873, J.A. Laurent, a French chef from the Ecole Supérieure Hôtelière de Paris, took over the Clarendon Hotel on Beach Road, which had previously been run by Mr Emmerson.

LEFT: Hotel de l'Europe (c. 1900).

MAISON F. PAUL & CO.

FRENCH HAIR DRESSING SALOON
NEW INSTALLATION
MECHANICAL BRUSHES.
FOUR SEATS.
JUST ARRIVED.

Pertumery from the best Makers of Paris and London.

Hats, stylish neck-ties and hosiery for Gentlemen.

FANCY GOODS
FOR LADIES AND GENTLEMEN.
43-A BATTERY ROAD.

26 96/5

TOP: Advertisement for the French hairdressing salon Maison F. Paul and Co., published in *The Straits Times*, 18 July 1895.

"Chic" hairdressing salons

In colonial Singapore, Parisian chic was very much in fashion. Having worked in London, Paris and Brussels, a certain Monsieur Paul opened a salon at the corner of Malacca Street and Raffles Place in 1892. Maison F. Paul and Co. dressed ladies' hair at a moderate price, for balls as well as for weddings and everyday receptions. Monsieur Paul's salon offered home services: a simple telephone call would bring a hairdresser to your home. Monsieur Paul also imported perfumes from around the world, and prepared wigs suited to each client.

A decade later, Gédéon Sabatier opened a hairdressing salon at Raffles Place: the Royal Hairdressing Saloon [sic]. He was married to a Japanese woman, Chio, and ran his salon with an assistant, Jules Muller. However it was not for his hairdressing skills that Sabatier would become notorious. He defrayed his chronic debts by trading in counterfeit bank notes. In 1913, he was arrested by the police, together with his wife and assistant. Chemicals, a printing press and samples of fake 1, 5 and 10 dollar notes were found in their apartment at No. 77, Prinsep Street. Sabatier and his accomplices were sentenced to five years in prison. Shortly after, Sabatier fell severely ill, lost his sight and died. The Royal Hairdressing Saloon was then bought by M.E. Castanier, a theatre fanatic who would make up and coif the local actors before their performances. It was Castanier who prepared the young ladies of the Convent of the Infant Jesus (CHIJ) in May 1914 for their play, *Christopher Columbus*, given in honour of Bishop Barillon.

The first large French companies

In 1909, Victor Segalen wrote about Singapore: "it unloads and re-loads." Indeed, Singapore is a hub, and the activities of the free port are of crucial importance. Most of the great shipping companies began to make port calls there: Messageries Maritimes, Chargeurs Réunis, Peninsular & Oriental Steam Navigation Company (P&O), Ben and City Lines, Nippon Yusen Kaisha.

Singapore was also a crossroads for trade in the neighbouring archipelagos. Capital began to flow in. The quay area expanded to accommodate the ships which grew in size. All of the quays were connected to conduits which supplied clean freshwater to ships in port. The port also provided warehouses for the storage of non-perishable goods such as alcohol and tobacco, as well as 'godowns', warehouses for temporary storage. The coal refuelling station, which was vital for the steamers, was opened in 1859.

OPPOSITE: Singapore-Coal Park-after sketches by M. Tetevuide, 1876. This is a view of a steamer docking at a coaling station in New Harbour.

The Messageries Maritimes

In the 1880s, a journey from Marseille to Yokohama took 42 days and 21 hours, and 39 days and 16 hours on the return journey, during the winter monsoon. Every two weeks, a ship would depart Marseille at 10am. A fleet of eight liners provided service on the Far East route. In the face of competition from other European companies, Messageries Maritimes chose to provide a higher standard of on-board service, which attracted a great number of English passengers.

The Singapore agency

Opened by Paul Brasier de Thuy in 1862, the Singapore agency of Messageries Maritimes was initially located on Flint Street, before moving to Telok Blangah in 1867, close to the premises of the Peninsular & Oriental Steam Navigation Company and within easy reach of the quays. Brasier moved into a property rented by the company at St James on New Harbour, close to the warehouses, the *entrepôts* and the port. The Brasier family, however, complained of the noise, even at night, around the docks where the coolies shouted incessantly. Brasier noted that an equally comfortable home could easily be found nearby, at a much lower rent. The nicest houses in Singapore could be rented at the time for between $60 and $100 per month. Fifty years later, however, in 1913, the Messageries Maritimes agency continued to rent the same premises.

The agency had commercial as well as technical functions. The loading and unloading of goods were the responsibility of the ship's captain. He would call upon a businessman who hired day-workers called coolies. Agency staff were always on the look-out for potential customers, both ships arriving in port and traders needing to ship their goods abroad. This work required a good knowledge of businesses in the region, as well as constant communications with the other agencies of the company. Agents also formed partnerships with producers and traders. They were furthermore required to attract passengers by offering reductions on ticket prices for large families. They promoted ticket sales via posters and classified advertisements, and published guides for the passengers.

FROM THE MESSAGERIES IMPÉRIALES TO THE MESSAGERIES MARITIMES

Founded in 1796 under the name Compagnie des Messageries Nationales, the company, operated mail coaches on behalf of the French State. The stagecoaches also sometimes carried passengers. Railways rapidly replaced horses, whereas the development of inter-Mediterranean trade and the colonisation of Algeria in 1830 created new requirements. In 1851, the company opened its first maritime route, between Marseille and the Italian port of Civatavecchia.

Besides the mail and goods, the company found itself carrying increasing numbers of passengers. Far Eastern routes were opened between 1862 and 1865. On 17 November 1869, it inaugurated the Suez Canal. In 1882, the company began operation to Australia, followed by New Caledonia and the New Hebrides.

During the First World War, the company's liners were transformed into hospital ships, and were also used to transport troops. A third of the fleet was lost during the conflict. This did not however prevent an "Around the World" route from being inaugurated in 1919 with the *El Kantara*, the first French vessel to pass through the Panama Canal.

Steamers became more modern with the introduction of diesel power. Interior décor was elaborate: luxurious saloons, comfortable cabins, vast dining rooms and refined cuisine all ensured that the journey became a veritable cruise. During the Second World War, the ships were once again requisitioned, leading to the destruction of half of the fleet. In 1949, the new liner *La Marseillaise* began operating on the Far East route. In 1977, the company was renamed Compagnie Générale Maritime.

TOP: Unloading goods from a French steamer at Borneo Wharf, 1907.

OPPOSITE TOP: Workers loading coal onto a French steamer, c.1910. This postcard was part of a menu for first-class passengers.

OPPOSITE BELOW: Official document recording Brasier's nomination as the interim Consul, 1883.

They normally also took care of harbour dues and customs fees but not in Singapore, which is a free port. In 1880, the agent noted in his report that Singapore's port infrastructure was still unsuited to the size of the Company's ships, and that the warehouses were too far from the quays.

The arrival of a vessel generated intense activity. The passengers would first of all disembark, followed by valuable packages. The agent kept a close eye on packages as they came off the ship, as the Company would have to pay compensation for any lost or stolen packages.

The port grew rapidly: 1913 saw the inauguration of King's Dock, the largest dry dock in the Far East. The Lagoon Dock basin, almost completed at the time, would be able to accommodate up to eight large vessels.

The agency was also responsible for dealing with any breakdowns on board ship, as well as for replenishing their coal supplies. Singapore was the fourth refuelling point on the route, after Port Said, Aden and Colombo. 1,750 tonnes of coal were required for a journey from Europe to Singapore.

Diseases and quarantines

The agent also had to deal with health issues and any quarantining which might be required. A report from 1913 states that Singapore's climate was debilitating for Europeans as well as "for the Indians and Chinese who form the principal population of the Straits Settlements. The mortality rate is dropping because the local Government is improving the living conditions of the working class on an ongoing basis: food is more abundant, water is better distributed, housing is more spacious and airier, and lastly, every means is being used to protect children from the frightening mortality. The illnesses which claim the most victims are malaria, tuberculosis, beriberi and dysentery; smallpox, cholera and plague only appear in the form of transient epidemics."

Staff

The local agent was provided with a clerk appointed by the Administrative Committee in Paris, as well as employees recruited locally by the agent himself.

PAUL BRASIER DE THUY (1829–1887)

Paul Brasier de Thuy was born in 1829 in Paris. He worked for the Messageries Impériales and was despatched to Singapore in 1862 to open the first agency there. His second wife, Camille Doumerc, accompanied him but died in 1867. They had two children, Josèphe Henriette Marie and Marie Joseph René.

Brasier lived for a long time in Singapore. The Brasier family was close to the missionaries and their children went to their schools. Brasier played a prominent role in colonial society. He was a member of the jury in the Court of Law in Singapore for several years, and played an important role with the Consul, as he was often asked to act as a witness when formalising the deaths of sailors passing through, clergymen or of any other French citizen deceased in Singapore.

On 5 April 1875, Brasier gave away his 17-year-old daughter in marriage to his chief clerk, Mr de Guigné, who, at the age of 26, was also the Deputy Chancellor of the Consulate. The bride gave birth to a daughter the same year, but passed away two years later. On 2 August 1887, he was awarded the Medal of the Green Dragon of Annam for services rendered to the French government of Cochinchina.

The Brasier family stayed in Singapore for a few more years. In June 1889, Brasier's son married the daughter of Charles Alfred de Bure, the Messageries Maritimes agent in Singapore.

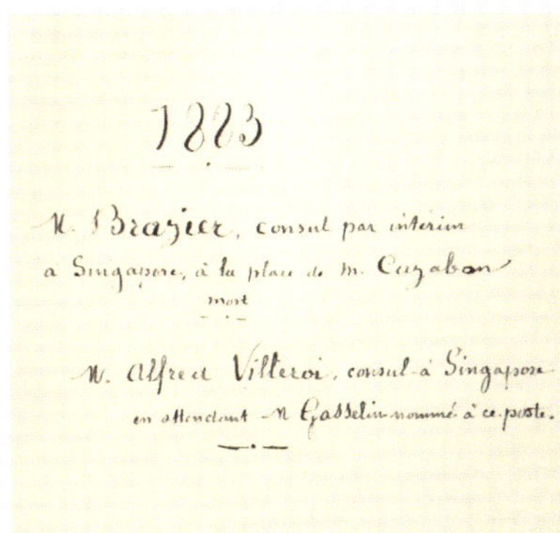
1883

M. Brasier, consul par intérim à Singapore, à la place de M. Cazabon mort

M. Alfred Villeroi, consul à Singapore en attendant M. Gasselin nommé à ce poste.

During his first years, Paul Brasier complained that he had too few expatriate staff compared to the other line agencies, forcing him to leave the agency under the control of local employees during the arrival or departure of a ship, as the agent and clerk were required to be on board. He also said that salaries were too low, given the cost of living in Singapore. "The cost of material goods," he wrote, "and rent have risen considerably here, and what might have appeared at one time to be relatively generous is barely sufficient today."

Supplies

The company staked its reputation on the quality of its services. In 1887, the agent noted that travellers in all classes were generally satisfied with the food, which they found more plentiful, varied and well-prepared than anywhere else. In 1917, Joseph de Courtois, the local agent, reported that Singapore Cold Storage provided the ships with meat, game, butter and other frozen items, mostly originating from Australia, but in ever-decreasing quantities, hence the constant increase in prices. Fresh produce and other supplies were provided by the local supplier Mohamed and Co. from the First World War onwards. Ice remained at the relatively low price of $15.50 per tonne.

A competitor to the Messageries Maritimes: Chargeurs Réunis

In the wake of the economic recovery following the war of 1870, the Fabre family founded the Compagnie des Chargeurs Réunis. Between 1884 and 1886, Chargeurs Réunis transported troops to Annam and Tonkin on behalf of the French Navy, and took on board passengers and goods for the return journey.

In November 1900, a regular route to Indochina was established. Steamers left Dunkirk on the 25th of each month, calling at Le Havre, Bordeaux and Marseille before passing through the Suez Canal, and reaching Colombo, Singapore, Saigon and Haiphong.

During the First World War, some vessels were converted into hospital ships or troop transports, while others became refrigerator ships, supplying the troops with meat. Regular services continued as well as they could, but the fleet suffered major losses during the war. In 1921, the Indochina route offered departures for Tonkin every 28 days, and every 14 days by 1930. In 1935, Chargeurs Réunis established a transport service in the China seas, mainly between Tonkin and Cochinchina, transporting coolies, and carrying loads of cement and phosphate.

Moine Comte, Chargeurs Réunis' first agent

Victor Charles Valtriny arrived in Singapore in 1854. He began to trade in wines and liqueurs, and then mineral water, and gradually built up an important position in 'trading'. He died in Paris in 1894. His son Émile took charge of liquidating his

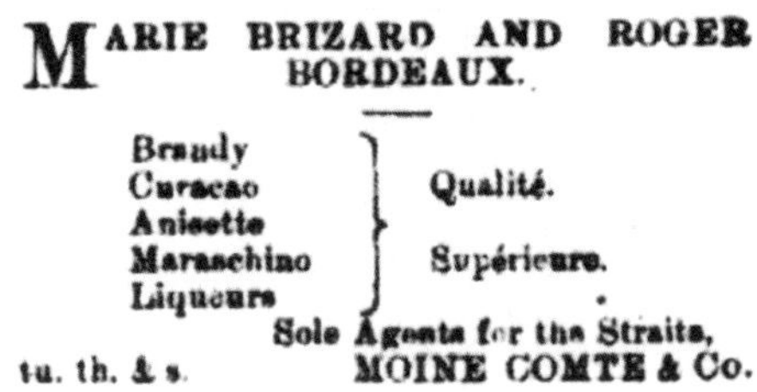

father's business, and Denis Moine Comte took over the business. He continued to import spirits and very quickly became the agent for Chargeurs Réunis. The Moine Comte company is one of the oldest in Singapore. It had its beginnings as Renard and Co. from 1840–2, and then became Valtriny in 1854, before it was renamed Moine Comte.

In 1906, Moine Comte was named an advisor on external trade to France. He was then working with M.C. Rousselat de Saint-Céran, who was later one of the first Frenchmen to leave for the front in August 1914 for the First World War. Denis Moine Comte also left Singapore and only returned five years later, on board the liner *André Lebon*. In 1923, Denis Moine Comte, who worked with Jacques Orner, handed over the business to Saint-Céran and C. Gayet, but the company continued to exist under the name of its founder, who also retained the right to establish a business in Marseille under his name. Denis Moine Comte died at the age of 70 in 1937, in Marseille. As a sign of mourning, the offices in Singapore closed for a day.

Pioneers in finance: The Banque de l'Indochine

The Banque de l'Indochine established its first branch in Saigon in 1875. There were two banks behind the project: Comptoir d'Escompte de Paris (CEP) and Crédit Industriel et Commercial (CIC). They wanted to develop banking in the Far East, and to create a private bank which could issue currency to facilitate trade in Asia.

The Banque de l'Indochine was an independent company whose shareholders were wealthy individuals. The trading of shares was not a common practice at the time, and the investment was thus provided by businessmen, financiers and rich avant-garde citizens, as well as the major French banks.

By 1875, the Banque de l'Indochine was an issuing bank as well as a commercial bank, issuing currency in Cochinchina and in the French Indies, a right which the French State had awarded it for a period of 20 years. It was also able to provide loans and to cash cheques. This system of colonial banks already existed in France, but this marked a first in the Far East, where French interests were at the time more or less non-existent.

In 1876, the first Indochinese piastre notes were manufactured with a single printed signature, that of the administrator. The branch director, who was responsible for the number of notes issued, as well as the cashier, who was in charge of verifying payments, had to sign each note by hand. By March 1881, they had already signed 17,000 notes each! Chinese traders, who were already familiar with English banknotes from Singapore and Hong Kong, valued these new notes. Between 1885 and 1898, the Banque de l'Indochine established branches in Vietnam, Cambodia, New Caledonia, Siam, Hong Kong and Shanghai.

TOP: Advertisement for Moine Comte, published in *The Straits Times*, 28 February 1895.

The Singapore agency

However, the Banque de l'Indochine was not the first banking institution to come to Singapore. The first bank to become established here was the Union Bank of Calcutta in 1840, followed by the Oriental Bank in 1846, which was the first to issue notes. Chartered Bank arrived in 1859, followed by Hong Kong & Shanghai Banking in 1877. In 1888, the Netherlands Trading Society became an agent for the Banque de l'Indochine, Fourteen years later, City Bank of America opened its doors here.

The opening of the Singapore agency of Banque de l'Indochine in 1905 was in response to the increase in transactions between the Saigon branch, the Malay Peninsula and the island of Java. These transactions were varied, as Singapore imported rice, fish, raw silk, salt, charcoal, straw, pork, exported jute sacks, betel nuts, cotton, oil, gambier, wax, machinery and various foodstuffs to Saigon. According to *1905–1985: 80 Years of History of a French Bank in Singapore* by Amina Tyabji and Joëlle Fabry, the main French exports to Singapore were spirits, watches, silk fabric, umbrellas and dairy products.

In 1905, Léon Housset, who held the position of interim director in Saigon, opened the agency at No. 31, Raffles Place, in former bank premises which he rented from Mr Sarkies. He had three French colleagues: Messrs. Pollet, Osier and Redon. French staff numbers varied between four and five people until 1914. The branch's capital was 500,000 Straits Dollars.

The bank's commercial activities expanded rapidly. The bank was a three-week journey away from its headquarters in Paris, and the steamers of the Messageries Maritimes carried documents back and forth. At the time when the bank opened its agency in Singapore, these were the *Tourane*, *Tonkin* and *Calédonien* (*Tonkin* and *Calédonien* would be requisitioned during the First World War to provide postal services) and the *La Seyne*, which operated the route approximately once a month.

TOP: Office of Banque de l'Indochine, at the corner of D'Almeida Street and Malacca Street, 1912.

BELOW: Note of 100 Piastres, Banque de l'Indochine. The piastre de commerce was the currency of French Indochina between 1885 and 1952. It was subdivided into 100 cent, each of which was worth 5 sapeque.

OPPOSITE TOP: Advertisement for Michelin, featuring Bibendum running with his tyre,1925.

OPPOSITE BELOW: Office of Banque de l'Indochine, Raffles Place, 1905.

Staff living conditions

Apartments were built for the staff on the second floor of the Raffles Place office. Mr Housset, the director, rented a house for his family on Mount Elizabeth Road. Electricity replaced the oil lamps, and fans were substituted for the *pankas*, large hand-drawn fans suspended from the ceiling. The director requested a two-horse carriage befitting his status. From France he ordered a full dining service, including Limoges porcelain decorated with small floral motifs. He also requested a doctor and a telegraphic address for the bank.

In 1912, as the office lease was expiring, the bank acquired a building at the corner of D'Almeida Street and Malacca Street, which was then pulled down to make way for a new structure.

Plans were drawn up by the architect Donald McLeod Craik, and the building was erected by a French company, Brossard et Mopin (Brossard and Mopin). The Banque de l'Indochine would remain in this building until 1959, although it only occupied the ground floor, renting out the remainder of the premises. The basement was rented to the Michelin company, who stored tyres there. The first floor was rented to Fraser & Neave, Singapore's oldest non-alcoholic beverage company. The second floor housed Evatt, a currency exchange agent, while the third housed the Messageries Maritimes.

Local staff were recruited from among the Vietnamese community, who had the advantage of speaking French and knowing the bank. Indians from Pondicherry found employment here as well, for the same reasons. By and large, the members of staff worked for the bank faithfully and remained with the bank for as long as 20 to 30 years before handing over their positions to their sons.

The bank's customers

The Banque de l'Indochine specialised in loans and import-export transactions. Its first customers were Chettiars, traders from Southern India, but doing business proved difficult as their property was in India, and their guarantees were rather difficult to assess. The French working in the import-export business and the shipping companies (businesses such as Clouët, Moine-Comte, Messageries Maritimes) were also among their customers. Almost all of the French companies in Singapore were customers of the bank: the Société d'Oxygène et d'Acétylène d'Extrême-Orient, Michelin, the Société des Matières Premières Tropicales (SMPT) which transported rubber from Indochina and Malaya for processing by Michelin,

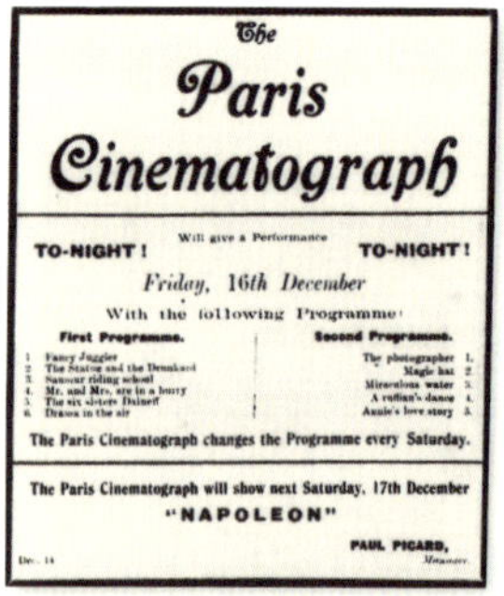

the Société française des Etains de Tekkah in Malaya, and the SOCFIN, founded by Henri Fauconnier. Chinese customers brought in by the *comprador* were initially thin on the ground, as they preferred to deal with the new Chinese banks whose employees spoke their language.

The Pathé Brothers Establishment

Charles Pathé, who in 1894 established a phonographic factory and shop in Paris, quickly realised the potential of the new industries of cinema and audio recordings. He went on to found Pathé Brothers Company with his brothers. Almost 60% of films and cinematographic equipment bore the Pathé logo.

In Singapore, where the entertainment industry was becoming established at the start of the century, Pathé cinematographic and recording products found a ready market. In 1904, the Lévy brothers, who had made their fortune in diamonds and were seeking ways to diversify their activities, imported films from companies such as Gaumont and Pathé. They also opened the first cinema in Singapore, the Paris Cinematograph.

PAUL PICARD AND THE FIRST CINEMA IN SINGAPORE: THE PARIS CINEMATOGRAPH

The first cinematographic projections in Singapore took place in the open air. The entrepreneur Paul Picard, together with the Lévy company, saw the potential of this new form of entertainment and opened Singapore's first enclosed cinema, the Paris Cinematograph. He rented a part of the Malay Theatre at No. 320, Victoria Street. The room was equipped with electric fans to ensure maximum comfort. Initially, Mr Picard was in charge of publicity and ticket sales as well as the music while the silent film was projected. Seat prices varied. A box seat cost a dollar, 60 cents for a reserved seat, and then 50, 30 or 20 cents for seats in categories 1–3. "Native ladies" paid 40 or 20 cents. The documentaries and feature films included *Le miroir de Cagliostro* by Georges Méliès, in 1899, and also *L'arrivée du train en gare de La Ciotat* by the Lumière brothers, in 1904. Other cinemas opened, including the French Cinematograph, the Matsuo Cinema, The Royal and Fernand Dreyfus' legendary Alhambra.

FAR LEFT: Movie poster *A Day At Singapore* by Gaston Méliès, George's brother, 1913. CENTRE: Georges Méliès (1861–1938). LEFT: The Lumière brothers, Auguste Marie Louis Nicolas (1862–1954) and Louis Jean (1864–1948).

In 1907, Mr Fernand Dreyfus was the sole representative for Pathé Brothers products in Singapore. At his shop at No. 19, Stamford Road, he sold cinematographic equipment, "talking machines", phonographs and records. He offered a catalogue of more than 20,000 titles in several languages. Observing the success of cinemas in Singapore, Dreyfus opened the Alhambra on Beach Road in December 1907. He screened Pathé films and documentaries exclusively. In 1909, he sold the business to the Chinese tycoon Tan Cheng Kee, but the Pathé Brothers Company retained a foothold in Singapore and its representatives, mostly Frenchmen such as Messrs. Maingaud, Huberdon and Donati, continued to sell records, films and cameras. By the end of the 1920s, however, against a background of economic crisis and increasing competition in the sector, the company closed down its Singapore branch.

Consular affairs: life in a diplomatic outpost

For Eugène Chaigneau as well as his successors, the main tasks of the French Consul were to represent France and to assist French citizens, whether they were settling in Singapore or passing through.

The consular services used the local press to keep abreast of local affairs and keep their countrymen informed about visa requirements, and in the event of war, mobilisation. The first newspaper to be printed in English in Singapore was the *Singapore Chronicle*, which appeared in 1824. In October 1835, the *Singapore Free Press and Mercantile Advertiser* also went on sale. On 15 July 1845, *The Straits Times* published its first edition, and the paper would sometimes include articles in French. Between April 1848 and May 1849, a bilingual English-French newspaper, *L'Observateur Français*, was available in Singapore. This paper, edited in Great Britain, was "a French journal of the political, commercial, and scientific news of the week."

The Consul of France also provided diplomatic representation for countries which had no official representative. For example, on 14 December 1914, *The Straits Times* announced that Belgian nationals were required to mobilise at the French Consulate. The issuing of visas was also the responsibility of the consular services. Visas had been instituted during the French Revolution to control entry into French territory, and remained compulsory prior to the signing of bilateral or international agreements. The French Consul, the Count of Bondy, in December 1914 published an article in *The Straits Times*, announcing that "all passports delivered to foreigners going to France or French Colonies by their own consul, must also be endorsed with the official visa and stamp of the French Consulate in Singapore."

The French representative also acted as a notary. Many liability claims were signed at the Consulate by Indian "renouncers" living in Singapore, most of whom

OPPOSITE TOP: Advertisement for the Paris Cinematograph, *The Straits Times*, 16 December 1904.

BELOW: Reproduction of an Administrative act, 1872.

OPPOSITE TOP: Postcard showing the French Consulate.

OPPOSITE BELOW: Tombstone of Joël Le Savoureux, located in the Garden of Memories of the Armenian Church.

had contacts with the Indian trading posts at Karikal or Pondicherry. The Consul also provided official confirmation of deaths, financial liquidations and the reading of wills.

Occasionally, the diplomatic delegation was also behind charity initiatives, such as in 1900 when the Consul, Mr de Jouffroy d'Abbans, organised a fund drive in aid of Indian famine victims.

The different addresses of the Consulate

The French Chancellery and Residence moved house repeatedly over the years. In the 1860s, the Consulate was located at No. 525, Victoria Street. During the 1900s, one of its location was at No. 8, Raffles Quay.

In his work *En Insulinde*, published in 1914, Etienne Lunet de la Jonquière, a military officer, described the Residence of the Consul and the offices on Raffles Quay: "We paid a visit to our very friendly Consul, Mr d'Abbans. He lives in a villa somewhere on the hill which overlooks the Governor's palace. His offices are however on the large quay which faces the open harbour where the sailing ships and cabotage steamboats anchor. What unluxurious premises! They simply occupy a floor in one of the buildings which in Saigon we referred to as 'compartments'. This we reached by passing through the workshop of a Chinese rattan cane trader on the ground floor. Here, five or six workers filled the building with a perpetual sound of castanets as they tied the canes into packages."

Daily life

As the years went on, the diplomatic mission gradually increased its staff. Maintenance staff were always recruited from the local population, but as administrative tasks required a knowledge of French, the Consulate recruited from the French-speaking Indian and Indochinese communities. Ramassamy Douressamy, for example, was originally from Pondicherry and was employed as a Chancellery clerk during the 1890s.

The daily life of the mission can sometimes be found recorded in newspapers. In the 1880s, Singapore experienced a high level of crime, and a curfew was imposed for a few months. On 11 May 1883, Consul Cazaban was robbed by a band of organised thieves who broke into his Everton Estate residence, almost opposite the Consulate's Chinatown offices on Neil Road. In 1892, Consul Emile de Gaspary was also burgled. The first time that this happened, a small piece of Indian furniture was stolen, followed by a sum of $110, and, finally, during a third burglary two weeks later, $185 and some jewellery disappeared. Only the Consul's Légion d'Honneur medal, a signet ring and some precious stones, which would have been harder to sell, were not taken.

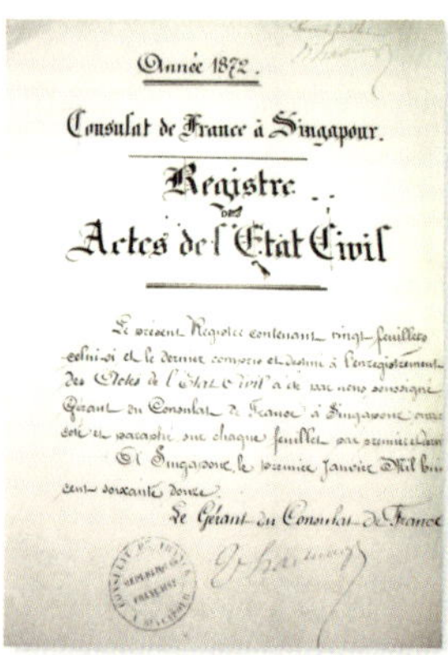
Année 1872.

Consulat de France à Singapour.

Registre des Actes de l'État Civil

Some Consuls died while in office. Consul Cazaban, who was despatched to take up the position of Chancellor at the Singapore Consulate in 1883, passed

away just three months later. He was 39, and was survived by his wife and children in France. According to his colleagues, "the illness to which he succumbed after three months of suffering can be attributed to Singapore's humid, debilitating climate as well as his constant, careful work." Similarly, three months after his arrival in January 1896, accompanied by his wife and daughter, Consul Joël Le Savoureux died as the result of malarial fever. Flags were flown at half-mast, the European community went into mourning, and the Consul was buried wrapped in the French flag. The headstones of Consuls Cazaban and Le Savoureux can still be seen in the Garden of Memories of the Armenian Church.

The Consulate fortunately also witnessed happier events. On 28 January 1889, the French Consul, Achille Raffray, married Miss Elizabeth Rutherfoord, a Canadian national, at the Church of the Good Shepherd in the presence of the entire French community.

Bastille Day and VIP visits

One of the highlights of the annual receptions calendar was 14 July, Bastille Day. In 1880, the Minister of the Interior ordered prefects and diplomats posted abroad to ensure that the date "is celebrated with as much colour as local resources permit." On this date, it was customary for the mission leader to assemble the French community as well as notable guests.

On 14 July 1906, two years after the signing of an agreement between France and Great Britain which aimed to reduce tensions between the two nations, the

British authorities worthily celebrated this "Entente cordiale". For the first time in the history of Singapore, a French event on a major scale was organised. The manager of the Sea View Hotel, located in Katong, Mr De Souza, organised a meal and dance in honour of the French national day. He rented a car from the Raffles Hotel, decorated in the French Tricolour, to provide transport for the guests. A French-style dinner was served, with the musical portion of the evening being provided by a local orchestra, the Town and Volunteer Band.

Receptions were also organised by the diplomatic mission to mark the arrival of important political figures. On 16 March 1902, on his return to France after serving for five years as Governor-General of Indochina, Paul Doumer and his family made a port call for a few hours in Singapore. They were welcomed by the British authorities and by the leading members of the French community: the Consul of France, Count d'Abbans, Bishop Bourdon, Father Couvreur as well as local businessmen such as Messrs. Moine Comte and Dupire, and Mr Tournaire of the Messageries Maritimes. After a meal at the Governor's Residence (the present-day Istana), Monsieur and Madame Doumer proceeded to Pasir Pajang to visit a gutta-percha factory. At 5pm, they returned to their ship, the *Sydney*.

The French religious presence

The opening of the Suez Canal was also a boon for the Catholic Church, which continued its expansion in the Malay Peninsula and Singapore. According to a British census in 1849, approximately 52,891 people lived in Singapore, and 3.5% of the population were Christian; in 1911, of the 300,000 inhabitants, only about 5% professed to a Christian faith. Nevertheless, the group of Catholic missionaries continued to perform their educational and evangelising duties with zeal. The parishes were well organised and the Catholic schools well known.

Churches for the Chinese and Indian communities

The different communities, be they Chinese (Hokkien, Teochew, Cantonese or Hakka), Indian or European, initially met at the Church of the Good Shepherd for services in English and Latin.

From 1870 onwards, Chinese Catholics and the few Indian Christians attended combined services at the Church of Sts Peter and Paul. These services were given in a Chinese dialect. Vicar Apostolic Barillon, in his report of 1914, which he sent to the MEP seminary in Paris, described the building: "The church and the steeple were constructed by Father Paris in 1869–1870. It comprises seven bays for the three naves, which are divided by immense hardwood columns ... The church's boundary wall was paid for, it is said, by Napoleon III ... The bell tower and the current rectory are the work of Father Galmel. As the church was not large enough, it was enlarged by Mr Vignol in 1891–1892. The massive columns

TOP: Léon Cazaban (1844–1883), Consul of France.

BOTTOM: Joseph Athanase Paul Doumer, commonly known as Paul Doumer (1857–1932). He was Governor-General of French Indochina from 1897 to 1902, and was elected President of the French Republic on 13 May 1931.

OPPOSITE TOP: Bishop Emile Marie Barillon (1860–1935).

OPPOSITE BOTTOM: View of the Cathedral of the Good Shepherd with a banner "Vive la France", which was put up by Reverend L. Lambert.

disappeared. The transept, sanctuary and sacristies were built. The old wooden framework was replaced by an iron framework." Stained glass was also imported from France and, in 1877, an organ by the famous French builder Aristide Cavaillé-Coll was installed (it was removed in the 1960s). The lilies which adorned the wooden pews also disappeared. The church was gazetted as a national monument in 2003.

The Indian Tamil Catholic community attended services at Sts Peter and Paul, but, as the number of worshippers reached almost 600 in 1882, it was decided that new premises were needed. Father Meneuvrier was responsible for raising funds, and for the construction of the new church. To this end, he called upon the architecture firm Swan and Lermit. The first stone was laid on 1 August 1886, on a plot of land donated by the colonial government on Ophir Road, and work was completed two years later. The new church, in the Neo-Gothic style, copied the form of the Basilica of Lourdes, and was named Our Lady of Lourdes in honour of the 30th anniversary of the apparitions of the Virgin Mary to Bernadette Soubirous. Its iron structure, imported from France, was in keeping with the architecture trend of the time (another example can be found at Telok Ayer Market, the present-day Lau Pa Sat).

In 1958, to mark the centenary of the apparitions of the Virgin Mary, Father Fortier imported stained-glass windows from France representing the 15 Mysteries of the Rosary. The church was gazetted as a national monument by the Preservation of Monuments Board in 2005.

The Catholic schools thrive

St Joseph's Institution (SJI)

Father Beurel's educational initiatives have endured. In 1885, the Brothers of La Salle, who had left the island because of infighting, returned. Brother Lothaire, having been a headmaster in London, Saigon and New York, took over the management of St Joseph's Institution. He focused on overcoming a number of internal problems as well as competition from the Protestants. At the turn of the 20th century, with the arrival of the Irish Brother Michael Noctor, SJI thrived. For 14 years, he placed his entire energy and passion into the service of the school. Three men helped him in this task: Tan Jiak Kim, a rich trader who headed the Straits Company; the Governor, John Anderson; and an extraordinary French priest, Charles-Bénédicte Nain, who was an amateur architect and put his talents to good use in the expansion of SJI. Over the 1880–1914 period, enrolment increased considerably. In February 1903, inspired by Saint Peter's in Rome, Father Nain added two semi-circular wings to the building, flanked by colonnades, and the new building was inaugurated by Bishop Fée. On 21 September 1912, grand festivities were organised to celebrate 60 years of SJI. The following year, a statue of Saint John Baptist de La Salle was placed in the centre of the main entrance. This was a gift from a Mr La Salle, a distant descendant of Saint John Baptist de La Salle.

In 1869, the Brothers welcomed 167 external students, of whom 25 paid for their schooling, and 55 boarders, of which 23 paid boarding fees. The template for the lessons was prepared in Paris for Brothers around the world. In Singapore, where no sports were played due to the heat, a number of Brothers found the time to draft their own textbooks. They were inspired by the lessons written by Brother Superior Philippe Bransiet, who added a touch of morality to each exercise, even in mathematics: "A careful child needs three pencils per week on average. A careless, scatterbrained child uses two every day. How much more would his family spend over a period of four years and three months if a dozen pencils cost 15 cents?"

Classes were held in English, but the dreadful accent of the French Brothers bothered Brother Michael so much that he pleaded with his boss not to send any more French Brothers! However, the Mission ignored his request.

Between 1900 and 1905, the number of students increased from 426 to 743. School hours were from 9am until noon, and from 1pm to 4pm. English, geography, history and mathematics were the main subjects taught, while some students learned French. Science was not offered as a subject, as there was no laboratory. At noon, the students bought food from

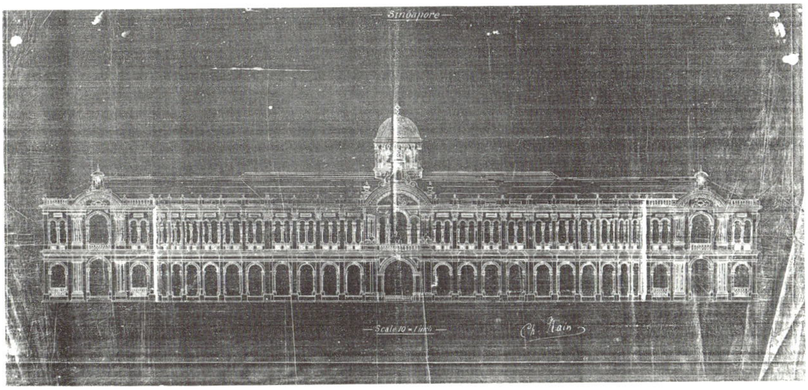

OPPOSITE TOP: Father Joachim Alexandre Meneuvrier (1858–1915).

OPPOSITE BOTTOM: School boys and food sellers, c.1908.

LEFT : SJI blueprint—Father Nain's design for the extension of St Joseph's Institution with arches and a large dome.

BELOW: View of SJI at Bras Basah Road, c.1915.

hawkers who were authorised to enter SJI. *Popiah* (spring rolls) or *rojak* (a local fruit-and-vegetable salad) could be purchased for one cent, a pack of *kachang puteh* (assorted savoury and sugared nuts) for a quarter of a cent, or a plate of *kway teow mee* (rice noodles) for two cents. Five cents was more than enough to buy the students a good meal.

The development of the Convent of the Holy Infant Jesus (CHIJ)

Opened in 1854, CHIJ gained in importance as the years passed. The Sisters managed to earn more money by enrolling more students, by selling needlework and by developing the orphanage. In 1872, they earned approximately $10,000 a year, which was sufficient for the school to function. In 1880, Mother Gaëtan, who returned from France with 17 young teachers, the majority of which were nuns, succeeded Mother Mathilde.

In 1881, the British government conducted its first inspection and decided to partly finance the school, with the caveat that public funds should not be used to proselytise. Religious instruction classes were therefore taught outside of school hours. In 1892, CHIJ received a donation of $10,000 from the government, a third of the sum required for the construction of a new building for boarding students. A rich Chinese, Cheang Hong Lim, donated $3,000. He also organised a charity

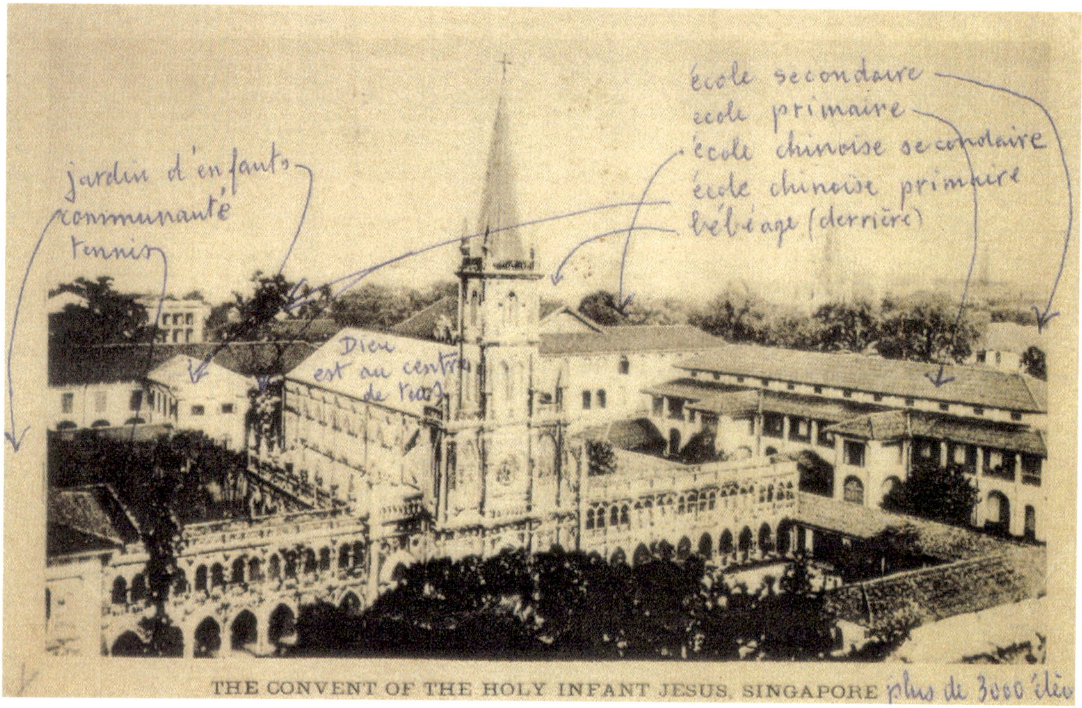

event which brought in $2,625. The Protestant community also made a donation, as an indication of the high esteem in which the Sisters' work was held. Numerous French Sisters arrived in Singapore to work at the Convent, and Sister Hombeline took over the running of the school in 1892.

On 4 July 1892, the new boarding building was inaugurated in the presence of Bishop Gasnier, the Governor and the Sultan of Johor, as well as the Consuls of France, Italy, Spain, the Netherlands and Russia. Sister Hombeline wrote in her diary: "It is one of the most beautiful [buildings] of Singapore ... Roofs are made of white painting boards ... Dormitory rooms are around 200 feet long and 30 feet wide, with an arch in the middle and a surrounding veranda."

The chapel, designed by Father Charles-Bénédicte Nain, is without doubt the most remarkable work of the period. It was inaugurated in 1904, when Sister Hombeline once again wrote: "Reverend Father Nain celebrated the first mass in this chapel he had built. Our Mother Mathilde came back the day before from Japan ... The cathedral choir sang during the liturgical ceremony." While the chapel was being built, changes were also being made to the education system. In 1904, the first class took its Junior Cambridge examinations, followed by Senior Cambridge examinations, which marked the French Convent's introduction to secondary education. The school continued to expand. In 1914, new classrooms were built with help from the government (a subsidy of $20,000) and were inaugurated by Bishop Barillon.

TOP: The Convent of the Holy Infant Jesus, 1920s. In this view of the convent, a sister identifies the various parts of the complex (clockwise from top right): Secondary school, primary school, Chinese secondary school, Chinese primary school, baby house, chapel, tennis court and children's garden.

FATHER CHARLES-BÉNÉDICTE NAIN (1870–1916)

Father Nain was born in 1870 at Farges, north of Lyon. He was ordained in 1894 and joined the order of the MEP. Passionate about architecture, he was also an adept draughtsman. Despatched to the diocese of Malaya, he served as a priest in a number of parishes, including that of the Good Shepherd in Singapore from 1909 to 1913, and left his mark on the colony's architecture. His first project was the CHIJ chapel. He was no doubt inspired by the churches of Mâcon and Fontaine, located close to his birthplace. The shape of the windows, the bell tower, the triforium as well as the pinnacles were in the very popular Neo-Gothic style. In 1903, the glass of the chapel, comprising more than 30,000 pieces, was ordered from Bruges artisan Jules Dobbelaere. On the capitals of the columns and the passages leading to the chapel, 648 different animal and plant species were sculpted. The wooden pews as well as the majority of the furniture were imported from Toulouse. Although the plans were signed by Father Nain, it seems that the works were entrusted to the architecture firm, Swan and Maclaren, which was well-known in Singapore at the turn of the century. Two of the five buildings which comprised CHIJ until 1983 were classified as national monuments in 1990: Caldwell's house and Father Nain's chapel, which was deconsecrated in 1983 and became Chijmes Hall. Today, the chapel, which is part of a dining-and-shopping complex, is rented out for classical music concerts and for wedding celebrations.

In 1903, Father Nain expanded St Joseph's Institution, giving it a baroque appearance and a resemblance to Saint Peter's in Rome. The building was declared a national monument in 1992 and, in 1996, the Singapore Art Museum (SAM) moved into the historic building.

During his ministry in the parish of the Good Shepherd, from 1909 to 1913, Father Nain also pushed for the building of a holiday home for the Brothers of the Christian Schools in Katong, a house which was converted into a school in 1933, under the name St Patrick's School. He drafted the plans and also built a new rectory, with the former building becoming the Bishop's residence. In 1912, he installed an organ in the Cathedral and, in 1913, connected the building to the electricity mains supply. He returned to France for health reasons, and died in Vichy in 1916, at the age of 40, while serving as a nursing officer.

TOP LEFT AND ABOVE: Father Nain and his drawing of the CHIJ chapel.

A former student who spent her entire school years at CHIJ before going on to teach there has left an account of her experiences. In a letter to a friend in rudimentary English, she reminisced about the French Sisters: "I was admitted into the CHIJ in 1911 at the age of four. The Lady Superior at the time was Rev Mother Hombeline (French). Rumour had it that she was a crippled child who was miraculously cured at Lourdes, hence the Grotto in the Convent, meant to

be a replica in miniature … In standard I, Madam St Eugene was the tiniest adult I'd seen, and French. And what's more, discipline went by the board. The pupils ran rings about her and nicknamed her Charlie Chaplin. But she was lovable."

Classes were taught in Malay and English, which always posed a problem with the Sisters, who came from France and spoke neither of these languages. These difficulties were reduced with the arrival of the Irish Sisters.

The Orphanage

The Ladies of Saint Maur also set up an orphanage and The Refuge, which took in women escaping from prostitution, forced marriages or poverty.

TOP: A group of girl boarders at the Convent of the Holy Infant Jesus at Victoria Street, c. 1915.

RIGHT: The orphanage of the CHIJ at Victoria Street, c. 1915.

OPPOSITE TOP: A CHIJ sister with an orphaned baby.

As soon as the orphanage was opened by Mother Mathilde in 1854, unwanted babies, wrapped in rags or newspapers, were placed in front of the door, which was soon named the Gate of Hope. The majority of these abandoned children were girls and, in 1892, 200 babies were left in the care of the Sisters, while in 1946, four to five children arrived at the orphanage daily.

The Sisters were devoted and became rather lyrical when describing in their diaries a day at the orphanage with the young children, whom they referred to as babies: "The great city clock has just struck seven. In the morning silence, tiny voices are immediately heard; the babies kneel on their beds and say their prayers ... These begin in English: Jesus, Mary, Joseph, I give you my heart and my soul, and then continue in Latin: *Ave Maria*, the Sister says, and immediately 30 little elves loudly reply: '*gratia plena ...*' We end with a hymn in French: '*O Jésus, notre divin Frère, Chef de la grande Eglise catholique et universelle!*"

When the children were no longer toddlers, they were sent from the nursery to the orphanage itself. The orphans, aged between 6 and 14, received primary education and, as they grew up, started learning the tasks which would make them the perfect household managers. "We then introduce her to a former student of the Brothers... If there is mutual approval, an agreement is rapidly concluded. Helped by her friends, the new fiancée creates her trousseau and her wedding costume. And soon, the banns are read."

Father Augustin Périé, who cared for the Christians on the plantations in the centre of the island, wrote in *Souvenirs Malay*: "When I wanted to help one of my Christians on Bukit Timah to marry, this is what I did. I went to Singapore to ask the Nuns for a girl, taking the young man with me. The Sisters would only bring a single person; the future spouses were brought in, chatted together for a few moments, after which they spent eight to fifteen days in reflection and prayer. After this time had passed, the young man would tell me his decision, and the young girl would tell her Mother Superior. If they agreed, the Mother Superior, the parents of the future spouses and myself would decide what to give for the wedding basket."

From August 1885 onwards, in addition to their teaching duties, the Ladies of Saint Maur also worked at the General Hospital. This was done at the government's request. They were admired for their boundless devotion, providing the sick of every nation and every faith with such enlightened, charitable care that the institution became widely known for its superior management. They performed this role until 1900. When the government offered them paid employment, the Sisters declined, as they preferred to retain their independence and maintain their status as volunteers.

Over more than a century of charity work, 85,000 babies were taken in and baptised by the Ladies of Saint Maur, 11,870 orphans brought up, and 9,627 adult baptisms performed in the hospitals.

THE RAFFLES SQUARE, SINGAPORE

IV.

An era of turmoil (1914–1965)

Although Singapore was not a major factor in the important decisions of the global powers, it was nonetheless affected by these. The two World Wars, the economic growth followed by the Great Depression of the 1920–1930s and decolonisation during the post-war years had repercussions for the island's small "French colony". Estimated at between 150 and 200 individuals and growing, the community was largely comprised of clergy, traders and diplomatic staff.

The First World War and the Singapore mutiny

In Europe, extensive systems of alliances were created in the late 19th and early 20th century. The Triple Alliance (Central Powers) consisted of the Austro-Hungarian Empire, Germany and the Ottoman Empire, while the Triple Entente Allies included, among others, France, the United Kingdom and Russia. The assassination of Archduke Franz Ferdinand in Sarajevo on 28 June 1914 was the spark that lit the Balkan powder keg, and August 1914 was marked by successive declarations of war between different European countries. On 23 August, Japan offered its support to the Allies by declaring war on Germany and, on 1 November, the Ottoman Empire joined the Central Powers. A French general mobilisation order issued on 2 August also applied to its population living abroad.

General mobilisation—Singapore's French community answers the call

French citizens of military age in Singapore were mobilised and were required to report at the French Consulate. On 14 August, these future soldiers left Singapore for Marseille on board the Peninsular and Oriental liner *Syria*. A witness to the scene recalled: "A small band of light-hearted men, cheering and waving

OPPOSITE TOP: Raffles Square, c.1926.

OPPOSITE BOTTOM: Raffles Square, c.1960.

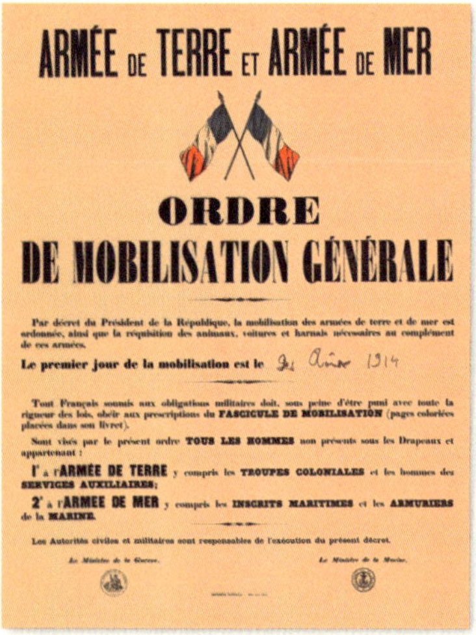

hats, handkerchiefs, their beloved Tricolour, anything they could lay hands upon, as they craned over the ship's rail for a last glimpse of all they were leaving behind. Enthusiastically, they called for cheers for England, for La Belle France … 'Their beloved Alsace', at the words hats were off, flags held on high, and then the band of the 5th Light Infantry mustered on the wharf, struck up the *Marseillaise*. Those who did not know the words did without them; the tune and the sentiment, *Vive la France*, *l'Angleterre*, *l'Entente Cordiale* were sufficient. The French tongue was heard on all sides, more fluently musical than ever in the excitement of the moment and one might be excused for thinking of some joyous fête, a gala day, rather than a leave-taking as solemn and serious as any in this world."

The 60 Frenchmen who answered the call-up included leading figures in the tiny community: Mr Dupire; Mr Hoberdon of the Pathé Brothers Company; Mr Ruinat of the Messageries Maritimes; the sons of Ayam brand founder Alfred Clouët, Clarence, who worked with his father and Francis, a planter; the sons of the Consul de Bondy, Pierre and Harold, both planters; Mr de Saint-Céran of Moine Comte; Alfred Bourrin and Georges Duchâteau, accountants at the Banque de l'Indochine. They were accompanied by a number of their countrymen from Java, Siam and the Federated Malay States such as Mr Fauconnier.

Clergymen such as Brothers Dezauney and Brigant of the Order of the Brothers of the Christian Schools, and Fathers Nain and Devals of the MEP were also sent to the front. "Everyone was gay and resolved to perform their duty bravely as soldiers, stretcher bearers or nurses," noted one report, "and if the French cause still requires fresh blood, they will die for her. After the war, we are confident that they will resume their respective careers."

During a stopover in Singapore, the writer André Bellessort described the atmosphere there and noted the lack of information from the Consul of France, Mr de Bondy, on events in France. He was also surprised by the good treatment given to German civilians. And he mentioned that many reservists returning to France were afraid of arriving too late, due to the length of the journey, and that by then, "everything would be over!"

Despite the distance between the battlefield and Singapore, the war affected business for a time. With the requisitioning or sinking of ships, goods no longer arrived and payments normally made by telegraph were delayed, affecting the entire economy. This pause was, however, short-lived. The manager of the Banque de l'Indochine, who remained at his post in Singapore, noted that from 1915 onwards, "the bank has re-established its activities in tin and rubber".

Collections in support of the troops were frequently organised by the French Red Cross, with festivals and ceremonies celebrating the friendship between

France and Great Britain. One event took place against the painted backdrop of an Alsace village, created by the French company Brossard-Mopin and Co.

Apart from the conscripted men, the Singapore population was not directly affected by the conflict yet. *The Straits Times* gave a daily account of events on the fronts in its '*French Consular Cables*' column. In the issue of 22 July 1916, the Consulate of France authorised the publication of a telegram from Paris dated 20 July: "... yesterday, we stormed some trenches south of the Somme, taking prisoners. The British withstood a massed attack north of the Somme and drove back the enemy who had penetrated Longueval and Bois Delville. Today, we attacked on both banks of the Somme, and carried the first German line, taking 400 prisoners. We penetrated a German trench in Champagne, bringing back prisoners ..." In addition, images from the war, sent from France by the Pathé company, were shown at the Palladium cinema before the main film.

As fighting raged in Europe and armies buried themselves in the trenches, life in Singapore remained relatively peaceful. Only the events of the Chinese New Year in February 1915 would remind Europeans in Singapore that they were at war. France, a British ally, would help the colony when it was in danger.

OPPOSITE: Poster announcing the general mobilization of the population, 1914.

BELOW: Advertisement for a French War Relief fundraiser, at the Victoria Theatre, *The Straits Times*, 28 December 1917.

The Sepoy Mutiny and the French vessel Montcalm

Against the backdrop of the First World War, Germany embarked on a campaign to destabilise the British Crown in colonial India, and found a willing participant in the Indian Ghadar independence movement. In October 1914, the Madras 5th Regiment of Native Infantry, a battalion of the Indian Army, was posted to Singapore to relieve the Yorkshire Light Infantry, which was to be sent to France. The new garrison was mainly composed of Indian Muslim soldiers under British command, and was housed in the barracks on Alexandra Road.

German prisoners had been interned in the Tanglin barracks and they may have started rumours that the Muslim soldiers were to be sent to the Turkish front, where they would have to fight their brethren. The harsh living conditions and meagre rations increased the discontent of the troops and, on 15 February 1915, in the midst of Chinese New Year celebrations when there was a slowdown, the Indian troops, known as sepoys, decided to mutiny.

At 4:30pm, General Ridout informed the Governor of the Straits Settlements, Sir Arthur Young, of the mutiny. Up to 600 Indian and Malay soldiers had taken up arms. A group of mutineers wanted to free the German prisoners and incite them to join, but only a few took advantage of the chaos and escaped. Another group of Indian soldiers made their way to Chinatown and Pasir Panjang, shooting at any Europeans that they encountered.

The British authorities had been taken by surprise and quickly called for assistance from foreign vessels in the Allied fleet to quash the rebellion. A Russian

Victoria Theatre

FRIDAY, JANUARY 4, AT 9.15 P.M.

French War Relief Fund

(Under the auspices of the French Consul)

OFFICIAL WAR FILMS

The only authentic pictures taken by the Cinematographic Service of the French Army.

NOTE:—The whole of the gross proceeds will be given to the above Fund.

Price $3, $2 and $1. Booking open now at Moutrie's.

cruiser and two Japanese warships answered the distress call. So did the French armoured cruiser *Montcalm* which had moored in Keppel Harbour some days earlier and departed after its band gave a concert in the Botanic Gardens; it turned back to help the British. On 17 February at 10:30am, French Admiral Albert Huguet landed with a force of 190 men. The French troops and a British regiment made their way to Seletar, where a group of the mutineers were holed up. Others had already crossed the Strait and given themselves up to the Sultan of Johor. Throughout the next day Japanese and English troops, assisted by the French, retook control of the territory. The women and children who had been evacuated to ships in the port were able to return home. On 20 February, while on patrol in the western reaches of the island, French soldiers found themselves face to face with a dozen mutineers. An exchange of fire resulted in one death among the mutineers, while the remainder abandoned their weapons and fled. On 23 February, the French garrison received thanks from Governor Young, who organised an official ceremony on the Padang. On this occasion, the Governor paid homage to the courage of all of the soldiers who had played a part in the events. A few hours later, the *Montcalm* sailed. In March 1918, Admiral Huguet was made a Knight of the Most Distinguished Order of Saint Michael and Saint George for his heroic actions.

TOP: 5th Indian Light Infantry, 1915.

OPPOSITE: The Cenotaph, c. 1935. This is a war memorial located within the Esplanade Park at Connaught Drive. It was built in memory of the 124 British soldiers born or resident in Singapore who died in the First World War, with a second dedication (but no names) added in remembrance of those who died in the Second World War.

The death toll of the brief revolt reached more than 50 and included British civilians. The mutineers were arrested and their court-martials began on 23 February. More than 126 sentences were handed out: 37 death sentences and 41 banishments, while the remainder received prison sentences ranging from one to 20 years. A few weeks later, life resumed its peaceful course.

The Sepoy mutiny raised British awareness of the need for conscription as well as a proper intelligence service. On 4 May 1916, Governor Young asked London to establish two new bureaux to be in charge of "criminal intelligence" and "criminal investigation". These intelligence and counter-espionage services, which were effectively put in place after the war, would become active throughout the 1920–1930s, notably in the fight against communism.

A duty to remember

The signing of the Armistice on 11 November 1918 marked the end of the First World War. Of those conscripted from Malaya and Singapore, some were dead, while others were injured, and scarred for life by what they had seen. To ensure that those who had fallen for their country were not forgotten, the British and French authorities encouraged the erection of monuments to the dead. Hundreds of memorials appeared in France and Great Britain as well as in the colonies.

The Cenotaph on the Padang

In Singapore, the British decided to build a cenotaph on the Esplanade, not far from the Padang. The foundation stone was laid during an imposing ceremony on the afternoon of 15 November 1920. The guests of honour included the island's Governor, Sir Laurence Guillemard, and Georges Clemenceau. After a first visit in October, Clemenceau expressed a desire to pass through the British colony a second time, before returning to India. The former French Minister of War participated in the cenotaph ceremony despite concerns over his health (he had contracted a bronchial illness in Java), and as a souvenir, he received a silver trowel from architect Denis Santry of Swan and Maclaren. Following the blessing of the foundation stone by the chaplain, the military band struck up the British and French national anthems.

TOP: Memorial tablet listing the names of Frenchmen from Malaya who died during the First World War.

The funeral monument was officially inaugurated by the Duke of Windsor on 31 March 1922. The cenotaph is a granite replica of the structure on Whitehall, in London. Two years later, a much smaller plaque was inaugurated, as the Saigon Cochin Chinese Association of World War Veterans wanted to honour their British comrades who had fallen on the battlefield.

On 14 July 1921, the Consul, Mr Noble, inaugurated a tablet dedicated to the "Frenchmen of Malaya, who died for France". British and French dignitaries as well as members of the French community attended this ceremony, and the Consul concluded his speech as follows: "Whenever our eyes turn to this tablet on which are inscribed these names, they will recall to us the sacrifices which have been made for France." The memorial plaque can today be found on the grounds of the Embassy of France on Cluny Park Road. The engraved names include Reverend Father Nain, a stretcher bearer and curate of the Cathedral of the Good Shepherd, who died at Vichy military hospital on 28 June 1916 (indicated as 1915 on the tablet by error); Charles Munie, from the Banque de l'Indochine, killed at Artois on 9 October 1915; Harold de Bondy, killed on 8 June 1918 in the forest of Villers-Cotterêts; and Julien Vuillaumié, of the Far East Oxygen and Acetylene Co. Ltd., killed after four months of fighting in the Vosges.

Memorial streets

In October 1928, the Singapore Municipal Council decided to name certain streets after British and French military leaders, or Great War battlefields. The Jalan Besar district, formerly a mangrove swamp, was the location chosen for Somme Road, Verdun Road, Foch Road and Marne Road as well as Petain Road. Oddly enough, French Road refers to the British Field Marshal, John French.

PETAIN ROAD

The Ongs, a Peranakan family, built shophouse-type houses blending European architecture and Peranakan style along Petain Road between 1926 and 1931. Sixty years later, the URA, Singapore's urban planning authority, decided to protect this heritage site so typical of its time. With the onset of the Second World War, Petain, a First World War hero, was no longer a figure of honour—he became Chief of State of the collaborationist Vichy regime and *The Straits Times* published letters questioning the appropriateness of Petain Road. A few decades later, abortive attempts were made to change the name of this Singapore street. Around the world, approximately 15 streets are still named after the Marshal, including one in Tremblois-lès-Carignan (Ardennes).

The interwar period

The 1920s was a decade of alternating periods of crisis and economic growth. Colonial society, which comprised around 100 French citizens (154 according to the 1921 census), saw its living conditions improve during this period. French companies continued to trade. The clergy, as numerous as ever, contributed to the development of Catholicism on the island, despite the rise of the communist movement. The Consulate of France was elevated to the level of a Consulate General in 1937.

Daily life of the French community

The city changed rapidly in the 1920s: cars became more numerous, and in 1925 the Singapore Traction Company began operations with trolleybuses and omnibuses. The first municipal power station was inaugurated in 1927 at St James, and electrical power and its various applications enabled the population to live more comfortably. The Cold Storage Company, established in 1903, began to sell new refrigerated products, which would also improve life in the tropics.

City Hall was constructed on the Padang in 1929, on the site of the Hôtel de l'Europe. A year earlier, the General Post Office had been inaugurated in the Fullerton Building. The port of Singapore, as active as ever, welcomed ships flying flags from around the world, enabling trade in tin, rubber and foodstuffs between the colonies of Asia and their home cities.

The Great Depression of 1929 had a relatively strong impact on Singapore, as the island was dependent on international commerce, which had begun to idle. In 1931, the colony saw a budget deficit, unemployment increased, and the impact was felt at every level of society. From 1934, the economy improved but did not return to pre-crisis levels of prosperity. Life in Singapore remained comfortable, however, particularly for the elite. In well-to-do areas, the Europeans and rich Asian traders lived in spacious homes surrounded by gardens and employed numerous household staff.

From a sporting and cultural point of view, the 1920s were marked by significant transformation. The number of clubs multiplied, and offered a wider range of sporting activities, such as swimming, tennis and golf. Radio first appeared in 1915, but only became popular in 1936 with the launch of commercial programming by the British Malayan Broadcasting Corporation. Entertainment venues such as New World, Great World and Happy World, which opened in 1923, 1931 and 1935 respectively, attracted Europeans as well as the local population with their cinemas, cabarets and boxing halls; they were the only places where the communities intermingled. It was also during this period that the Raffles Hotel became the key venue for colonial soirées, while the Seaview Hotel was the place to be on Sundays.

The small "French colony" enjoyed good living conditions. Very often, the men worked for French businesses that had taken root at the end of the previous century. The women, meanwhile, spent their days at the Tanglin Club. At the start of 1939, a small circle, which called itself the Centre Intellectuel Français de Malaisie, was formed at No. 20, Mount Elizabeth (not far from the current site of Mount Elizabeth Hospital). Its aim was to promote cultural exchanges between the different European communities and the French community. For $2 a month, a member was granted access to a library of classical and modern works of French literature, and could attend conferences, meetings and film screenings. On 15 July 1939, the Centre Intellectuel organised a French fête, where the 200 guests listened to a speech by the French Prime Minister, Edouard Daladier, broadcast from the Indochinese radio station, Radio Saigon, as well as sketches by the comedian Sacha Guitry. A performance of extracts from plays by Molière and a dance party provided a finale to the fête.

As the Centre's membership expanded from 130 to 200, its president planned the construction of a clubhouse on the grounds of the Consulate General of France, at No. 5, Gallop Road. A few months later, however, the outbreak of the Second World War would put an end to this "French centre" project.

The French community also came together to welcome visiting dignitaries.

Georges Clemenceau visits Singapore

On 18 January 1920, after resigning from his position as President of the Council in France, Georges Clemenceau retired from political life. At the age of 79, with no official mandate, the elder statesman was now in a position to satisfy one of his greatest passions: travelling. Thoroughly enjoying his new-found freedom, Georges Clemenceau, also known as "the Tiger", decided to make a long journey through South and Southeast Asia, which would last from September 1920 to March 1921. To keep him company on this long tour, he brought along a Corsican friend named Nicolas Pietri, who would later be the executor of his will, and Mr Turpault, an industrialist from Vendée. During his stopover in Singapore from 17 to 22 October, Clemenceau was received as a head of state, because he symbolised victorious France in the eyes of the Allies and the entire world.

17 October saw the arrival in Singapore of the French liner bearing Clemenceau. From its upper deck, the view of the port made a powerful impression on him. At Johnston's Pier, a large crowd of officials, admirers and gawkers awaited his arrival excitedly. He was met by the Governor, Sir Laurence

TOP: The Raffles Hotel, 1927.

OPPOSITE: Clemenceau and the missionaries of Singapore.

Guillemard, who was of French ancestry and fell under the spell of the old man. Clemenceau had left Marseille as an ordinary citizen, but was received with fanfare in Singapore. He telegraphed his family with the following words: "We arrived this morning. Slightly disconcerted by an official reception which exceeded any we might have expected … Singapore is a marvel." The following morning, he was at the Consulate of France with Consul Danjou. He met with the Fathers of the MEP, as well as with French bankers, engineers, traders and miners, who came from Perak for the occasion. Governor Guillemard wrote in *The Times*: "The charm of his manner was irresistible, his gay humour was infectious, his courtesy won all hearts, and in two days he was the idol of Singapore."

On 19 October, he visited the Raffles Museum and the General Hospital. Being very interested in Chinese culture, he also made an impromptu visit to a Chinese temple on Balestier Road. He was then received by the French community at the Tanglin Club, and finally attended a banquet held by the Chinese community in his honour. Mr Durnerin, director of the Banque Industrielle de Chine and representing the French community in Singapore on behalf of Mr Moine-Comte, who was absent due to an illness, welcomed him with these words: "*Monsieur le Président*. The French colony in Singapore is happy to be able to present to you its admiration and gratitude. Three years ago, the news of your coming to power rang through our trenches like the promise of a finally, truly liberating war. A few months later, in the spring of 1918, as we fought foot by foot for the soil of the Ile de France and Picardie, your name was inextricably linked to that of Foch, and we fought the war with an easier heart, knowing that you would be able to protect the rear as the front advanced. Today, this task has been accomplished, and we salute you as the author of this return, which, with clenched teeth, our youth had

awaited so long. For all of the nations of Asia and Europe which have come together in Singapore, you are the organiser of Victory and the Giver of Peace. However, for us French nationals living in the shade of the British flag, you have even greater significance: I am referring to the precursor of the Entente Cordiale which you now see in action. *Monsieur le Président*, assembled here are representatives of the various communities of Singapore. In their presence, please allow me to express, to the Government of the Straits Settlements, to the British colony, to the Chinese Community and to the other allied or amicable communities, our gratitude for the support which has been so willingly given for six years to everything that is French."

The next day, Clemenceau plunged into the heart of Chinatown. Accompanied by Messrs Pietri and Turpault, as well as by the French Consul, Mr Danjou, he was fortunate to be guided by Dr Lim Boon Keng, a medical doctor like Clemenceau. Clemenceau appreciated the animation of a busy people, listened to the diversity of dialects and took an interest in the architecture of the shophouses. A fierce opponent of opium consumption, Dr Lim showed Clemenceau its harmful effects by taking him to an opium den. They also paid a visit to two Chinese schools. According to press reports, Clemenceau met dignitaries from the Indian and Malay communities too.

BELOW: Clemenceau inaugurating Clemenceau Avenue.

LIM BOON KENG (1869–1957)

Born in 1869 into a family of Straits-born Chinese in Singapore, Lim Boon Keng was the first Chinese to be awarded the prestigious Queen's scholarship in 1887. He then went to Edinburgh to take up his medical studies. Upon his return to Singapore in 1893, he opened a practice in a small shophouse on Telok Ayer Street. With a Dr Robertson, he also opened a dispensary to treat the many patients suffering from cholera in 1897. He became involved in local politics, and held a number of important positions in the colonial administration (on the Legislative Council, Municipal Commission and Chinese Advisory Board, among others). In 1911, he met Dr Sun Yat-Sen and became involved in the events in China at the time. Besides his political commitments, Dr Lim also launched campaigns to fight opium use in Singapore, and also played a role in the development of Chinese and English education for young Chinese. During the Second World War, he headed the Overseas Chinese Association and was ordered by the Japanese to exert control over the Chinese population of Syonan-to. He died in 1957.

On 22 October, he was received at the French Catholic institution of the Convent of the Holy Infant Jesus. In the speech he gave to the young girls, mostly Asian or mixed-race orphans, he spoke about the war and the Entente Cordiale.

Singapore did not wait for the departure of "France's Grand Old Man" to commemorate him. In his presence, with great pomp and circumstance, the authorities inaugurated Clemenceau Avenue, the longest and largest of Singapore's avenues. Singapore was thus the first city in the world to name one of its major arteries after Clemenceau.

The ceremony symbolically marked the end of Clemenceau's official stay in Singapore. This would not be his last stay in the colony, however, as Clemenceau decided to stop in Singapore once again on his homeward journey. From 15 to 23 November, Clemenceau re-visited the colony, and it was he who laid the first stone of the memorial monument (Cenotaph) for the First World War. Almost a century later, Clemenceau's statement to the press at the time is prescient: "Yours is a wonderful country, and I am almost ashamed to have received such kindness. I shall not forget this. In truth, the way in which I have been welcomed in Singapore has gone straight to my heart … Here reigns a real atmosphere of satisfaction shared by all races. You have no beggars in the city. I even asked … when the time would come when, everywhere on the streets, the people of Singapore will spend their money without counting."

Clemenceau was not the only French hero to visit Singapore. In December 1921, Marshal Joffre made a port call of a few hours as part of a world tour which brought him to the United States and then to Asia. In 25 August 1939, the Governor General of Indochina, Jules Brevie, also passed through Singapore.

ANDRÉ MALRAUX

Born in 1901, André Malraux began writing articles on artists from a very young age. In 1923, he embarked on an expedition to Cambodia with his wife Clara. He was arrested for the theft of a bas-relief from the Banteai Srei temple in Angkor, and was sentenced to prison. French literary circles managed to obtain his release. In 1925, the couple decided to once again head for Indochina to establish a newspaper. They called in at Singapore where Clara rediscovered "Chinese haste mixed with the Malay slide, and the slow lengthening of the Hindu stride." Clara , who spoke English fluently, would return from Saigon to Singapore to negotiate the purchase of articles on world news from *The Straits Times* for their newspaper, *l'Indochine*. This second Indochinese sojourn was also unsuccessful—the newspaper only published a few issues. Inspired by the Far East, André Malraux published *La Tentation de l'Occident*, *Les Conquérants*, *La Voie royale* and received the Prix Goncourt in 1933 for *La Condition humaine*.

During their port calls in Singapore between 1923 and 1931, the Malrauxes stayed at the Raffles Hotel. In 1965, Malraux returned as French Minister for Cultural Affairs, and he wrote in his *Antimémoires*: "The Raffles has changed a lot; but as before, the rickshaw pullers play Chinese cards on the pavement. Bicycles have replaced the shafts of the rickshaws. When I came here the first time, I wasn't even 25 years old. Asia—and my destiny—lay before me."

André Malraux has joined the ranks of literary figures such as Joseph Conrad, Rudyard Kipling and Somerset Maugham who have been honoured by the Raffles Hotel by having a suite named after him.

The French business community

During the economic crisis of 1929, some companies struggled and even closed up shop, for example, the Pathé company. In contrast, business was flourishing for the Banque de l'Indochine, the Messageries Maritimes and the construction company Brossard-Mopin. Other companies decided to move to Singapore, and entrepreneurs continued to try their luck there.

The Ballereau economic report on French-Malaya trade

On 5 February 1932, the Consul of France to Singapore, Mr Ballereau, submitted a report to the Sub-directorate of Commercial Relations in London that laid out in great detail the nature of trade between Malaya and France, and provided commentary on trading conditions. France only accounted for 2.4% of all Malaya/Singapore trade. It mainly sold brandy, liqueurs, wine, French foodstuffs (in small quantities, as these were very often considered luxury products), and manufactured products (such as perfumes, tyres and tiles). On the export side, Malaya mainly sold foodstuffs (tapioca, pineapple, sago) and raw materials (copra, rubber, tin) to France.

The Consul explained why, in his view, France was not a major economic player: the prices of French products were too high, competition was stiff (a "Buy British" campaign was bearing fruit), and some articles became the targets of counterfeiters. He mentioned the case of Vichy water: "These have had a relatively major success, as the English like it as a last drink of the evening, after spirits. Two Singaporean businesses, who are specialists in sodas, lemonades and sparkling waters, produce Vichy water using Vichy salts and natural mineral water from a source in Malaya, which they sell under the name 'Natural Vichy Water' and 'Artificial Vichy Water'. The Consulate of France has protested in vain against this abuse of the word Vichy. The final decision of the court cases currently underway is doubtful."

Nor did French companies make the effort to adapt to the local market: the packaging and the few publicity materials were in French, as were their prices! The Consul concluded his report by proposing that the French government assist French entrepreneurs by providing them with information on local markets.

The Banque de l'Indochine

The Singapore agency of the Banque de l'Indochine opened in 1905. Ten years on, it continued to occupy the same building at the corner of D'Almeida Street and Malacca Street, which was built by the French business Brossard-Mopin. The building was connected to the electricity network in 1915 and, in 1923, a lift was installed. At the time, staff were housed in rented apartments or in a hotel, but during the economic crisis of 1920, rents increased and housing became less affordable. In 1921, those difficult times began to subside, and the opening of the Causeway to Johor in 1923, linking Singapore to the Malay Peninsula by road, provided a springboard for rejuvenated trade. The economy picked up, and the

OPPOSITE: Clara and André Malraux. The couple came to Singapore many times and usually stayed at the Raffles Hotel.

TOP: Advertisement for Vichy water, *The Straits Times*, 4 November 1940.

LEFT: Bungalows of the Banque de l'Indochine, Mount Elizabeth, c.1923.

bank bought a plot of land on Tanglin Hill to build a house for its manager. The residence was situated in a fashionable district of the city, and had its own tennis court. Three bungalows were built for expatriate staff on Mount Elizabeth Road, on the current site of the Mount Elizabeth Hospital. These houses were two-storey structures, enabling better ventilation, and had large verandas. In 1925, garages were added; by then the French members of staff drove their cars to work, and the bank had acquired several cars including a Fiat, a Buick and a ten-horsepower Citroën.

Local employees continued to be recruited from Indochina, and Indians from Pondicherry. Some worked at the bank from generation to generation, such as the members of the Selvanathan family and M. B. Rajam, who was decorated in 1961 for 35 years of service in the company. In 1915, the bank had 12 employees—in 1940, it had 23.

After 1914, the bank issued more and more loans to the Chinese, who became its largest group of clients. Tan Boon Liat was one of the best known clients, and formed a partnership with the Société Lorraine de Rotin. His family was educated in the European manner, and were part of Singaporean high society. Dr Lim Boon Keng was also an important bank client.

Until 1929, trade between Indochina and Singapore grew continuously due to the rice, rubber and tin trade for which Singapore had become a veritable hub. In 1906, 60% of global tin production came from Malaya's mines, and this material transited through Singapore. France was one of the main importers. Products from Java, the China Sea region and the Pacific also passed through Singapore, transforming the port into an exceptional trading centre.

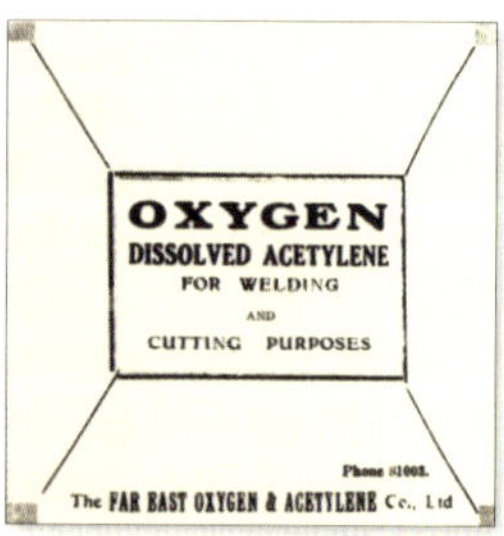

The Great Depression of 1929 had some impact on the Banque de l'Indochine. Some major clients went bankrupt. Moine Comte merged with another company, and Chesnot became the agent for Michelin. The bank continued to invest in property, including buildings on Holland Road and Bukit Timah Road, fashionable areas at the time even though they were far from the town centre.

Far East Oxygen and Acetylene Co. Ltd.—Air Liquide

The late 19th century was a time of technological innovation. Georges Claude, a graduate of the Ecole Supérieure de Physique et Chimie Industrielle, developed a method of liquifying air and separating it into nitrogen, oxygen and carbon. Together with businessman Paul Delorme, he founded Air Liquide, Société Pour L'Etude et L'Exploitation des Procédés Georges Claude in 1902. In 1907, Air Liquide took its first exploratory steps and established an operational base in Japan. Its branch in Singapore was established later, in August 1911, where it was called Far East Oxygen & Acetylene Co. Ltd. The company was initially represented by Moine Comte & Co. Its workshops were located at No. 45, Robinson Road. In 1917, the Singapore branch was no longer represented by Moine Comte, but the company retained its premises on Robinson Road and continued to grow.

In 1930, the company opened a factory at No. 851, Pasir Panjang Road, which produced gases used for welding and metal cutting. In 1932, the company established a free school for welding apprentices and in 1939, a new factory opened in Tiong Bahru. The following year, the company opened the Oxygen Sports Club. At the end of the Japanese occupation, it was one of the first companies to reopen for business.

The Brossard-Mopin construction business

Founded in 1906 and based in Saigon, the Brossard-Mopin construction company opened a number of offices in the Far East and played a considerable role in the Chinese, Indochinese and Malayan markets. It pioneered the use of reinforced concrete in Asia which, unlike steel, is highly resistant to local climate conditions and requires little maintenance. The Hanoi railway station, the 6,000 metres of docks in Saigon and the city's market are all the work of Brossard-Mopin.

The company's Singapore offices were inaugurated in 1912. Initially located in Gresham House on Battery Road, the company moved to Raffles Place in 1924, into the French Bank Building, a building constructed by Brossard-Mopin. In 1932, it moved to No. 69 E, Geylang Lorong 1. Thanks to the high reputation of its engineering architects and its competitive prices, the French company won numerous contracts.

Over a period of two decades, it was responsible for more than 140 different construction projects: the Kallang Bridge in 1916, Eu Court apartments in 1920, Saint Teresa's Church in Kampong Bahru in 1926, the Mercantile Bank Building on Raffles Place, the Capitol Theatre in 1928 and the FMS Railway station in Tanjong Pagar. In 1930, the company took on the renovation of the Hajjah Fatimah mosque, built in 1846 on Beach Road, and modified part of the prayer hall and the dome. The main material used for the minaret was reinforced concrete. The mosque was gazetted as a national monument in 1973.

The Telok Ayer Methodist Church is one of the oldest Chinese Protestant places of worship, and was designed in 1924 by Swan and Maclaren. The building blended European Art Deco style and other Asian-inspired architectural elements, such as the pagoda-shaped roof and the "five-foot way" typical of shophouse designs. Brossard-Mopin won the contract with a tender of $46,000. On 19 January 1924, the first stone was laid, and work was completed by Christmas; the Church, became a national monument in 1989.

OPPOSITE TOP: Advertisement by Far East Oxygen and Acetylene, *The Straits Times*, 25 April 1931.

OPPOSITE BELOW: Founders of Air Liquide.

TOP: Advertisment for tiles by Brossard-Mopin, *The Straits Times*, 13 October 1921.

BOTTOM: Advertisement for concrete lawn rollers by Brossard-Mopin, *The Straits Times*, 15 October 1925.

Numerous advertisements in the local press at the time mention a Brossard-Mopin warehouse where it was possible to buy French tiles, cement and even rent a steamroller, for example to smooth out a tennis court, for a mere $30! The French company employed Indochinese and Indians from Pondicherry at its offices, and Chinese, Malays and Indians on its work sites. Recruited from France or Switzerland, the firm's engineers held management positions and were sometimes responsible for drafting plans. Thus, Pierre-Henri Barrière managed the Singapore office until 1926 and played an active part in the city's life as a qualified juror. In 1912, he also built a kind of ship with a concrete structure—somewhat of an innovation—which would provide a connection between Johor and Singapore until the construction of the Causeway in 1923.

Brizay Construction Ltd.

In 1926, Emile Brizay, a 26-year-old engineer, answered a job advertisement placed by the Brossard-Mopin company. The company was looking for an engineer familiar with pre-stressed concrete to work in Malaya. Although he spoke no English, Brizay was hired and arrived in Singapore. He worked on all kinds of worksites: hotels, bridges, shops, churches and banks. In 1927–8 alone he was responsible for three projects: St Teresa's Church, the Fresh Food Store (which later housed the Singapore Cold Storage) and the Mercantile Bank building.

Soon he decided to establish his own business. In September 1929, he opened offices in the town of Segamat, in Johor, and won many contracts from the Public Works Department due to his competitive prices. In 1934, he crossed the Causeway and moved back to Singapore. Noting the island's housing shortage, he became a developer-builder. He registered his business under the name Brizay

EMILE BRIZAY (1900–1983): A TALENTED ENGINEER

Emile Brizay was born in Nantes on 25 February 1900. At the age of 16, he joined the army; only after his death did his family discover his Croix de Guerre in the back of a drawer. In 1926, he moved to Malaya and, three years later, married Madeleine Dyonnet, who would bear him four sons. The family settled in Singapore in 1934. In June 1940, Brizay refused to surrender to the Japanese and joined the Resistance. A fervent Gaullist, he headed the Free French Committee in Singapore. With the Imperial Japanese Army at the gates of the city, Brizay left for Australia, where he offered his services to General Casey, a deputy of General MacArthur, who named him Consultant Engineer to the Chief Engineer of the US Army in Melbourne. He oversaw the construction of wooden hangars and warehouses in Sydney, Darwin, Townsville and many other sites. With the end of the war in 1945, he returned to Malaya to help rebuild the country. Many of the bridges that he had built had been destroyed. In 1948, he returned to France for good, and died in 1983. Emile Brizay successfully combined imagination, an ability to adapt and an entrepreneurial spirit throughout his life.

Construction Limited, with the lawyer Ramsay Wilson as president. He then bought a six-hectare area of land close to Holland Road, split it into 14 plots and built houses there between 1935 and 1938, the first of which he kept for himself. The city council decided to name the area Brizay Park.

TOP: View of Brizay Park, *The Straits Times*, 15 March 1936.

BELOW: Advertisement by Optorg, *The Straits Times*, 14 August 1936.

In 1979, Professor Jon Lim paid homage to Brizay, and described the property: "Perhaps one of the finest examples of off-formwork rests with the roof ventilators at Brizay Park Homesteads. These are shaped like inverted champagne glasses and consist of slots between alternating concrete panels in order to draw up induced ventilation from below under strong wind conditions."

In 1940, Brizay won the contract for the new Ford factory, the first automobile assembly line in Southeast Asia. Brizay designed and constructed an immense building more than one hectare in size at Bukit Timah. Rather than using a steel framework, he decided to use reinforced concrete. Here too, the façade contained Art Deco styling elements. In October 1941, Ford took possession of the premises. Two months later, the Japanese invasion began, and the English signed their act of surrender inside the building. During the occupation, the building's assembly lines were used to build trucks. In 1946, Ford regained possession of its plant, and remained there until 1980. The rear of the building was demolished in 1997 to make way for the Hillside condominium. Nine years later, the remainder of the renovated building was gazetted as a national monument and became a museum dedicated to the Japanese occupation during the Second World War, entitled "Memories at the Old Ford Factory".

The Optorg Group

The Optorg group was established in 1919 by a major textiles company in northern France to develop its wholesale trading activities across the globe. In 1936, the trading company established itself in Indochina. Its first offices in Singapore also opened in the same year. The company imported cotton, wine, liqueurs, fertiliser, hardware and chemical products.

The Optorg company also represented the Compagnie des Chargeurs Réunis in Malaya and Singapore. In 1937, Paul Clerc became manager, and the offices moved to No. 124, Robinson Road. Clerc was a noted figure in Singapore. Born in Paris, he joined the army and received a Croix de Guerre at the age of 19. In 1920, he joined the company of his brother-in-law, Malcolm Béranger, in Malaya. Clerc was internationally known as an amateur tennis champion, having won the championship title in Malaya in 1927, and he was also the Deputy President of the Singapore Lawn Tennis Association. He was decorated by France with the Croix de la Résistance for his bravery during the Japanese Occupation of Singapore. He was also one of the founding members of the Alliance Française in 1949. In 1953, he received the medal of Knight of the Legion of Honour after 33 years of service in Singapore. The Optorg group continued to grow and

FRENCH KNOW-HOW DISPLAYED DURING THE MALAYA-BORNEO EXHIBITION IN SINGAPORE (31 MARCH–8 APRIL 1922)

In the tradition of the universal exhibitions that were held in the mid-19th century, Sir Laurence Guillemard, the Governor of the Straits Settlements (1921–1927), wanted, "for the first time in history, to bring together representatives of all classes from the two important Malayan countries under British influence (the Malay Peninsula and Borneo), so that by personal meeting, by interchange of ideas and discussion of matters of interest to each, considerable mutual benefit and a revival of local trade could be stimulated." The site was the newly reclaimed district of Telok Ayer and the main entrance faced Robinson Road. On entering, three large avenues opened up to visitors: Guillemard Avenue, dedicated to commercial stands, Raffles Avenue, mainly focusing on businesses with electrical and mechanical products, and Borneo Avenue, devoted to the sciences, medicine and restaurants. There was also a stadium and a large stage to welcome the guests of honour. Each day, visitors were offered a programme of cultural and sporting activities.

The traders of the French community participated in the Exhibition, whose highlights were described in *The Straits Times*: "The visitor is attracted by the piquant exterior of the French pavilion, in which is grouped the exhibits of not one but a number of local French firms showing the ramifications of the industries in which our friends of the Entente Cordiale are engaged ... Messrs Brossard and Mopin show a reinforced road surface which might well engage the attention of our Municipal Commissioners as well as machine-made joining from Tonkin. Messrs Beyer and company show a fine collection of French perfumes, Moine Comte and Cie have a delightful exhibit of Lyon's silk, while Pathé Brothers are represented by a comprehensive display of cinema projectors, and everything, from the proverbial anchor down to a needle, in the area of cinema. The M.M. Cie is also represented and the Fauconnier Posth by a most interesting collection of rubber goods, even a rubber elephant!"

gradually focused on the African continent, where today it is a specialist in the distribution of machinery, trucks and motor vehicles.

The religious missionaries remain active

The censuses of 1921 and 1931 indicated the continued predominance of the Buddhist, Taoist and Confucian religions (72.6%). Nonetheless, the Catholic community expanded from 22,000 members in 1904 to 41,000 in 1922. During the interwar period, the MEP continued to play a very active role in the Catholic community in Singapore. The French bishops of the MEP, Bishop Barillon, from 1904 to 1933, and Bishop Devals from 1934 to 1945, encouraged the construction of churches and invited new congregations to move to Singapore.

Bishop Barillon and the Chinese Catholics

In 1904, Father Emile Barillon was ordained as Bishop of Malacca, and took up his duties in Singapore two months later. He managed a team of about 40 priests, mostly French, as well as three local priests who worked across Singapore, which was divided into four parishes. Bishop Barillon aimed to develop structures for training teachers and the catechists who would come to assist the missionaries. In 1920, he opened the Minor Seminary of Saint Francis Xavier in Upper Serangoon to provide better training for the local priests.

Squeezed into the Church of St Peter and St Paul, the Chinese Catholic community began to feel cramped with the arrival of large numbers of Chinese Catholic migrants. To address the space crunch, the Church of the Sacred Heart was built in 1910 for the Hakka and Cantonese communities. In October 1923, Reverend Father Mariette was given the task of building a new place of worship. In 1925, he acquired a green-field site close to Tanjong Pagar in Kampong Bahru, on Bukit Purmei. The drawings of Father Ouillon, inspired by the Sacré Cœur in Paris, served as a plan for constructing the new church, to be named St Teresa of the Infant Jesus. Brossard-Mopin and Paul Brizay carried out the works. White and positioned on a hill, the church does resemble the famous basilica.

Unfortunately, the construction of the church was marred by a tragic event. While Father Mariette was performing a tour of inspection on the evening of 13 March 1928, he was killed by a falling wooden plank. He was buried in the Bidadari cemetery. After two years of work, on 7 April, Bishop Perrichon blessed the building in the presence of more than 6,000 people. To beautify the site, in March 1930, a first Way of the Cross was purchased from the French company A. Nouvelist; later, a coloured statue of St Teresa would arrive from Lisieux. This was replaced in 1983 by another statue representing Christ ascending to heaven. The French stained-glass windows represent the life of St Teresa and were donated

OPPOSITE: Cover of the official guide to the Malaya Borneo Exhibition, 1922.

TOP: Father Emile Mariette (1863–1928).

LEFT: Church of St Teresa, consecrated on 7 April 1929.

BISHOP ADRIEN DEVALS (1882–1945)

Born to a farming family in the Aveyron region, Devals entered the Minor Seminary in Rodez and joined the MEP in June 1900. In September 1906, he left for Malaya, where he was assistant to the rector, and then the curate of the Church of the Assumption in Penang, where he ministered to the Europeans and Chinese in the parish. In 1912, while on a posting to Singapore to care for the Hokkien community there, he ran into difficulties with anti-Christian Chinese secret societies who vandalised the church. The same year, he returned to France following the death of his father. He stayed in France until the outbreak of the First World War in 1914, when he first served as a nurse, then as an interpreter in a munitions factory with Chinese workers. In 1920, he returned to Malaya. In Penang, he contributed towards the construction of new churches and schools. He was appointed Bishop of Malacca in Singapore in 1934, where he planned to promote Catholicism and Catholic Action. His plans came to a halt with the Japanese invasion of the Malay Peninsula. He passed away in 1945 in the agricultural colony of Bahau, in Malaya.

in 1931 by the MEP procureurs (who oversee administrative tasks), Father Ouillon and Father Couvreur, and a generous Chinese donor, Mr Wee Cheng Soon.

Bishop Devals and Catholic Action

In April 1934, Father Adrien Devals was ordained as Bishop of Malacca in the Church of the Assumption in Penang by the Vicar Apostolic of Bangkok, Bishop Perros. He soon moved to Singapore and focused on the renewal of the Catholic faith. Following the teachings of Pope Pius XI, he developed Catholic Action programmes to further involve Christians in the life of the Church, and invited religious orders to open more schools in Singapore. In 1935, the Carmelites from Bangkok, a contemplative order, opened a monastery in Singapore. Mother Teresa of the Angels, accompanied by three Sisters, founded the institution of the Carmel of Christ the King in Kampong Bahru, beside the Church of St Teresa.

In 1936, Bishop Devals established the *Malaya Catholic Leader* newspaper with the assistance of Father Cardon. He reported the conditions of the clergy in 1939: "The recruitment and training of our local clergy is continuing normally in our seminaries in Singapore and Penang. We have 21 priests, all animated by the best missionary spirit and working with a zeal which exceeds all praise; this however remains a small number relative to the work, which increases year by year."

Continuing the educational mission

The SJI and CHIJ remained two very reputable establishments where teaching was provided in English, which enabled students to get jobs in the offices of the government or in the major trading businesses upon graduation. During the economic crisis of the 1930s, school fees rose and became unaffordable for many families. In order not to deprive needy children of their education, the missionaries opened new schools where lessons were taught in Chinese and Tamil, with a smattering of English. Upon his return to Singapore, after serving France during the First World War, Father Bécheras of the MEP, who was in charge of the parish of Sts Peter and Paul, founded two boys' schools near the church on Queen Street—one Chinese and the other English—as well as a girls' school in the district of Serangoon. He learned Teochew, Hokkien, and then Mandarin.

Following a dispute with a school inspector in 1927, Father Bécheras had to fight for the very existence of his English school. Without government support, he completed the construction of an elegant building comprising spacious, airy classrooms. He also provided training for the teachers, and organised courses for former students to complete their studies and prepare them for a career in education. In 1936, he added a two-floor school block and, in 1937, converted the establishment into a secondary school. "The problem of educating our Chinese Catholic children has now entered a new phase," wrote Bishop Devals, adding: "English is no longer sufficient for the younger generation. Relations with China require them to gain a thorough education in their mother tongue." In 1939, the school was named the Catholic High School.

In 1936, Bishop Devals visited Bangkok and was impressed by a school run by the Brothers of St Gabriel, whom he invited to move to Malaya and Singapore.

OPPOSITE BELOW: Father Edouard Bécheras (1879–1957).

BELOW: View of St Joseph's Institution, c. 1930.

They took over the management of the Holy Innocents' Boys' School in Upper Serangoon, where the school still stands today. Bishop Devals gave them 18 acres of land in Bukit Timah, close to the Church of St Joseph, to establish a business school. However, the project was halted by the Japanese invasion in 1942.

Charity in times of crisis: a priority

The Fathers of the MEP continued to provide assistance to those most affected by the economic crisis. Singapore's government had little interest in the disadvantaged classes and left the task of working with the disenfranchised fringes of the community to wealthy benefactors and the churches.

Bishop Devals called on two French orders, the Little Sisters of the Poor and the Order of the Good Shepherd. In 1935, a delegation from the order of the Little Sisters of the Poor in Singapore established St Theresa's Home to take in elderly people who had been abandoned. Land for this purpose was purchased by Bishop Devals on Derbyshire Road. The building was simple, even austere. However visitors were very impressed with the way in which these "European Mothers" took care of the elderly. In 1937, thanks to a donation of more than $60,000 from the local entrepreneur Aw Boon Haw, the sisters built a much larger hospice on Thomson Road, which could take in up to 300 people. On 18 May, the new centre was opened in the presence of the Governor, Shenton Thomas. The Sisters provided "full residential care, free medical facilities, physiotherapy and recreational activities for the elderly, regardless of race, gender or religion." Upon their departure from Singapore in 2003, the Catholic Welfare Services took over management of the centre.

In order to help young girls "in distress", Bishop Devals also called upon the Order of the Good Shepherd. The Sisters arrived in 1939 and founded their 352nd home. Located on Punggol Road, the Good Shepherd Home was placed under the responsibility of Mother Marie de Saint Liguori Burke. The Sisters welcomed young girls who had had a bad start in life (such as orphans or prostitutes); they also ran a school on the site of the Church of Our Lady of Lourdes, which served the Tamil community. After the war, the British government provided the Order with land on Thomson Road.

The Malaya Catholic Leader: A newspaper serving Catholic Action

At the instigation of Bishop Devals, the first English-language Catholic weekly was launched in Singapore in January 1935: the *Malaya Catholic Leader* (*MCL*). The 20-page issue was sold, at a price of ten cents, by young choristers who went from door to door in the different parishes. Close to 3,000 copies were sold weekly.

The editor was Father René Cardon of the MEP. The editorial line reflected the principles defined by Pope Pius XI as part of Catholic Action, which aimed to ensure the participation of the laity in the functioning of the Church itself in order to address anticlericalism and the dwindling influence of Catholicism. The main articles focused on the dogma of religion and provided advice on how to be a good Catholic. There was also information on Catholic communities around the world. The *MCL* informed the French community, which was made up of many clergy, on what was happening back home. Some articles had a political bias: an article in the issue of 1 February 1936 explained the role played by the French Communist Party in the Front Populaire coalition against the Church.

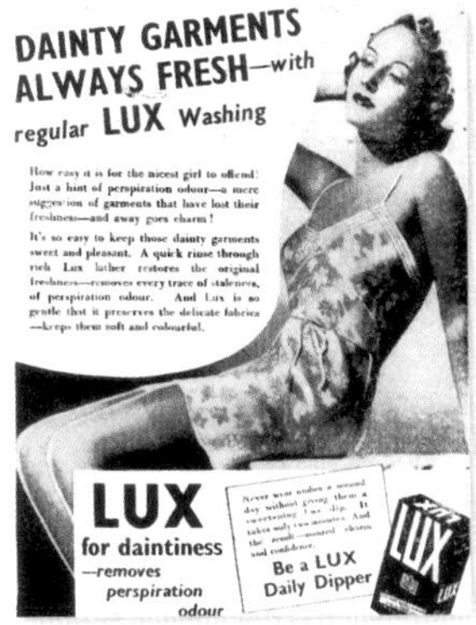

The weekly also contained updates on the buildings that the Church was constructing. Readers could contribute to the paper by sending letters, photographs, or announcements for weddings and obituaries.

To keep the price of the newspaper low, Father Cardon solicited donations and advertising. Some of the ads would be surprising today: Tiger beer, Craven A cigarettes, washing power and soap brands such as Lux, whose advertisement featured a rather lasciviously posed pin-up.

During the Second World War, the *MCL* stopped publication. The Japanese occupiers prohibited its publication and the Catholic community had other priorities: surviving these troubled years.

The 1920s and 1930s constituted a relatively lively period for the Catholic Church. The atheist communist movement grew, notably in Asia where it was sometimes embraced by the anti-colonial movement and secret societies. The British authorities in Singapore regularly had to deal with resurgences of communist activity in the Straits Settlements, and Catholic places of worship were sometimes vandalised and required police protection.

The 1930s: Joseph Ducroux, a communist revolutionary in Singapore

In 1917, the October Revolution brought Lenin to power in Russia where he established a proletarian dictatorship in accordance with the Marxist-Leninist ideal. Lenin fervently hoped that this revolution would spread across the globe. During the 3rd International in Moscow in 1919, communist delegations met to establish the Comintern to put Lenin's ideas into action.

This revolutionary organisation was intended to facilitate the creation of communist parties around the world, and specifically in the various colonial territories. The communist parties called for independence for colonised countries and adopted an anti-imperialist, nationalist and revolutionary approach to establish a "new democracy". Faced with this "Red peril", France and the United Kingdom united their efforts to eliminate such movements. A Frenchman, Joseph Ducroux, played an important role in the Comintern network in Asia and notably in Singapore, even though he only paid a brief visit.

OPPOSITE TOP: Masthead of the *Malaya Catholic Leader*, official Organ of Catholic Action.

OPPOSITE BOTTOM: Father René Cardon.

TOP: Advertisement for Lux, in *Malaya Catholic Leader*, 27 July 1940.

Ducroux was born in 1904 into a family of winemakers in Belleville-sur-Saône (Rhône). After completing his secondary studies with flying colours, he obtained a scholarship and left for Bristol to study commerce and English. Two years later, he was recruited by travel agency Thomas Cook in Paris. In 1923, he joined the French Communist Party and became a member of the Seine Federation of Communist Youth. In 1925, he was arrested by the French police while distributing political leaflets against the Rif War in Morocco. His political commitment did not falter, however, and he continued to write articles for communist newspapers under a *nom de plume*, Dupont. He followed the revolutionary movements in Egypt and India closely and was asked by the Comintern to lead an operation in Asia. The British and French security forces were already aware of his political activities, and for the time being, the two forces worked together.

Between 1926 and 1930, Ducroux made several trips to Moscow to be trained as a Comintern agent. Gradually, his mission became focused on organising the budding communist movement in India. He also learned to encrypt messages, while continuing to write articles under his Dupont pseudonym.

In June 1930, he obtained a passport. He then attempted to obtain a visa to enter British colonies in the Far East, but failed. He decided to assume a new identity, and took the name Serge Lefranc. At the end of 1930, with a false passport in his pocket, he boarded the Trans-Siberian for China. His aim: to reach India while covering his tracks from the British authorities.

Ducroux made his way to Shanghai in February 1931, where he met the agent Hilaire Noulens, the secretary of the Pan Pacific Trade-Union secretariat, a Comintern agency in Shanghai. He also met Communist leader Ho Chi Minh in Hong Kong and the main Vietnamese communist leaders.

In April 1931, Ducroux, under the name Serge Lefranc, entered Singapore. He stayed at the Raffles Hotel and then, four days later, rented an office. Officially, he was working as the representative of a French company, Etablissements Cidlo, which specialised in forestry equipment, among other things. He went to the French Consulate, at the time under the directorship of Mr Ballereau, and met a consular agent who recommended that he get in touch with the French Moine Comte company.

The British authorities tracked the actions of "Serge Lefranc" closely, as they already knew his true identity. From May onwards, British police surveillance was stepped up. René Onraët, the director of the Special Branch of the Criminal Intelligence Department (CID), rented premises opposite the offices of Ducroux, which provided a hideout for two CID agents who monitored the daily movements of Ducroux and his visitors. Ducroux's Indian office assistant was called in for interrogation. He agreed to collaborate with the police by passing on the letters that he had been asked to send. Onraët thus intercepted six or seven letters. Written in French and in coded language, these were opened, decoded, and then

TOP: Joseph Ducroux (1904–1980).

OPPOSITE BELOW: René Onraët on the cover of the *Malayan Police Magazine*, January 1936.

sent on to their recipients in Shanghai, Hong Kong and France, in order not to arouse Ducroux's suspicion.

On 1 June 1931, at around 4:30pm, Ducroux was arrested in Singapore together with 14 Chinese and 1 Indian, all suspected of being communist agents. Police also raided premises in Geylang, Tanglin and Cairnhill and seized a print shop that published communist literature and leaflets. When Onraët searched Ducroux's offices and home, he found a large amount of money, business cards printed with the name Serge Lefranc, communist literature and an address book. The latter contained contact information for Noulens in Shanghai and for Ho Chi Minh in Hong Kong and the address book provided conclusive evidence of their involvement in the communist movement. Ho Chi Minh, who was using the pseudonym T.V. Vong, was arrested in Kowloon, Hong Kong on 6 June, and Noulens in Shanghai on 15 June 1931.

The media and the British authorities trumpeted Ducroux's arrest. Internationally, the case had major implications in the fight against the spread of communism in Asia. The Special Branch had stopped the MCP (Malayan Communist Party) and ICP (Indochinese Communist Party) in their tracks.

MR RENÉ ONRAËT AND THE LEGION OF HONOUR

In 1932, the Consul of France in Singapore, André Ballereau, recommended that the British officer René Onraët be awarded the French Legion of Honour. He wrote: "The discovery of documents on the person and in the papers of Lefranc, alias Ducroux, are thanks to his skilful intervention, and has enabled the arrest of the Indochinese communist leader Nguyen Ai Quoc (alias Ho Chi Minh) and that of Noulens." The French diplomat added: "Mr Onraët is of French origin. His naturalised British father was a police officer in central India. His mother is French." But the British authorities opposed the nomination on the grounds that as a servant of the British Crown, Onraët could not receive recognition from another nation.

René Henry de Solminihac Onraët was born in India in 1887. After completing his studies in England, he joined the Straits Settlements police force in 1907. He also worked for the British services in Malaya. While posted to Penang, he married Muriel Purghope in 1914. In 1922, he was appointed superintendent and director of the Criminal Intelligence Department, later to be called the Special Branch. This service, established following the Sepoy mutiny of 1915, was mainly responsible for intelligence and counter-espionage services. Onraët became the Inspector General of the Police of the Straits Settlements in 1935. In 1939, he returned to Great Britain to enlist in the British army. Two years later, he retired with the rank of Major but continued to work for the Colonial office. After the end of the war, the British Military Administration asked Onraët to re-establish the Special Branch.

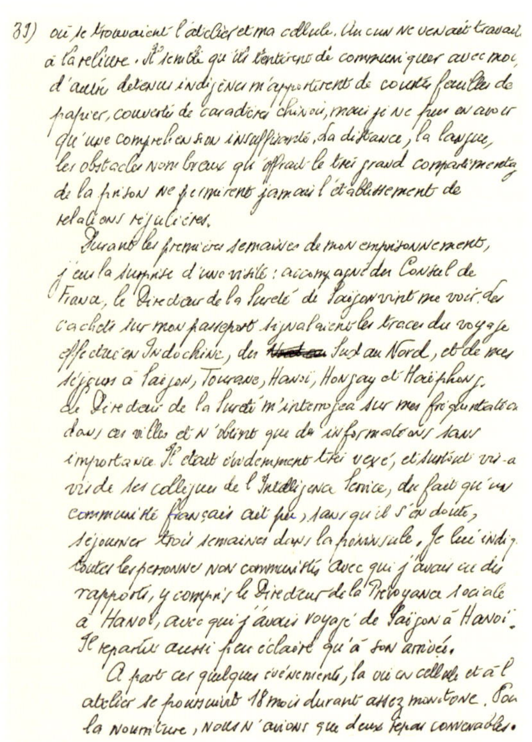

31) où se trouvaient l'atelier et ma cellule. Aucun ne venait travailler à la reliure. Il semble qu'ils tentèrent de communiquer avec moi, d'autres détenus indigènes m'apportèrent de courtes feuilles de papier, couvertes de caractères chinois, mais je ne pus en avoir qu'une compréhension insuffisante. La distance, la langue, les obstacles nombreux qu'offrait le très grand compartimentage de la prison ne permirent jamais l'établissement de relations régulières.

Durant les premières semaines de mon emprisonnement, j'eus la surprise d'une visite : accompagné du Consul de France, le Directeur de la Sûreté de Saigon vint me voir. Les cachets sur mon passeport signalaient les traces du voyage effectué en Indochine, du ~~[illegible]~~ Sud au Nord, et de mes séjours à Saigon, Tourane, Hanoï, Hongay et Haiphong. Le Directeur de la Sûreté m'interrogea sur mes fréquentations dans ces villes et n'obtint que des informations sans importance. Il était évidemment très vexé, et surtout vis-à-vis de ses collègues de l'Intelligence Service, du fait qu'un communiste français ait pu, sans qu'il s'en doute, séjourner trois semaines dans la péninsule. Je lui indiquai toutes les personnes non communistes avec qui j'avais eu des rapports, y compris le Directeur de la Prévoyance sociale à Hanoï, avec qui j'avais voyagé de Saigon à Hanoï. Il repartit aussi peu éclairé qu'à son arrivée.

A part ces quelques événements, la vie en cellule et à l'atelier se poursuivit 18 mois durant assez monotone. Pour la nourriture, nous n'avions que deux repas convenables.

At his trial, Ducroux denied any involvement in communist activities. Speaking in perfect English, he presented himself as a businessman whose only contacts were of a professional nature. However, he did admit to his false identity (Serge Lefranc), and explained this was due to the need for references to do business with the Moine Comte company. After a four-day trial, the judge sentenced Ducroux to 18 months in prison. Others who were arrested at the same time received much harsher sentences.

Ducroux was released in December 1932, a week early. His prison sentence was combined with a lifetime ban from Singapore, and he was accompanied to the port docks by the British police. He departed for Saigon, the closest French destination to Singapore, where the French police were awaiting him. He was taken to the central prison, under arrest for using a false identity. At the same time, a campaign was launched to demand his repatriation to France. He received a one-year prison sentence for falsifying his identity documents, but was allowed to serve his sentence in the Saint-Pierre prison in Marseille, France.

On 3 November 1933, Ducroux was once again a free man. After a brief stay on the Côte d'Azur, he returned to Paris and continued with his political activities. He got married and worked as a translator for Editions Sociales Internationales, the French Communist Party's publishing house, of which he was director from 1944 to 1955. Following internal purges after the death of Stalin, Ducroux, considered a pro-Stalin element, was brutally dismissed. He then worked for the French Communist Party-affiliated Banque Commerciale de l'Europe du Nord until his retirement.

In an article "*Singapore: how did everything start?*", he discussed his experiences in Singapore: "This serious failure in Singapore represented a real turnabout in my political life. My international career which had started so well in China and in Moscow had ended. Another career, only in France and at a lower and reduced level was to follow." He died in Paris in 1980, aged 75.

The Consulate becomes a Consulate General

TOP: Extract from Joseph Ducroux's diary.

OPPOSITE: André Ballereau, French Consul, 1937.

Downgraded to a vice-consulate from 18 August 1916 to 15 July 1918, the Singapore mission regained its consulate status at the end of the First World War.

Fourteen years later, the Consul, Mr Ballereau, began negotiations with Paris to transform the Singapore mission into a Consulate General; he finally won the day in 1937. The mission's administrative duties remained identical, but its diplomatic role gained importance. This change in status indicated the importance that Singapore was gaining on an international level, particularly for France.

Indian and Indochinese staff continued to handle administrative tasks, such as secretarial, translation, and maintenance work. In 1929, Mr Samy Marimoute, in recognition of his 35 years of service as a factotum, received a bronze medal of honour, an award given for services rendered to France. Positions of responsibility remained in the hands of a growing French staff.

The Consul had to regularly remind the British colonial authorities of the French presence in the colony. In a letter dated 25 July 1932, Consul Ballereau recounted his journey to Malacca on the occasion of the silver anniversary celebrations of Father François of the MEP. He wrote: "I felt it necessary to attend the celebration events as much to please Father François as to underline his French nationality and that of his colleagues in the Missions Etrangères de Paris … A French flag had been installed in the seat of honour at the last moment because I had expressed a desire for this … After speeches in English and Chinese, I spoke in French, as a reminder that the Missions Etrangères and Father François himself are French and to claim for France the right to be proud of the good which her sons have disseminated in the Far East, and particularly in Malaya."

The Consul General and his team continued to perform the main functions of a foreign diplomatic post: civil registrations, notarial services and visa issuance. He also sent reports to the French embassy in London, to which the Consulate General reported.

In March 1939, the diplomatic mission moved to Nos. 5 and 7, Gallop Road. The two "black-and-white" houses were respectively named Atbara and Inverturret. Located near the Botanic Gardens, Atbara was designed in 1898 by R.A.J. Bidwell of the Swan and Maclaren architecture firm. It is the oldest "black-and-white" type

CRIME OF PASSION AT THE CONSULATE GENERAL

On 28 November 1939, the body of a young Chinese man, Goh Teow Hoon, was found in the servants' quarters at the Consulate General. This was a crime of passion. The young man, enamoured of Wee Ah Wah, the cook's wife, twice attempted to kiss her. She rebuffed his advances, and he then stabbed her twice with a knife. Hearing the attack, the wife of the Consul General Mr Pingaud called for help. Upon arrival at the scene, Police Inspector Francis Goodship took statements from various witnesses, and also searched Goh's room, where he discovered a tin of caustic soda. The Inspector then decided to head to the cook's room, where he found the young man's body with traces of soda on his lips. Two weeks later, the medical examiner concluded that this was a case of suicide by poison.

house in Singapore. Bidwell developed an architectural style which adapted the English traditional home of the start of the century to a tropical environment. In 1906, in the same neighbourhood, he also drafted the design for Inverturret.

The consular mission was also responsible for welcoming visiting dignitaries and sailors making port calls, and facilitating contact between them and the members of the French community. After a first visit in 1933, the training vessel *Jeanne d'Arc* returned to Singapore in November 1937. Consul Ballereau and his team organised meetings between the British authorities, the French military and residents. A tour of the city and sporting activities were also planned. Commander Auphan hosted a tea dance for 400 guests on board the ship.

In June 1939, Consul Pingaud welcomed the military personnel participating in the Singapore Defence Conference, an event which took place over three days in the gymnasium of the Tanglin Barracks. More than 50 officers of the British and French armies discussed plans for cooperation between their naval bases in the Far East. Tensions between the fascist powers and liberal democracies were increasing as much in Europe as in Asia, and war loomed.

The Second World War

TOP LEFT: "Black-and-white" house, Atbara, French Consulate, Gallop Road.

TOP RIGHT: "Black-and-white" house, Inverturret, French Consulate, Gallop Road.

OPPOSITE: Pierre Boulle (1912–1994). He was a French novelist largely known for two famous works, *The Bridge over the River Kwai* (1952) and *Planet of the Apes* (1963).

On 3 September 1939, Great Britain and France officially declared war on Germany. The population in Malaya heard radio retransmissions of the speech by British Prime Minister, Neville Chamberlain. He announced the expiry of the Franco-British ultimatum following Nazi Germany's invasion of Poland, and war began on European soil.

The defence systems in Singapore were focused on repelling a sea-borne attack. The British were also determined to retain control of the air, and 360,000 men were assigned to defend the colony. Winston Churchill had warned that the Empire's resources would only enable it to retain locations of vital strategic importance, while others would be sacrificed. Singapore, "an impregnable fortress", constituted a key bastion of British defences. In 1939, a journalist from the *Singapore Herald* described Singapore as "a new, bigger and better Gibraltar, one of the most formidable concentrations of naval, military and strategic power ever put together anywhere."

September 1939–December 1941: A distant war

Following Chamberlain's announcement, the European population in Singapore sprang into action. The German Consul General, Dr Adolf Windecker, informed his countrymen of forthcoming internment. Many had already left for Java in the Dutch Indies. They were joined by a few Italians, despite their country's neutrality in the first weeks of the conflict.

The French mobilisation order in Malaya and Singapore

On 4 September 1939, the French Consul General Pingaud issued a press statement: "Every Frenchman knows where his duty lies, following the order for general mobilisation, the first day of which was Saturday, the first Frenchmen all over the world are rallying to the colours and it is expected that those under the age limit of 49 years will return to France and stand shoulder to shoulder with their countrymen and allies to fight for the cause of the freedom of mankind." On 7 December 1939, the Indian "renouncers" were reminded to register with the French authorities, as were all other French citizens living in Malaya.

The writer Pierre Boulle recorded his registration in his book, *Aux sources de la rivière Kwai*. At the time, he was a planter in Sungei Tinggi, 80 km from Kuala Lumpur.

In November 1939, he finally received his call-up papers from the French Consul, who was responsible for the assignment of young people in Singapore, Malaya and the Dutch Indies. Pierre Boulle was assigned to Saigon. Before proceeding to Indochina, he passed through Singapore and described his encounter with Consul Pingaud: "At Singapore, the Consul received us with a monocle screwed into the eye. He noted with a sigh that times were hard and his funds limited, so that he couldn't refund us our travelling expenses from Kuala Lumpur to Singapore—not that we had even asked him to!—but that he nevertheless considered it his duty to give us first-class tickets from Singapore to Saigon. This question of funds seemed to be his main concern at the moment. He stressed the point again and apologised for having to make us travel on a small cargo boat, the *Maurice Long*, on which the fares were less expensive than on the big liners. We took leave of him, without pointing out that in the *Maurice Long*, which was assigned particularly for the transport of pigs and dried fish, there was neither first nor second class."

A French resistance network forms

In June 1940, events in France came to a head. After the "phoney war" and the start of the Battle of France on 10 May, on 17 June Marshal Pétain announced his intention to request an armistice. The next day, General de Gaulle issued his famous call for resistance from London, in which he declared that the war was not over. On 22 June, in another speech that was widely broadcast, he declared: "I invite all Frenchmen of the land armies, naval forces, and air forces, I invite the engineers and specialist workmen of the armament industry who may find themselves on British territory or who can go there to join me for this purpose. I invite the leaders, soldiers, sailors and airmen of the French forces of the earth, sea and air, wherever they may find themselves, to get in touch with me. I invite all French people who wish to remain free to listen to me and to follow me."

As Singapore was British, the war effort was in full swing. For most of the island's French community, joining the Free French movement appeared the natural thing to do. But some of the French decided to follow Marshal Pétain and his collaborationist Vichy government, and departed for French Indochina. Others were unsure of the best course of action, and decided to wait and see.

Following a meeting at Montoire in October 1940, in which Pétain committed himself to collaboration with the Nazis, General de Gaulle, now in Leopoldville in the Congo, set up the Council for the Defence of the Empire. In the name of France, this Council exercised all of the powers of a government at war over all French territories resisting the Nazis, or which would in future join in the fight. Free French Committees were established in other territories. *The Straits Times* of 29 October reported the founding of liberation committees for Malaya and Singapore, headed respectively by Mr de Langlade, the general manager of SOCFIN, and Mr Emile Brizay, Architect Engineer. Singapore soon became the headquarters for the Free French network in the Far East. The committee's mission was propaganda and intelligence gathering in Southeast Asia to assist Free France and Great Britain. In Singapore, men who sided with Free France wore an armband to show their affiliation.

The Singapore Free French Committee

The Singapore cell, under the leadership of Brizay, was extremely active. It was responsible for receiving the numerous Frenchmen arriving from China, Hong Kong or Indochina who wished to head for London or Africa. The local press mentioned some of the new recruits, such as former sailors who had joined the Gaullist movement: "During their stay, all were housed at the Marine Hostel at the expense of the Free French committee who also provided them with pocket money as most of them were penniless. Their passages to Britain were also provided by this committee. Free French women attended to the men's clothing and supplied them with a good deal of light and warm clothes."

Following an 18-month stay in Indochina, Pierre Boulle obtained permission to return to Malaya in July 1941. The next month, in Singapore, he decided to join the Free French Committee. He underwent military training from the British Intelligence Service in a school called the Convent, hidden away in the jungle, where he learned to blow up bridges, derail trains and handle explosives.

In December 1941, Brizay was asked by the British Air Vice-Marshal to build aircraft hangars. Brizay proposed a wooden structure, assembled using nails. He won the contract to build some 150 of them—but they would never be put to use, at least not by the English.

A TOUS LES FRANÇAIS

La France a perdu une bataille!
Mais la France n'a pas perdu la guerre!

Des gouvernants de rencontre ont pu capituler, cédant à la panique, oubliant l'honneur, livrant le pays à la servitude. Cependant, rien n'est perdu!

Rien n'est perdu, parce que cette guerre est une guerre mondiale. Dans l'univers libre, des forces immenses n'ont pas encore donné. Un jour, ces forces écraseront l'ennemi. Il faut que la France, ce jour-là, soit présente à la victoire. Alors, elle retrouvera sa liberté et sa grandeur. Tel est mon but, mon seul but!

Voilà pourquoi je convie tous les Français, où qu'ils se trouvent, à s'unir à moi dans l'action, dans le sacrifice et dans l'espérance.

Notre patrie est en péril de mort.
Luttons tous pour la sauver!

VIVE LA FRANCE !

GÉNÉRAL DE GAULLE

An active commitment towards Indochina

As the situation in France deteriorated rapidly, and the Japanese threat to French Indochina increased, the Service de Renseignement Intercolonial (SRI) stepped up its activities. Its aim was to provide regional information on Japanese advances. The Frenchmen of the SRI established regular contact with the British Intelligence Service in Singapore. This rear-guard action by the men of the Gaullist movement in Singapore enabled them to play a part in the war effort. The British received warnings about the movements of the Japanese fleet. Boulle, now involved in the resistance movement, held a desk position as he awaited a mission. In September 1941, a member of the resistance movement met him at the Adelphi Hotel to offer him his first mission: to go to Indochina with a tonne of explosives and train young recruits. After two days at sea, the crew received a coded message. The next day, the message was finally deciphered: "Indochina alerted. Japanese keeping close watch on rendezvous point. Return immediately." The mission was aborted, and the little boat returned to Singapore. Boulle returned to his office job, which he described as increasingly monotonous.

An active commitment focusing on the hunt for spies

The Liberation committees also worked to hunt down Vichy (Nazi-supporting) agents. Following the end of the Battle of France in June 1940, pro-Vichy elements arrived in Singapore, including Commander Maurice Lenormand who attempted to send two secret letters to Shanghai, without going through official channels. His mail was intercepted, however, and Lenormand was captured and sentenced to death by the British and French resistance.

A symbolic commitment

On Armistice Day (11 November), the Free French Committee participated in a memorial ceremony at the Singapore Cenotaph. On the Padang, before British officials, Brizay placed a wreath in memory of those who had fallen during the First World War. On Bastille Day, a large portion of the French community met at the Cathedral of the Good Shepherd for the requiem mass held by Father

TOP: The "Appeal of 18 June"—General de Gaulle's call to all French men and women to unite in the Resistance, 1940.

BOTTOM: The French flag with the Cross of Lorraine, emblem of the Free French.

Cardon, a WWI veteran. Meanwhile, Mr Baron, the propaganda representative of the Free France movement in the Far East, planned to celebrate the French national day, and brought together his members at the Raffles Hotel.

A financial commitment

The Free French committees organised various activities to raise funds for the Gaullist movement. On 4 July 1940, the Europeans in Singapore organised an auction, including sales of champagne at a dollar a glass. More than $3,000 was raised by the auction, and donations were also made.

Other initiatives were more modest but highly symbolic. In December 1940, when the war fund was set up, a resident of Singapore suggested organising an auction of the emblem worn by the men of the Free French Committee (the Tricolour and Croix de Lorraine). He set a reserve price of $50.

The colony's European women, as part of the Groupement Féminin Interallié de Malaisie, also played a role in the war effort. Approximately 30 British, French, Polish and Czech women met twice a week at the Centre Intellectuel Français at Mount Elizabeth to knit clothes. In December 1939, they managed to ship 221 pullovers, 25 pairs of socks, 10 pairs of gloves, 10 scarves and 55 pillow cases.

A regularly requested commitment

Thanks to press articles and radio messages from Malaya and Saigon, Singapore's small French community were kept abreast of happenings in mainland France. In September 1939, the BBC started a French-language service. Brizay adapted this concept in Singapore, and the 30-minute programme which he produced included five minutes of advertising and music, a ten-minute news bulletin in French and 15 further minutes of entertainment. The programme was broadcast several times a day.

The French missionaries during the first years of turmoil

At the time when war broke out, a large proportion of the French community comprised clergymen. Conscripted missionaries were instructed to proceed to Indochina. The speed of events and the French defeat would render this mobilisation pointless. In December 1940, Bishop Devals wrote: "We are here with the English and see no hope other than in their victory for the recovery of France and freedom in Europe."

"Business as usual"

Far from the battlefront, life continued in Singapore with a certain nonchalance. The British authorities did not want to alert the population to the possibility of hostilities in the region. Lieutenant-General Arthur Percival, in his book *The War in Malaya*, described Singapore on his arrival: "An atmosphere of unreality hung

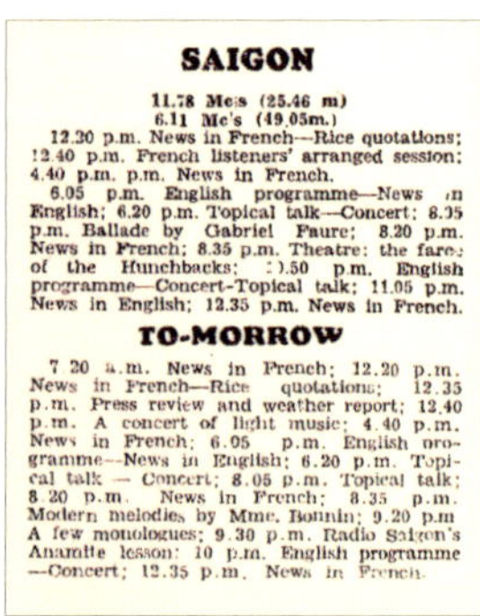

SAIGON

11.78 Mc/s (25.46 m)
6.11 Mc's (49.05m.)

12.20 p.m. News in French—Rice quotations; 12.40 p.m. French listeners' arranged session; 4.40 p.m. p.m. News in French.

6.05 p.m. English programme—News in English; 6.20 p.m. Topical talk—Concert; 8.05 p.m. Ballade by Gabriel Faure; 8.20 p.m. News in French; 8.35 p.m. Theatre: the farce of the Hunchbacks; 10.50 p.m. English programme—Concert-Topical talk; 11.05 p.m. News in English; 12.35 p.m. News in French.

TO-MORROW

7 20 a.m. News in French; 12.20 p.m. News in French—Rice quotations; 12.35 p.m. Press review and weather report; 12.40 p.m. A concert of light music; 4.40 p.m. News in French; 6.05 p.m. English programme—News in English; 6.20 p.m. Topical talk — Concert; 8.05 p.m. Topical talk; 8.20 p.m. News in French; 8.35 p.m. Modern melodies by Mme. Bonnin; 9.20 p.m A few monologues; 9.30 p.m. Radio Saigon's Anamite lesson: 10 p.m. English programme —Concert; 12.35 p.m. News in French.

TOP: Progamme list of Saigon Radio, published in *The Straits Times*, 23 January 1941.

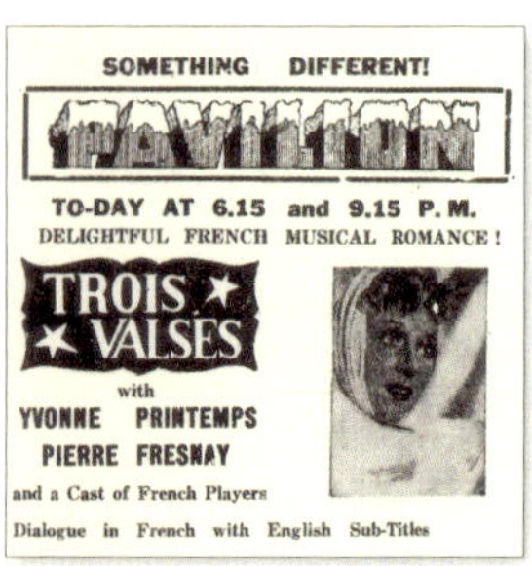

BOTTOM: Poster of the French movie, *Trois Valses*, at the Pavilion Cinema (31 October 1940).

OPPOSITE: Lieutenant-General Arthur Ernest Percival (1987–1966). He was a British Army officer and a veteran of the First World War. He built a successful military career during the interwar period but is most noted for his involvement in the Second World War, when he commanded the forces of the British Commonwealth during the Battle of Malaya and the Battle of Singapore.

over Malaya. In the restaurants, clubs, and places of entertainment, peace-time conditions prevailed. Having just come from England, where austerity had already become the fashion, I must confess to rather an uncomfortable feeling when provided with an almost unlimited amount of food in the hotels and restaurants." Classical music concerts were put on, and cinemas remained open. At the Alhambra cinema, on Orchard Road, the adventure film screenings were preceded by news reels. For example, on 17 July 1941, before a screening of a film starring Humphrey Bogart, the audience viewed the first images from the Pathé and Universal studios of British and Free French forces entering Syria, as well as a "speech to the French Empire and the review of the Free French Forces somewhere in Africa", as the film's publicity posters advertised.

The Consulate General of France and Vichy

With the establishment of the Vichy regime on 10 July 1940, the Third Republic disappeared and was replaced by the French State. The new regime did not encourage dissent, and diplomatic staff generally remained loyal to the new government. According to historian David Bobin, only from May 1941 onwards did diplomatic staff really start to desert the Pétain government, when the Vichy state embarked on a policy of rapprochement with Nazi Germany.

In Singapore, it appeared that Consul General Pingaud initially adopted a wait-and-see attitude. From the financial contributions that he made and his participation in ceremonies at the Cenotaph, the Consul General of France appears to have favoured the Gaullist movement. In October 1939, his wife co-chaired the General Committee of the Malaya Patriotic Fund with the British Governor, Shenton Thomas. She also ensured that the French played a part in raising funds to fight the Axis forces.

December 1941–February 1942: the war reaches Asia

On 30 August 1940, the Japanese Imperial Headquarters and the Vichy government signed a treaty allowing the Japanese army to use the French colony's airfields in Indochina, and permitting 60,000 Japanese soldiers to be stationed in Tonkin. In exchange, Japan recognised Vichy's territorial integrity and French sovereignty over Indochina. The Thai government, sensing the weakness of the French government, decided to recover territory in Cambodia and Laos which it had lost to the French in the 19th century. Through its representative Lieutenant-Colonel Jiro Saito, Japan capitalised on the conflict and imposed its presence across Indochina. In July and December 1941, Vichy and Tokyo signed new agreements for the "common defence of Indochina". Cochinchina became a stationing and transit base for Japanese soldiers. Malaya and Singapore were only a few hours' flight from Indochina.

LUCIEN GOUDARD

Born in the Creuse region in 1898, Lucien Goudard was in Malaya when the Second World War broke out. Working for the Société des Mines d'Etain in Kinta, Perak, he joined a group of French volunteers, the Local Defence Corps. He participated in the retreat through Malaya and travelled more than 700 km to arrive in Singapore in January 1942. During the bombing of the town, he helped evacuate many injured and attempted to protect the Convent of the Holy Infant Jesus. He was taken prisoner by the Imperial Japanese Army and was sent to Saigon where he remained free, but under surveillance. He found employment in a garage and soon joined a resistance network called *Testanière*. He passed food and medicine to a camp of British prisoners and helped a number to escape; he also guided a number of British aviators to the Chinese border. After the war, he received the King's Medal for Courage in the Cause of Freedom from the British Governor, Sir Franklin Gimson—one of the few Frenchmen to receive this distinction. He was made a Knight of the Legion of Honour in 1950.

On 6 December 1941, the Imperial Japanese Army launched an attack on the US naval base of Pearl Harbor, in Hawaii, bringing the United States into the war. On the night of 7 December, Japanese forces landed on the beaches of Kota Baru, in northern Malaya, and Singora, in Thailand. A few hours later, aircraft flew over Singapore and bombed Raffles Place, Chinatown and Seletar. Hong Kong and the Philippines also suffered their first bombings on the same night. On 9 December, General de Gaulle declared war on Japan. The Second World War had expanded across Asia.

The Malayan campaign

The Japanese army moved very rapidly across Malaya. Allied regiments composed of British, Australian, Asian and French volunteer troops (including Lucien Goudard) attempted to resist them. On 1 December 1941, the battleships H.M.S. *Prince of Wales* and H.M.S. *Repulse* were sunk in less than an hour as they sailed to intercept the Japanese fleet at Kota Baru and Singora. Japanese air raids became constant, and the situation in Malaya and Singapore worsened day by day. By 10 February, more than 30,000 Japanese soldiers had reached Johor. British forecasts of a Japanese attack from the sea had turned out to be inaccurate. Instead, the Japanese had made their rapid advance through Malaya on carts, on foot and by bicycle.

The evacuation of Singapore

The number of refugees in Singapore increased in tandem with the advance of the Japanese troops. The inhabitants of the Malay Peninsula arrived in the port city by the thousands, and the population soon swelled to one million. One eye-witness remembered: "The island of Singapore [was] swarmed with people with nowhere to go. Wherever you went, you saw people with suitcases or bundles sitting by the road-side wherever they could find some shade, clustering around water taps or begging for food from passers-by." A curfew, from 9pm to 9am, was introduced at the start of February. An atmosphere of insecurity swept across the island. On 4 February 1942, the population living along the Strait of Johor was evacuated southwards.

Lieutenant-General Arthur Percival was responsible for managing the evacuation of Singapore's civilian population. The issue was raised at a relatively late stage, because evacuating the European community would indicate to their Asian counterparts that the British colonial power was in dire straits. In December 1941, the authorities organised an initial evacuation on a voluntary basis, without much success. A second departure was organised in January 1942. Some 5,200 European women and children departed, while 4,800 remained in Singapore. The evacuees to Australia included Brizay's wife and four children. Brizay himself left Singapore in February 1942 on a Dutch ship.

The Allied-flagged *Félix Roussel* and its convoy left Bombay on 23 January 1942 carrying troops to defend Singapore and to aid in the evacuation of civilians.

BELOW: European women and children evacuating from Singapore, 1941.

On 5 February in the late morning, the *Félix Roussel* was approximately nine miles from Singapore when it was overflown by a formation of 27 Japanese aircraft. The ship was struck by two bombs between its chimney stacks, starting a fire, which the crew rapidly brought under control. The *Empress of Asia*, another ship in the convoy, was much more severely damaged. The *Félix Roussel* docked in the evening, and its troops and equipment were unloaded. The port and town were under air raids day and night. Several gangways were positioned, and women and children boarded without any proper count being made. On the evening of 6 February, the ship sailed. Louis-Robert Cadars, a young service lieutenant remembered: "Shortly after leaving Singapore's harbour in the depths of the night, we managed to join the other transports thanks to a providential fog bank. With great difficulty, the convoy reformed and finally left the trap formed by the Bangka and Sunda Straits. The escorts were fewer than on the inbound journey. As soon as possible, the upper decks were first of all freed of the crowd of women and children who had found themselves trapped there, as the interior rooms were also packed in the same way. Every space had been used, including the corridors which were transformed into temporary dormitories. After this, passengers were finally properly accommodated in the facilities and cabins which had been provided for the transport of troops. In addition, the journey lengthened endlessly due to the numerous course changes which the lead escort was forced to order. Water and food were beginning to run out much faster than expected. We however made port safely." The *Félix Roussel* repatriated more than 1,100 women and children to India.

RIGHT: A family mourns the death of a child.

OPPOSITE: Shinozaki Mamoru (1908–1991). After the war, he wrote a book entitled *Syonan — My Story*, which gives an insight into the Japanese Occupation of Singapore.

On 13 February, a final evacuation order was given, but it came too late. Many Europeans did not manage to leave Singapore when the "Tiger of Malaya", the Japanese General Yamashita Tomoyuki, brought the "impregnable fortress" to its knees on 15 February 1942. Operation Matador, the British military operation to counter the Japanese invasion, was a miserable failure. The human cost of the Malaya campaign was 3,506 dead on the Japanese side, and approximately 7,500 dead on the Allied side. The Japanese took almost 130,000 prisoners and possession of an almost intact naval base, as well as warehouses containing tin and rubber, among other goods.

February 1942–September 1945: The French on Syonan-to

General Yamashita Tomoyuki's 25th Army completed the Malayan campaign in 70 days rather than the 100 days expected by Japanese military headquarters. Percival, the British Lieutenant-General, signed the capitulation in the hangar-like spaces of the Ford factory. Singapore was renamed *Syonan-to*, "the Island of the Light of the South", and Malaya became "*Malai*" in December 1942. Clocks were put forward by an hour and a half to be on the same time as Tokyo. British currency was replaced with a new currency which soon became known as "banana money" because of the fruit on the bills. Shops were required to display Japanese signs, otherwise soldiers were allowed to plunder them.

The new Japanese colony was run under a dual military and civilian administration. In March 1942, Colonel Watanabe Wataru, in charge of military administration, listed the following priorities: maintaining order, controlling the country's wealth, and guaranteeing a certain degree of economic self-sufficiency for the occupation army. Odate Shigeo was a representative of the civilian administration, and held the position of mayor. One of his first decisions was to free Shinozaki Mamoru, a former Press Attaché of the Japanese Consulate to Singapore, arrested by the British in September 1940 for spying. Shinozaki would hold various positions in the Japanese civilian administration, including those of Chief Officer of Education and Chief Welfare Officer.

In February 1942, the press came under Japanese control. A new English-language newspaper appeared: the *Syonan Times*, which became the *Syonan Shimbun* (or *Syonan Sinbun*) in December 1942. The few Frenchmen still remaining on Syonan-to could only read news which had passed through the sieve of the Japanese censor. Major national events in Vichy France, Allied countries, and Indochina received regular coverage.

Singapore's concert halls and entertainment venues re-opened in April 1942. In the cinemas, news images focused mainly on the benefits of the Japanese occupation as part of the Greater Eastern Asia Co-prosperity Sphere, a policy

aimed at creating a self-sufficient block of Asian countries around Japan. Radio focused on programmes propagandising the glory of Japan. Japanese '*nippon-go*' courses were regularly broadcast in order to 'Japanify' the population.

In occupied Singapore, the different populations of the island were not treated identically. Among the Europeans, the Swiss, citizens of a neutral country, and the French, who were considered Allies due to the Vichy regime, were required to wear an armband—a total of almost 200 people according to the Swiss Consul, Heinrich Arbenz. French buildings were neither vandalised nor taken over.

The Consulate General closes its doors

The official diplomatic position of the French mission remained unclear, and very few documents can be found to deduce exactly when the consulate closed. Following the British bombing of the French fleet at Mers-El Kébir on 3 July 1940, diplomatic relations between France and Great Britain were severed. Despite this, administrative documents confirming the continued activities of the consular mission in Singapore can be found, such as the document drawn up for the wedding of Mr Guy Soniam de Schompre, the manager of the Free French network in the Far East. Furthermore, the Consulate General of France was still listed in the Straits Settlements directory for 1940, albeit with a post box as its address.

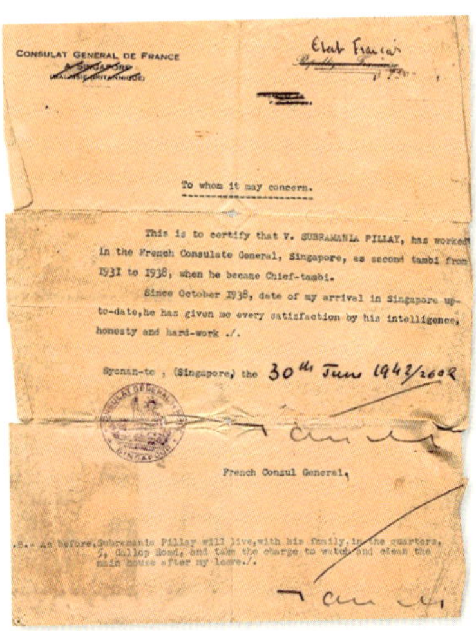

CONSULAT GENERAL DE FRANCE

État Français

To whom it may concern.

This is to certify that V. SUBRAMANIA PILLAY, has worked in the French Consulate General, Singapore, as second tambi from 1931 to 1938, when he became Chief-tambi.

Since October 1938, date of my arrival in Singapore up-to-date, he has given me every satisfaction by his intelligence, honesty and hard-work ./.

Syonan-to , (Singapore) the 30th June 1942/2602

French Consul General,

N.B.- As before, Subramania Pillay will live, with his family, in the quarters, 5, Gallop Road, and take the charge to watch and clean the main house after my leave./.

On 24 January 1942, the readers of *The Straits Times* learned that Jacques Pingaud "is no longer authorised to exercise his consular functions." A month later, the Japanese military authorities issued an order to close all consular missions in Singapore. According to the accounts of employees at the Banque de l'Indochine, the French were required to leave Singapore in June, because the Occupation force did not want to have too many "mouths to feed". Yet, on 30 June 1942, the Consul signed a letter of recommendation for one of his employees, on a modified letterhead on which "French Republic" had been replaced with "French State". The letter certified that the employee had worked as a *tambi* (handyman) for the Consulate and that he and his family could stay in the compound to maintain the premises. Due to the conflicting evidence, there is no confirmed date as to when the consulate actually closed.

The first days of the Occupation

During the first days of the Occupation, chaos reigned in certain parts of the town, where instances of rape and pillage occurred. Plunderers were arrested, their heads cut off and displayed throughout the city. An atmosphere of insecurity and violence hung over the island. On 14 and 15 February 1942, Japanese soldiers massacred the injured and members of staff at the Alexandra Hospital. From 15 February to 3 March, the Japanese military police *Kempetai* set up identity checkpoints, mainly for the Chinese and Eurasians, and arrests increased. On 17 February 1942, the European civilian population whose homelands were at war against Japan were assembled on the Padang and taken to internment camps. The prisoners of war, nearly 100,000 men, were also interned. As a Japanese official, Shinozaki was responsible for issuing a "Good Citizen card"—a "protection card" for individuals considered "good citizens". These were distributed to foreign nationals including the Swiss, Germans and Thais. As for the French, Shinozaki mentioned in a 1973 interview: "The French position was very delicate. In British time they belonged to De Gaulle but when Japan came they turned Vichy. But it was quite difficult to separate the two. I treated all French as Vichy and gave them all cards."

OPPOSITE TOP: Postcard with an image of Japanese soldiers and the "banana currency" used in Syonan-to.

OPPOSITE BOTTOM: Letter from the French Consul in which "French Republic: has been replaced with "French State", 30 June 1942.

Frenchmen in Changi Prison?

On Monday 16 February 1942, the Imperial Army ordered the entire European population to assemble on the Padang the following morning. Nationals of neutral or allied countries were exempted, but some French nationals were interned. These were the resistance fighters who had been unable to leave Singapore in time, or planters who had been captured during the Japanese advance through the Malay Peninsula.

The European civilian population of Malaya was interned in Changi Prison, and later at the camp on Sime Road. According to Japanese historian Nakahara Michiko, the names of a number of French women were on the register of the Civil Internment Camp at Changi, drawn up in March 1942. A browse through the various eye-witness accounts of former prisoners of war also reveals French-sounding family names. The manager of the Banque de l'Indochine, Mr de Courseulles, was imprisoned at Changi over the 1942–1945 period for his work as a resistance fighter. While filing a Legion of Honour request for Roger Dillon-Corneck, manager of the Tekkah mines in Perak, the Consul General of France, André Guibault, wrote in 1952: "Arrested by the Japanese in May 1942, he was incarcerated in the prison at Changi for working in the resistance in the State of Perak, until 30 June 1942, when he was deported to Indochina where he was placed under house arrest in Saigon."

During their years in prison, the interns organised many activities. In her memoirs, *Diary of a Girl in Changi*, Sheila Allan remembered that French courses started at "Changi University" on 19 June 1942, at the same time as Dutch and Spanish courses. Conferences, and films such as Terrence Rattigan's *French Without Tears* also distracted the prisoners from sickness, hunger and death.

The testimony of a Vichy man

The French Commander Maurice Lenormand, who had been arrested and sentenced to death by the British and French resistance fighters, recounted his adventures in a series of seven articles titled "*British bullying of Vichy National*". Published in the *Syonan Times* between 26 March and 14 April 1942, the Vichy supporter wrote: "I give below full information concerning my troubles since my arrival at Singapore on June 7, 1941," justifying his actions in the following way: "I am doing so heartedly and openly since my story will be the best way to enlighten at last those French people still stubbornly believing in the good feelings of the English towards the French, and at the same time the 'de Gaullists' who, for their part, have tried to divide France in order to rule it."

He had left Indochina for medical reasons, and moved to Shanghai to infiltrate the city's Free French Committee. Upon arrival in Singapore, on 7 June 1941, he infiltrated the Gaullist movement easily. On 26 June, he was arrested, the victim of a plot, so he claimed. He explained: "On June 26, I handed over a letter—without any importance—to a member of the Free French committee to post it as I was not well and had to stay in bed: of course I asked him to put a stamp on it and left it open for the Censorship." He was refused the assistance of a lawyer or the Consul of France. Interned in a civilian prison, he was brought before a judge on 16 July, who explained the main charge against him: the suspected despatch of letters to Indochina which compromised the Free French movement. The session was then adjourned.

On 19 September, Mr Baron, the head of the Gaullist movement in Singapore, met the prisoner in a bid to enrol him in the Free French movement. Lenormand refused. He embarked on a hunger strike on 20 November. Ten days later, he was transferred to the General Hospital, where he remained bedridden until 9 December. He was then taken back to the prison where he learned that his execution had been set for Tuesday 17 February 1942. On that day, Japanese soldiers released him.

The French clergy and the Bahau agricultural colony

In February 1942, when the Japanese occupied Singapore, the diocese of Malacca comprised 83,000 Catholics under the leadership of a single bishop, 50 priests (including 23 locals), 182 Brothers, 401 Sisters and 68 schools with a total of 27,000 children. With Singapore's transformation into Syonan-to, the schools came under Japanese control. As Chief Officer of Education, Shinozaki was responsible for the reorganisation of education system. The schools re-opened in April 1942, the start of the school year for Japanese students. English disappeared from the curriculum, and was replaced by Japanese, called *nippon-go*.

St Joseph's Institution

As Japanese troops advanced through the Malay Peninsula in December 1941, Singapore's defences sprang into action. St Joseph's Institution's dormitory building was converted into a hospital by the British armed forces, and all of the city's schools closed down. The SJI classrooms were requisitioned by the Red Cross, while the institution's main courtyard was used as a cemetery.

When the Japanese occupied Singapore, the SJI was renamed the Bras Basah Boys' School, and the Brothers were forced to share the premises with a detachment of Japanese soldiers. The new government opened primary classes for each ethnic group (23 Malay classes, 2 Indian, 5 Chinese and 2 mixed). Brother Joseph remained director until 14 December 1943, after which he was imprisoned. Mr Jing of the Raffles Institution took over the running of the school. The curriculum saw drastic revisions, and singing, gymnastics, theatre, arts and crafts, drawing and Japanese became the new subjects. Later, the students took up gardening, as they needed to grow their own food to survive. In 1943, the student enrolment dropped from 551 to 221; by 1944, the school had only 62 students.

Convent of the Holy Infant Jesus

In December 1941, when the first Japanese bombs fell on Singapore, the Convent of the Holy Infant Jesus was not spared. Chaos reigned. Fortunately, it was the

LEFT: The ground in front of SJI in Bras Basah Road became a vegetable garden.

Christmas holidays, and few children were on the premises. The buildings however housed the Sisters of the Good Shepherd and the Carmelites, as well as orphans—a total of several hundred people. Believing that the Japanese would respect such premises, the Mother Superior, Mother Saint-James, ordered an enormous red cross to be placed on the buildings which had been converted into a hospital. Contrary to expectations, the school became a target for the Japanese. The windows of the chapel were partly destroyed, and the orphanage and the main entrance were hit.

During the Occupation, the school was renamed the Victoria Street Girls' School. The Japanese performed frequent checks to ensure that the Sisters were not hiding British soldiers on the premises, and they verified that none of them were English. All of the Caucasians were required to wear an armband identifying them as not English. This did not prevent Japanese soldiers from knocking on their door to ask for girls one day, while mass was being celebrated in the chapel by Bishop Devals. He immediately brought the service to a halt and made it known to the soldiers that they were in a religious building and certainly not in the right place to find "girls". Frustrated, the soldiers contented themselves with taking the school's car and bus.

With a shortage of teachers, the Japanese organised abbreviated courses to train future teachers. The CHIJ grounds became a campus, where the students learned Japanese national songs, watched propaganda film screenings and played lots of sports. The Sisters grew vegetables and fruit for consumption.

CHIJ also enjoyed a certain prestige among the Japanese officers posted to Singapore. The daughters of the Imperial family had been educated in the schools founded by Mother Mathilde at the start of the 1870s, as the Ladies of Saint Maur were the first Catholic missionaries to settle in Japan.

BELOW: Bombing on Bras Basah Road, February 1942.

The Bahau agricultural colony

In August 1943, as the Japanese military forces came under increasing pressure, they struggled to maintain supply lines. The Japanese authorities put in place an evacuation plan under which 300,000 people were required to leave the city. The Japanese intended to establish agricultural colonies as part of the "Grow more food" programme. To simplify this task, Shinozaki, as Chief Welfare Officer, decided to establish two organisations to manage the Chinese and Eurasian communities. These were the Overseas Chinese Association (OCA), presided over by Dr Lim Boon Keng, and the Eurasian Welfare Association, managed by Dr Charles Paglar. The first agricultural colony was developed at Endau, close to Mersing in the State of Johor, which welcomed Chinese volunteers who cultivated the fertile land. Harvests were intended for their own consumption. Endau was managed by the OCA, and a guarantee was obtained that there would be no Japanese in the camp—this 'New Syonan' saw the arrival of its first convoys in September 1943 and, thanks to the favourable conditions, the Endau experiment got off to a relatively successful start.

Hearing the good news from Endau, Bishop Devals and Herman De Souza, a representative of the Eurasian community, decided to meet Shinozaki to discuss the establishment of another agricultural colony, for the Eurasian and Catholic community of Singapore.

In the meantime, the State of Negri Sembilan had already launched its own agricultural programme, and specifically invited the population of Syonan-to to come and settle. The *Kempetai* regularly harassed the Eurasian population; living conditions were harsh, with hyper-inflation, the black market and the lack of food making daily life a testing experience. In his 1973 interview, Shinozaki explained the situation: "The Eurasian community had consulted me sometimes, they wanted to get out of Syonan because they were closely watched by the *Kempetai*. But we could not accept them into Endau because Endau was a OCA project supported mainly by their own money. If the Eurasian community wanted to get out of Syonan, then they must select another site. Although Negri Sembilan had opened up many new farming lands, they were mostly small areas. To be able to accept a big community a larger area was required and that was Bahau. I was rather anxious about the conditions in Bahau but Bishop Devals of the Roman Catholic Church and Mr Herman De Souza Sr were very much interested in seeing Bahau for themselves. If they were satisfied with it, they said, they wanted to move the convent as well as the Catholic people there. So they went to investigate the place to form their own judgement. After a few days they reported back to me that it was good enough, roads had been opened and big huts built. The people could stay in the big huts first and later build houses of their own, and some of the huts could be used as a church and convent. But I thought a more important thing was to find out if there was a good source of water. It was a hilly place and not suitable for rice growing. But they said: 'Never mind, we don't eat so much rice. It can be supplied by the state. We want to go there.'"

After the meeting, Shinozaki contacted the authorities in Negri Sembilan to start off the project. According to other sources, Bishop Devals simply accepted the Japanese offer, or had no other choice but to do so. Regardless, the religious leader decided to leave for Bahau, especially as it looked likely that Singapore would become a battleground; an early departure was imperative.

TOP: Settlers clearing jungle land in Bahau's Mukim VI camp.

OPPOSITE: Settlers clearing the site for the erection of the Bachelors' camp in Bahau's Mukim VI camp.

The first group of colonists left Singapore on 29 December 1943. After a train journey from the Keppel Road railway station to the town of Kuala Pilah, the group travelled several hours by truck before completing the journey on foot. These were mainly men, responsible for clearing a plot of land for their families, who according to the Japanese would join them later. Bishop Devals, a number of Brothers from SJI and Shinozaki made the journey with the team of 150 young Catholics, which also included a number of doctors and experts in agriculture and construction.

The tasks they faced were enormous: an access road and bridges were required, and the land had to be cleared. A wooden chapel was built. Prayers and masses were organised to help the colonists surmount these difficulties. Father Philippe Meissonnier (MEP) was in charge of the Bahau parishioners. In three months, the Brothers cleared over three hectares of land and began to grow onions, peanuts, aubergines, beans and sweet potatoes, as well as bananas and papayas. They attempted to grow rice, maize and sugar cane as well as raise ducks, which were hardier than chickens.

In May–June 1944, Bishop Devals also organised the departure of the Sisters from CHIJ. Mother Saint Charles Delbarre, now head of the institution, selected 5 Sisters and 20 orphans to embark on a difficult new life in the Malay jungle. These included teenage girls to protect them from harassment by the Japanese soldiers. The younger children, aged five years and below, were left in Syonan-to with Chinese families, while the remaining students returned to their homes.

Mr J. Oehlers, a dentist, his wife and their baby Michael were included in the second convoy on 14 February 1944. He hoped to open a practice in the Bahau colony. In his 2008 memoirs, he recorded daily family life in Bahau and his first

encounter with Father Bécheras (MEP), who was in charge of the community: "When I had completed my two weeks' work, the priest in charge, Father Bécheras, a slim man with a pointed beard, came to me and thanked me. He said that he had a present for me and produced a 50ml Yeast Vite bottle filled with the liqueur Dom. I was hesitant to accept it, but on the insistence of the good father, I finally did so. Dom was like gold in Bahau." He often treated the children and Chinese Catholics in the camp of sub-district Mukim V. On 13 June 1945, the *Syonan Shimbun* claimed that almost 10,000 people now lived in the agricultural colony, which produced sufficient amounts of vegetables.

Despite being in the middle of the jungle, the Brothers of La Salle and the Ladies of Saint Maur did not forget their vocations as educators. Two Brothers and two Sisters set up a small school.

Working on relatively infertile land, the lack of hygiene and malnutrition, and diseases such as malaria and beriberi made life very difficult. The Sisters and orphans were even encouraged to eat a stew of grass and snails as tapioca, sweet potato and *kangkong* crops were insufficient. In order to eradicate malaria, quinine was distributed, but it proved ineffective. Funerals took place on a daily basis, and between 300 and 1,500 people did not survive the harsh living conditions, particularly children and the elderly. More than 300 Eurasian families and 400 Chinese Catholic families—or close to 3,000 people—lived in Fuji Village, the other name given to Bahau, which meant "pretty village" in Japanese.

Bishop Devals left the bishopric affairs in the hands of his Vicar General, Father Michel Olçomendy, so that he could devote himself exclusively to the Bahau camp. He made several round-trips from Bahau to Singapore to raise funds to help the camp's development. Proceeds from boxing matches, which were very

BELOW: Signing of the Japanese surrender document, in the Municipal building, 12 September 1945.

OPPOSITE: Philippe François Marie, Comte de Hauteclocque, is known as General Leclerc.

popular at the time, were donated to the Bahau cause. Information was regularly published in the *Syonan Shimbun* to encourage Catholics to move to Bahau.

Despite the bishop's diabetes and his age, he helped with the construction of bridges and land clearing, until he was injured one day. The wound rapidly worsened, and he was rushed to the hospital in Seremban. An amputation was performed, but gangrene set in. The clergyman passed away on 17 January 1945, at the age of 62. A requiem mass was held in the Cathedral of the Good Shepherd and the city's entire Catholic community and leading Japanese dignitaries attended his funeral.

On 3 September 1945, British and Canadian soldiers from the Force 136 resistance network arrived in Bahau. The Union Jack was hoisted, and food and medication were parachuted in.

September 1945: Liberation

Following the dropping of two atomic bombs on Hiroshima and Nagasaki, on 6 and 9 August 1945 by the Americans, Emperor Hirohito announced his country's capitulation on 15 August. Two days later, Shinozaki made an official announcement, to the effect that the Emperor had decided to cease hostilities. On 21 August, the Singapore media announced the Japanese surrender. The

Bahau colonists found out about the end of hostilities from a clandestine radio station deep in the jungle.

Allied troops stepped into action. Under Operation Tiderace, Lord Louis Mountbatten, the Supreme Allied Commander in Southeast Asia, expected Malaya to be recaptured by 28 August. Following the surrender of Penang, the fleet proceeded to Singapore and reached the Raffles Lighthouse on 2 September. On 4 September, British and Japanese representatives met secretly on board H.M.S. *Sussex* to draft a re-occupation agreement for the island and the territories of Southeast Asia. The next day, British and Commonwealth warships entered the port of Singapore and took control of the territory. Troops landed to cheers from the crowd. On 6 September, more than 34,000 people were freed from the internment camps. On 7 September, *The Straits Times* ran the headline "Singapore is British again". The French battleship *Richelieu*, which formed part of the liberation convoy, arrived on 11 September. While passing through the Strait of Malacca, a mine exploded under its hull, slowing its progress. On 12 September 1945, Lord Mountbatten and representatives of the Allies received the Japanese surrender at City Hall, ten days after the unconditional surrender signed on the SS *Missouri* in Tokyo. Representatives from the Netherlands, the United States, Australia, China and other countries participated in the ceremony. To represent France, General de Gaulle despatched General Leclerc, who was accompanied by Captain Merveilleux du Vignaux, commander of the *Richelieu*.

The ceremony began at 10:30am with an inspection of the British, Australian and Indian guard of honour by Lord Mountbatten. The former prisoners of war as well as the civilian population were on the Padang when the Japanese generals arrived at the Government Building, escorted by soldiers of the Allied forces. The pillars of the building were draped in the flags of the victorious nations. At 11:10am, General Seishiro Itagaki signed the act of surrender in the name of General Hisaichi Terauchi. Lord Mountbatten emerged from the City Hall and gave a speech to the waiting crowd. A Eurasian, Sheila Allan, described the morning of Wednesday 12 September in her memoirs: "This morning was the Victory Parade, it was the formal surrender by the Japanese officers … After the ceremony was over, the flag was hoisted while the band gloriously and thrillingly played 'God save the King' followed by French, Dutch, Chinese and American anthems. Heard speeches—had photo taken. We cheered and danced and cheered ourselves hoarse. There was dancing in the streets, we were mad, gloriously madly happy."

The road to independence

The end of the Second World War saw the birth of a new world order, as European colonial imperialism gradually made way for international relations dominated by the US and Soviet superpowers, who would face off in the Cold War from 1947 to 1991. The 1945–1965 period constituted a crucial stage in Singapore's quest for independence. France, having left Indochina in 1954 after eight years of war, began to seek a more important role in Singapore's economic growth. In this respect, it relied on the island's small French community, which in 1956 numbered approximately 175 people.

Changed circumstances: the BMA makes way for a new civilian administration

The British Military Administration (BMA) remained in charge of the colony until March 1946. The priorities of Lord Mountbatten, posted to Singapore, were to restore law and order, fight the corruption which permeated the administration and private sector, rebuild the port and its docks which had been destroyed by Allied bombing, and to restore the gas, power and water supplies. The BMA quickly took matters in hand, but living conditions only saw a slight improvement. The cost of living increased rapidly, and unemployment remained a major issue. In December 1945, after more than 6,000 workers demonstrated on the Padang to demand improved food rations and better salaries, the BMA prohibited any unauthorised public gathering. Some people responded to this unpopular decision by joining the Malayan Communist Party (MCP) or the Pan-Malayan Federation of Trade Unions.

The British military requisitioned the offices of the Cathay Building on Handy Road for their offices. They shared the premises with the Allied Command, as well as the French Liaison Mission. In January 1946, the Liaison Mission placed an appeal to French residents in Malaya and Singapore in the local newspapers: "French citizens whose goods or property in Malaya suffered loss or damages because of the Japanese are requested to send related information to the Cathay

RIGHT: The Malayan dollar, re-introduced in 1945, with the portrait of the King George VI.

building." On 21 June 1946, Consul Gabriel Morand announced the reopening of the Consulate General of France in the offices of the Cathay Building.

In London, the Colonial Office, which was in charge of Crown colonial policy, had decided to separate the management of Singapore from that of the Malay Peninsula as early as the end of the Battle of Malaya. On 1 April 1946, the Straits Settlements were dissolved and Singapore became a wholly separate Crown Colony with a civilian administration overseen by the Governor, Sir Franklin Gimson. The Peninsula meanwhile became the Malayan Union, with Kuala Lumpur as its capital.

In the new political structure, the management of Singapore's currency, higher education, immigration, taxes and civil aviation remained at the "pan-Malayan" level. Governor Gimson was given the responsibility of leading the territory towards greater autonomy, as well as developing a national consciousness among the different ethnic groups. In March 1948, a new constitution established an Executive Council and Legislative Council, and the Rendel Constitution of 1955 provided the local authorities with even more autonomy. In 1957, Malaya became independent. In 1959, the British authorities granted Singapore full internal autonomy. The first elections to the Legislative Assembly on 30 May resulted in an overwhelming victory for the People's Action Party (PAP) led by Lee Kuan Yew, and Lee became the island's Prime Minister. On 31 August 1963, he proclaimed Singapore's independence before associating it with Malaya 15 days later, after a referendum. This Federation of Malaysia would last two years.

The French and Singapore's economic development

The new Prime Minister and his party moved rapidly to raise Singapore out of its developing nation status. At the end of 1960, Lee announced policies to attract foreign investment and encourage foreign corporate participation in key industry sectors such as petrochemicals and shipbuilding. In August 1961, the Economic Development Board (EDB) was established following advice from UN experts. Its purpose was to identify and attract investors, using all means necessary. Among the French businesses located in Singapore, the Messageries Maritimes and Banque de l'Indochine remained firmly entrenched.

The Banque de l'Indochine

After three years of idling during the Japanese Occupation, the Banque de l'Indochine gradually rebuilt its business under the directorship of Mr de Courseulle. After a particularly tough year in 1946, business improved, but in 1950, with France's decolonisation process in Southeast Asia and instability in the rubber and tin markets, the bank went through difficult times. After 1959, it moved to the Nanyang Building on Robinson Road. In 1962, it was awarded full licensed

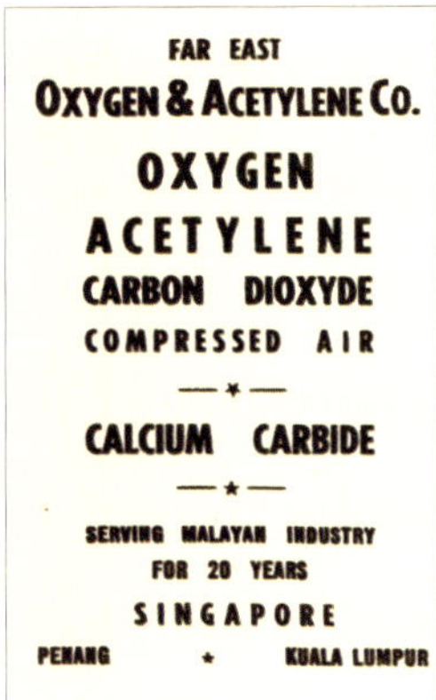

bank status, enabling it to operate in any currency—the only French bank in Singapore to benefit from such advantages. During the 1960s, the bank mainly worked with local import-export companies and businesses active in the metalworking and timber sectors.

The Far East Oxygen and Acetylene Co. Ltd.

Following the departure of the Japanese, Air Liquide, active in Singapore since 1911, was one of the first businesses to reopen. In 1949, in the swimming pool at the Lido, René Laude tested new diving equipment which would enable divers to remain underwater for up to two hours. An article in *The Straits Times* underlined the importance of the company to Singapore: "Since 1927, the Far East Oxygen and Acetylene Company, an affiliate of the big French concern L'Air Liquide, has worked among the true pioneers of Singapore and Malaya industries … Though F.E.O.A.C. fields of activity may not be well known to all, everyone has seen its silver and blue lorries, loaded with cylinders, or its mysterious oxygen trailers moving slowly on Singapore's roads." The company was also involved in the Jurong Industrial Park project, which opened in 1969.

The Clouët company and the Denis Brothers

After the Second World War, Ned Clumeck, the son of Victor Clumeck, Alfred Clouët's partner, restarted the business. Shortages in Europe did not make trade any easier, but through his connections with the British, he was able to buy up surplus military equipment which had accumulated on the docks. He acquired an American batch of pilchards, cooked in tomato and canned in oval tins under Ayam Brand. In his premises at No. 33, Wallich Street, he affixed a red label with a green border (the company's colours) on the white tins. The product became a firm favourite among the Chinese, but he faced stiff competition from American companies Del Monte and Morjon.

A. Clouët and Co. nevertheless continued to grow, but its foodstuffs business gradually became smaller than the construction materials, hardware, plumbing fittings and sanitary ware which Alfred Clouët had fortunately begun to sell.

In 1953, the Denis Brothers, active in Indochina since 1862, bought A. Clouët and Co. from Ned Clumeck. Pilchards had vanished from the coastal areas of California, but they obtained supplies from South Africa instead, thus ensuring the continuity of their products. Construction materials always comprised a major segment of the business; for example, they built the first mosaic factory in Malaya. The company's Singapore headquarters remained in their magnificent property at No. 51, Holland Road, until it was purchased by the government. The company now has its offices on Tagore Lane.

The name Alfred Clouët has not been forgotten, for it endures in the names of the Denis Brothers' distribution companies: Clouët Trading Pte. Ltd. in

THE DENIS BROTHERS

Etienne Denis (1799–1879) was initially a master mariner, but decided to set up his own business. He built a 227-tonne schooner which he named *La Mouette* and, in November 1862, established the Compagnie des Frères Denis, an import-export company, in Saigon. His sons, Alfred, Emile, Gustave and Alphonse, came to assist him. After an initially difficult start in the new country, the family venture eventually bloomed. In 1874, the company moved into a grand building in the centre of Saigon.

Alphonse, the youngest son, eventually took control of the company. After a modest start in rice and pepper trading, the company grew spectacularly into an industrial group that today incorporates well-known brands such as "Taureau Ailé" and "33 Export". In 1959, when Malaya and Singapore were separated, the Clouët company, bought by the Denis Brothers, established a branch in Kuala Lumpur while retaining its Singapore offices at No. 33, Wallich Street. Today, the Denis Brothers group remains a family-owned business, and the vision of Etienne Denis is alive and well.

The Ayam brand also continued to grow, and is today a leading brand in canned goods and other foodstuffs, with a range of more than 100 different products, which are sold in every food retailer in Singapore, Malaysia and Borneo. The brand is also expanding in Europe, and particularly in France.

Singapore, A. Clouët and Co. (KL) Sdn. Bhd. in Malaysia and A. Clouët (Australia) Pty. Ltd. in Australia.

From steamers to aircraft

The journey from Europe to Asia, which took three months before the Suez Canal opened, was reduced to one month with the canal's completion, and shrunk again with commercial aviation. The first long-haul flights were by no means direct: seven or eight stopovers and several days of travel were required.

OPPOSITE TOP: Advertisement for Far East Oxygen and Acetylene, *Singapore Free Press*, 9 March 1974.

OPPOSITE BOTTOM: Gate of Holland Road office, A. Clouet and Co.

LEFT: Aviation meeting (Race course), March 1911. It featured the exploits of Joseph Christiaens, nicknamed the Frenchman.

TOP: Advertisement for Air France, *The Straits Times*, 22 October 1950.

BOTTOM: Advertisement for UTA, Air France, *The Straits Times*, 17 January 1965.

OPPOSITE TOP: Advertisement for French Simca cars, *The Straits Times*, 11 November 1959.

OPPOSITE BOTTOM: Advertisment for the Optorg Company (Malaya) Ltd, showing French products sold in Singapore. *The Straits Times*, 11 November 1959.

Singapore, a maritime traffic hub, also became a stopover for long-haul air transport routes. The island's first flight took place at Farrer Park in 1911, in a biplane piloted by Joseph Christiaens, a Belgian who had become known as "the Frenchman". In 1923, the Singapore government decided to build a seaplane base at Sembawang, close to the Royal Air Force base. The first regular civilian flights started only in 1930, however. In 1931, Sir Cecil Clementi declared that he wanted to transform Singapore into "one of the largest and most important airports in the world". In December 1933, Imperial Airways extended its weekly flights from Rangoon to Singapore via Bangkok. An inaugural flight left London on 9 December and arrived on 19 December in Singapore. In 1935, Qantas inaugurated a Darwin–Singapore route, marking the start of foreign flights. In 1937, a civilian airport with a grass runway opened in Kallang. Daily flights started between Singapore and Kuala Lumpur, Ipoh and Penang.

Air France

Air France was established in 1933 as the result of the merger of four major airlines and the Aéropostale airmail service. The company started a weekly Marseille–Saigon service, which required 3 different aircraft, a car and no less than 16 stopovers and took 9½ days. The length of these stopovers varied from the length of a breakfast to an overnight stay in a hotel for passengers, allowing time to complete mechanical checks or refuel the aircraft.

In 1945, French civil aviation was nationalised and the entire network was entrusted to Air France. A Paris–New York route started the following year. In November 1949, Air France provided a weekly Saigon–Singapore service. The company was represented by Messageries Maritimes, and tickets were issued at No. 66, The Arcade. The number of flights increased, reaching five flights per week to Tahiti and Australia, via Saigon, Bangkok or Rangoon, with the purchase of 24 Caravelles, an aircraft which could transport up to 90 passengers. In August 1959, Air France ordered 17 Boeing 707 airliners for its Far Eastern routes, including Singapore and Malaya.

UTA

TAI (Transports Aériens Intercontinentaux), established in 1946, was a division of French shipping company Chargeurs Réunis. It began its first flights in the early 1950s, flying from Paris-Orly to Indochina and Africa and in 1963 merged with Union des Transports Aériens (UTA) and Union Aéromaritime de Transports (UAT). On 1 June 1964, a UTA Douglas DC-8 landed in Singapore at the civilian airport at Paya Lebar (opened in 1955), eight miles northeast of the city centre. This was the world's longest air route, linking Paris to Los Angeles via Singapore, Noumea and Tahiti. McDonnell Douglas DC10 aircraft delivered to UTA from 1973 onwards served Singapore on the Far Eastern route four times weekly.

The development of air transport, which enabled faster movement and the transport of perishable goods, benefited commerce. The almost daily connections to Indochina were also of great benefit to the business of French traders.

Conquering the Singapore market

The few French nationals in Singapore participated in events that showcased not only French culture but also the country's products and know-how. Some events were organised by the local authorities, while some were initiated by the French government, represented by its diplomatic delegation. The year 1950 marked the first "French Week" in Singapore. On this occasion, the Alliance Française organised an exhibition at the British Council Hall of more than 300 images of France and Indochina, as well as 100 art photographs and 50 posters. Amateur thespians from the French community also gave a performance of *English Without Tears* at the Victoria Theatre.

During the first "French Commercial Fortnight" in Singapore in May 1965, a supplement dedicated to Franco–Malaysian cooperation was included with *The Sunday Times*. Advertisements for French products appeared together with articles on the sharing of technology between the two countries.

Edouard Hutte, the Consul General, wrote about the aim of this Commercial Fortnight in Singapore: "France is already well-known here for her capabilities in technical aid in the development of the new industrial site of Jurong. French firms from all economic sectors have submitted tenders in order to increase the productive potential of Singapore. The French Commercial Fortnight is intended for the general public, which is naturally interested in the practical side of French production, either in consumer goods, such as foodstuffs, ready-made dresses or in luxuries such as haute couture, lingerie and perfumes. Consequently, some social events are forecast, notably the screening of French films which are praised all over the world. Also the Alliance Française of Singapore, whose main concern is to teach French and to prepare students to whom scholarships in France are awarded, is contributing to the aim of bringing together the two countries. The French Commercial Fortnight endeavours to create contacts, and to make the range of French quality products better known."

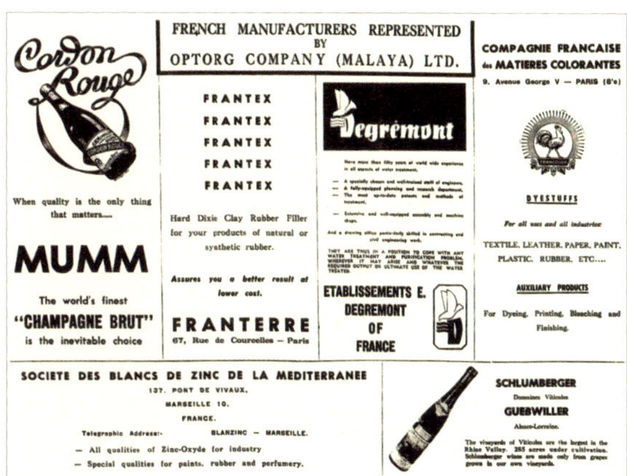

During the two weeks, 60 shops offered French products at promotional prices, with some major retailers decorating their windows in the French Tricolour. Restaurants offered French dishes, wines and cheeses. Two fashion parades by Carven were also planned at the Goodwood and

Cathay Hotels. Screenings of the Jacques-Yves Cousteau documentary, *Le monde sans soleil* (A World Without Sun) and Jacques Demy's *Parapluies de Cherbourg* (the Umbrellas of Cherbourg) were advertised at the Cathay Cinema.

The transition of the MEP in Singapore

Following the death of Bishop Devals in 1945, Father Michel Olçomendy of the MEP temporarily took over the duties of the Bishop of Malacca. In 1947, he was officially ordained, and held the position until his retirement in 1977. Originally from the Basque country, he guided the Catholic community through the tumultuous period of independence and the emergence of the new Singaporean nation. Together with the entire Catholic clergy, he dealt with the British authorities and the growing communist movement, and also maintained cordial relations with the new party in power, the People's Action Party.

In 1950, Marist Brothers arrived in Singapore, at the request of Bishop Olçomendy and Father Bécheras, to oversee education at the Catholic High School, which had opened in 1937. The school's priorities and philosophy remained unchanged, but training focused on bilingual education.

In May 1954, strikes and riots broke out in Singapore. Chinese students demonstrated in the schools and on the streets. They were protesting against the overcrowding of Chinese schools, and their often incompetent teachers. Their teachers earned a third less than those in English schools and the Chinese students

could not enter the University of Singapore; anyone wishing to continue with higher education had to go to Beijing. The communists also began to organise in the Chinese schools, and these were the scenes of serious disturbances. The Catholic High School was also affected, and Father Bécheras expelled 75 troublemakers. The next day, he sat with his long white beard, old colonial helmet and cane in a chair at the school's entrance. He had appointed himself gatekeeper, and barred entry to both the expelled students as well as activists from other schools. Press campaigns were organised against him, he was caricatured in the papers, but he stood firm and his school remained calm. His composure during those difficult days contrasted with that of the headmasters of the other Chinese schools. Governor Sir John Nicoll visited to congratulate him: "Not only have you acted well, but you have also shown us the way."

In May 1957, illness forced Father Bécheras to return to France temporarily. On 30 September, in Marseille, he suffered a fall just before boarding a ship bound for Singapore, but embarked nonetheless. He died on board on 7 October. His body was brought back to Singapore and thousands of Christians accompanied him to his final resting place.

Since 1992, the Catholic High School campus has been located at No. 9, Bishan Street 22, and a statue of Father Bécheras has stood there. In 1958, the Marist brothers established their own school, the Maris Stella High School at No. 25, Mount Vernon Road. They also opened a kindergarten on Flower Road.

Numerous initiatives

In 1948, Bishop Olçomendy reinitiated the project to establish an Industrial School, which had been put on hold because of the war. The Brothers of Saint Gabriel founded the Boys' Town School, for boys from disadvantaged families aged 11 to 18. The idea for the school came out of a meeting between Brother Vincent of the Brothers of Saint Gabriel and W.T. McDermott, an Australian philanthropist. They met during the Japanese Occupation in the detention camp at Changi, where Brother Vincent was held prisoner. After liberation, the project took shape thanks to the moral and financial support of McDermott.

The Brothers of St Gabriel opened many schools, including Assumption English School, Boys' Town, St Gabriel's Primary and Secondary School, Montfort Junior, and Montfort Secondary School. In 2004, the Brothers founded the St Gabriel's Foundation to continue their work.

OPPOSITE TOP: Bishop Michel Olçomendy (1901–1977).

OPPOSITE BELOW: Police riot squad, 1950s.

TOP: Sculpture of Father Bécheras, in front of the clock tower of the Catholic High School.

Gathering of priests involved in the *Malaya Catholic News*. (From left) Frs. J. Charbonnier, J. Ho, A. Christophe, L. Lee, P. Abrial, Archbishop M. Olçomendy, J. Ting and a Marist Brother Principal of Catholic High School.

In 1950, Bishop Olçomendy resurrected the idea of a Catholic newspaper. Thanks to the efforts of Father Meissonnier, and assisted by a few laypersons, the *Malayan Catholic News* once again saw the light of day in July 1950. In 1974, two magazines were available: the *Catholic News* for Singapore, and the *Malaysian Catholic News* for Malaysia. *The Catholic Hour* programme was broadcast on the Singapore airwaves three times a month. In 1955, the *Hai Sing Pao*, a newspaper in Mandarin for the Catholic Chinese community, appeared.

The British authorities established the Social Welfare Department in June 1946 to assist people who had suffered during the war, and then embarked on longer-term initiatives, such as improving sanitation in Chinatown. The Social Welfare Department founded a number of educational establishments. The Order of the Good Shepherd also continued to assist the disadvantaged. The Sisters moved to Marymount (Thomson Road) in the 1950s with the help of Bishop Olçomendy. They ran a shelter for children in need and established the Marymount Convent School. They opened kindergartens, the Good Shepherd Centre in Yishun, a shelter for battered women, their children and household employees ill-treated by their employers, and the Rose Villa for single mothers in need. They also worked in close collaboration with secular associations.

The Consulate General of France

During the war, the Consulate was forced to move out of its "black-and-white" houses on Gallop Road, and reopened its offices in the Cathay Building on Handy Road after liberation.

THE WAR IN INDOCHINA AS REPORTED BY THE SINGAPOREAN PRESS

Indochina was a major issue for France throughout the 1946–1954 period. With the departure of the Japanese in September 1945, Ho Chi Minh proclaimed the independence of the Democratic Republic of Vietnam. This triggered a war which would last for almost eight years, and only end with the signing of the Geneva agreements on 21 July 1954, following the French capitulation after the battle of Dien Bien Phu. A number of articles described the evacuation of French civilians from Vietnam who transited through the port of Singapore. One journalist wrote: "A small piece of France sailed into Singapore yesterday morning, and left last night for Marseille, home and peace. It was the new French liner-troopship *Edouard Branly*. Aboard were Catholic nuns, businessmen, pretty Parisians, soldiers and one French poodle. The *Edouard Branly* left Saigon two days ago and its 506 passengers, most from Hanoi and Haiphong, are learning again how to relax."

French West African troops on their way to Indochina, *The Straits Times*, 27 July 1950.

In 1948, however, the owner of the Cathay Building repossessed the premises. Radio Malaya, the Dutch Liaison Unit and the French Consulate all had to find new premises. Atbara and Inverturret once again became the home of the French delegation and remained so for the next 50 years.

From 1958 onwards, some departments reported to the Embassy of France in Kuala Lumpur. The delegation's mission was to promote the image of France on a cultural, economic and technological level. Press articles appeared, giving a general overview of the French presence and accompanied by texts which extolled French technological and commercial successes. This was complemented by advertisements for French companies that were based in Singapore.

Following agreements between Malaya and France in 1962, French citizens no longer needed visas for stays of less than three months. This policy remained in place until Singapore gained independence in 1965.

The receptions at the Consulate General, which were the responsibility of the diplomatic delegation, continued their annual cycle: Bastille Day celebrations, medal awards and visits by dignitaries were all events that were much appreciated by the small French community.

On New Year's Day 1953, the French community of Singapore attended an awards presentation. Mr Meyffreys was awarded the medal of the Legion of Honour by the Consul, A. Guibaut, for his more than 30 years of service in the

Ministry of Foreign Affairs. The other medal awarded that day was to Colette Meffre. Mrs Meffre, born in Toulon in January 1924 and married at the age of 18 to an employee of the Messageries Maritimes, received a bronze medal of the Famille Française for providing the nation with five boys over a period of ten years, including one boy born in Singapore in June 1951. In October of the same year, the Consul recommended a Legion of Honour award for Mr Crosnier, aged 59. The agent for the Messageries Maritimes, he was also the longest-serving member of the French community in Singapore.

TOP: Somerset Maugham visiting the Alliance Française of Singapore in 1959.

The Alliance Française: the initial years

On 1 September 1949, a branch of the Alliance Française of Malaya opened in Singapore. This was managed by Paul Clerc of the Optorg group, and comprised about 50 members and around 20 students. The courses, which were free, consisted mostly of French conversation lessons. These took place twice a week and were provided by—amongst others—a young Briton, Mr Clayton, "more of a Francophile than a Francophone", in the words of one student. Numerous Britons from the naval base participated in the cultural and social activities at the Alliance Française, as well as many Dutch visitors who had left Indonesia after independence in 1949.

An annual fee of $20 enabled members to attend film screenings as well as participate in the activities of the "French Club", as the institution was also known. A theatre club put on a play by Tristan Bernard, *L'Anglais tel qu'on le parle*, at the Dutch Club. French language and culture at the time were at a particular disadvantage, and French was only rarely taught in a few private schools. In the 1960s, conversation courses and an advanced French literature and civilisation course were offered to the students at the Alliance Française. With a larger subsidy from France, the Alliance was able to grow—it even hired a secretary.

Like many institutions, the nascent Alliance Française of Singapore faced difficulties in finding suitable premises. In 1949, the Alliance was located at No. 394, Orchard Road, the current site of the Lucky Plaza shopping mall, and consisted of a single room which served as a classroom, library, secretarial office and reading room. The following year, a neighbouring garage was converted into a classroom. In 1954, the Alliance moved into three air-conditioned rooms on the third floor of the Laidlaw Building (now the Bank of China), close to the former Central Post Office on Battery Road. The premises comprised a library, a bar and a number of small classrooms. Although it had no licence, the Alliance was allowed to sell alcoholic beverages, and Madame Rudet, the wife of a French resident, sold sandwiches *à la française*.

When the owners took back the premises in 1957, the classrooms were transferred to Penang Lane, above the Peking Restaurant. These four rooms were insufficient for the increasing number of students, and the charcoal used to roast the suckling pigs in the restaurant below often made the air unbreathable. In 1960, the Committee decided to rent a large colonial house at No. 23, Chatsworth Road. The committee organised fêtes and banquets there which soon became extremely popular. In 1962, Lee Kuan Yew and S. Rajaratnam were two of the many dignitaries who visited the Alliance Française before independence.

A DIRECTOR OF THE ALLIANCE FRANÇAISE REMEMBERS 1960S SINGAPORE

To commemorate the centenary of the Alliance Française publication, *Lien*, Jean Caudmont, its Director from 1961 to 1963, provided a lengthy description of Singapore at that time: "Singapore was a blossoming city in the actual sense of the word, before it became so in the figurative sense. From Mount Faber, views extended not over a sea of concrete but over a verdant, indescribably-nuanced ocean which blanketed the entire Chinese town. The vast majority of the island was still covered in forests, jungles and marshes from which emerged a few Malay houses built on stilts. Monkeys, snakes and scorpions reigned there with impunity (tigers, so numerous at the turn of the century, only disappeared in 1937). The fauna sometimes invaded human homes. The town was characterised by its low houses, where no skyscrapers reached for the heavens. The port reached the shore and a forest of masts extended from Collyer Quay to Shenton Way which, as yet unencumbered by buildings, was merely an immense parking area. Parking was anyway free in almost all of the streets, and paid spaces were rare. At the mouth of the Kallang River, in the Chinese port, hundreds of junks could be seen, and sizeable numbers were still being built in the neighbouring shipyards.

At the start of the 1960s, Singapore had not yet succumbed to the tourist 'invasion'. The rare visitors came from calling vessels, stayed a single day and slept aboard the ship. First-class hotels could be counted on the fingers of one hand, whereas the others, equally few in number, offered affordable prices. The general atmosphere evoked that of a novel by Joseph Conrad or Somerset Maugham (who visited the Alliance Française in 1959 for a signing). The old town was literally 'Indochinese'; Sago Lane still retained its traditional social function while Bugis Street, already a well-known 'sailor's street', had yet to become a tourist-trap. Trishaws were a cheap, convenient mode of transport rather than a way of fleecing tourists. Each ethnic group retained their traditional attire, and cheongsams rubbed shoulders with saris, dhotis, and sarong-kebayas. ... Singapore was still merely an extension of the Malay Peninsula and in the evenings, we liked to go and enjoy satays or crabs in the large suburban village that was Johor Bahru."

The French consul Mr Hutte making a speech at the General Assembly of the Alliance Française of Singapore board in 1964.

V.

A Relationship Reborn (1965–2011)

Singapore's fortune stemmed primarily from its function as an *entrepôt*. In colonial times, its location at the mouth of the Strait of Malacca gave it a vital role as a trading platform between the Indian Empire and the Far East. During the interwar period, Singapore was the centre for the export of tin and rubber from Malaya. In the 1950s, it remained dominated by trade and activities connected with the British naval base.

Following its separation from Malaysia on 9 August 1965, Singapore had to rethink its economic and social policy. The city would within a few short years become a global city, and achieve spectacular economic success. Development was a priority for the Prime Minister, Lee Kuan Yew, who took office in 1959. The island would need to open up to the world in order to compensate for its minute domestic market. In a few decades, Lee and his ministers enabled Singapore to metamorphose from a developing nation to a wealthy, developed country. France played a role in this expansion, by expanding bilateral agreements in the economic and cultural arenas, and by encouraging its companies to establish businesses there. The last half century has seen exceptional growth in the French presence, from a population of 225 in 1967 to 9,106 in June 2011.

OPPOSITE TOP: Seafront skyline of Singapore, c. 1965.

OPPOSITE BOTTOM: Present-day skyline of Singapore, as viewed from Marina Bay Sands SkyPark.

BELOW: The national flag, first adopted in 1959 and reconfirmed when the Republic gained independence on 9 August 1965.

Laying New Foundations (1965–Late 1970s)

Singapore's appearance changed rapidly, shifting from a coastal town with villages and shophouses to a metropolis criss-crossed by communication routes and crammed with industrial zones. The Singaporean government took all necessary measures to bring about the industrialisation of the fledgling nation. France played a role in this, both in the financial and industrial sectors. In 1970, on the occasion of his state visit to Paris, Prime Minister Lee explained to President Pompidou and Prime Minister Chaban-Delmas: "I welcome French business and old European

culture in Singapore to offset the other cultures. Singapore is going half American and half Japanese. More French industrialists, businessmen and executives would be welcome. All industrialists from all the developed countries are welcome to play a part in Singapore's rapid industrialisation."

"From third world to first": Lee Kuan Yew

Prime Minister Lee set in place a development policy, which over the years has proven extremely effective.

An economic model

Singapore was already a trading hub, but competition from Malaysia and Indonesia forced it to develop its industrial capabilities. The city-state planned its transformation in detail, and called upon a team of administrators who were both highly qualified and well-paid, and thus unlikely to be corrupt. In 1961, Lee established the Economic Development Board (EDB), a government body that encouraged foreign investors to set up shop in Singapore. He called on experts from the United Nations, and in particular Albert Winsemius, a distinguished Dutch economist who had played a major role in the economic reconstruction of his homeland after the Second World War. From 1965 until his retirement in 1984, Winsemius visited Singapore several times a year. Together with the ministers of finance Lim Kim San, Goh Keng Swee and Hon Sui Sen, he is responsible for the Singapore economic miracle. Their approach was to offer multinationals financial incentives to start businesses in Singapore. From 1967 onwards, these companies received "pioneer certificates", which exempted them from taxes for a period of five years.

These companies needed solid local infrastructure. The industrialisation plan for the Jurong Industrial Estate started in 1961. By the end of the 1960s, a strip of marshland covered in mangroves along the West Coast and Jurong was transformed into the island's first industrial zone for manufacturing textiles, toys and wooden articles. The French textiles company Montagut, famed for its "*fil lumière*" synthetic yarn, appeared on the Singapore market in 1967 and began to develop the China market as early as 1979. In 1968, the statutory board Jurong Town Corporation (later renamed JTC Corporation) was formed to develop and manage industrial estates.

In 1972, a second industrial zone was established by consolidating seven islands around Jurong. This was named Jurong Island, and specialised in steel and petrochemicals, which ranged from refining to derivative products. It is administered by JTC. At the end of the 1970s, 32,000 people were employed in 264 factories and a hundred more factories were under construction. The French-owned Far East Oxygen Company, a member of the Air Liquide group, which had been established in Singapore since 1911, moved to Jurong and sold its services to the shipyards as well as to the medical sector. By 1974, the company had 250 employees. The Entreprise de Recherches and d'Activities Pétrolières (ERAP, part of the Total group), which was engaged in geological studies of the region, also benefited from the infrastructure recently built by JTC.

The government also embarked on the task of providing housing for its population by setting up the Housing Development Board (HDB) in 1960. The buildings which were erected were often inspired by the designs of the Swiss architect Le Corbusier. Apartments were partly subsidised by the State and became affordable to low-income Singaporean citizens. This prevented financial speculation and wage inflation, and enabled Singapore to benefit from an inexpensive labour force. In 1966, the population of the overcrowded Chinatown area was dispersed to more peripheral areas, where new towns such as Toa Payoh were built. *Kampongs*—villages—gradually disappeared from the landscape.

OPPOSITE TOP: Lee Kuan Yew, 1959. Lee was the first prime minister of Singapore from 1959 to 1990.

OPPOSITE BOTTOM: Advertisement for Air Liquide in *Singapore Trade Industry Magazine*, January 1970.

LEFT: Construction of HDB flats replacing Kampong Kuchai, off Lorong 3 Geylang, 1973.

The government also invested in education and training for its labour force. The opening of numerous technical schools ensured an increasing supply of skilled employees. This development policy rapidly bore fruit: in the 1970s, more and more companies relocated their factories to Singapore, where production and labour were cheaper. The increase in the number of foreign companies rapidly reduced the unemployment rate, which had reached 10% in 1959, but fell to 4.5% in 1973.

A number of companies in the electronics sector took an active interest in Singapore's inexpensive labour force. One of them was the French company Thomson-CSF, the result of a merger of the electronics divisions of Thomson-Brandt and the Compagnie Générale de Télégraphie Sans Fil (CSF). It moved into Singapore at the start of the 1970s, targeting the aviation and telecommunications sectors. Twenty years later, the company called on the Point Architect architectural firm to build its new premises. Architect John Fung described them: "Another building completed by my office was the headquarters for Thomson Consumer Electronics at Toa Payoh. This building was subsequently acquired and renovated by Singapore Press Holdings and it now serves as their HQ." In 2000, Thomson-CSF became Thales.

Against the background of the Cold War

Against an international landscape marked by the Cold War, in which the USSR and the USA faced off while avoiding direct confrontation, Singapore supported the American side. Like Thailand, the country served as a rest and recuperation base for GIs; this also contributed to the country's economic growth. In 1967 Indonesia, Malaysia, the Philippines, Thailand and Singapore decided, with US support, to form the Association of South East Asian Nations (ASEAN). This organisation promotes mutual economic growth and development, while stemming the area's communist movements. ASEAN membership enabled Singapore to develop closer cooperation with its neighbours, which comprised one third of its foreign trade.

Sectors for priority development

In 1964, the government established the Port of Singapore Authority (PSA). The shipyards doubled in capacity. In January 1968, the British announced plans to close down their naval bases over the next three years. This was a tough blow for Singapore, because the British bases provided employment for 25,000 Singaporean workers and generated 20% of the country's GNP. Following the departure of the British troops, the base

SINGAPORE, AN R&R BASE FOR THE US MILITARY

During the Vietnam War, Singapore and Bangkok were considered R&R bases—rest and recuperation stations for US soldiers. This was the backdrop which the writer Paul Theroux used for the adventures of his hero Jack Flowers in his book, *Saint Jack*, published in 1973. A few years later, the book was made into a film by Peter Bogdanovich working with French producer Pierre Cottrell. English journalist Ben Slater describes Cottrell's arrival in Singapore in February 1978: "Cottrell jumped into a taxi and gave instructions to the driver to go to the Shangri-La. As they headed into town, the taxi driver made an offer, which under the circumstances Cottrell couldn't refuse, to see some girls performing a "cucumber show". Since Saint Jack was going to be dealing with Singapore's sex industry, Cottrell felt that research might as well begin as soon as possible." The book was extremely controversial, and knowing that the government would never issue the necessary permits, the filmmakers disguised the project as *Jack of Hearts* and submitted a watered-down script to the authorities. Cottrell's crew included several Frenchmen: sound engineers Guillaume Sciamma and Jean-Pierre Ruh, cameraman Bernard Prim, assistant director Denys Granier-Deferre and editor Sophie Cornu. *Saint Jack* premiered in New York in April 1979 and shortly afterwards, *Jack le Magnifique* appeared on French screens. The Singaporean authorities banned the film, which they felt projected an unfavourable image of Singapore, and only lifted the ban in 2006.

Ben Gazzara (centre) as Jack Flowers in *Saint Jack* by Peter Bogdanovich, 1979.

and docks at Sembawang were returned, and Singapore very rapidly became one of the world's leading ports.

In 1966, Singapore established its own shipping company, the Neptune Orient Lines. The French Messageries Maritimes, which had had a base in Singapore since 1862, remained afloat into the 1970s. By entering into partnerships with two Italian companies and two Japanese companies, the company was able to provide the longest routes in the world, running via the Arctic and Antarctica. One of its ships left from the major Mediterranean ports for the Far East every 24 days. In 1973, the company moved to the 10th floor of Shing Kwan House, on Shenton Way. Gérard Clément was the company's manager for Singapore and Malaysia. In 1977, the company merged with Compagnie Générale Transatlantique and was renamed Compagnie Générale Maritime. A year later, it became Compagnie Maritime d'Affrètement (CMA) and in 1995 became France's leading maritime container transport company.

Other French companies such as Michelin and SMPT (Société des Matières Premières Tropicales), already long-term residents in Singapore, continued their activities in the region by using the island as an *entrepôt* hub.

The Singaporean government implemented major projects to improve its transportation infrastructure. Bus companies were established, and in 1974,

OPPOSITE TOP: Advertisement for Thomson, in *Le Lien*, June 1982.

OPPOSITE CENTRE: Advertisement for Messageries Maritimes in *The Sunday Times*, 2 May 1965.

OPPOSITE BOTTOM: SMPT workers moving rubber cargo at Phillip Street.

Singapore Bus Service (SBS) received its first buses with a French Berliet chassis. These were named *The Spirit of Singapore*. Some French makes of cars were also available in the city, such as Renault, Citroën, and Peugeot.

Singapore hoped to develop into a major financial city, and the Development Bank of Singapore (DBS) was founded in 1968 in order to assist the island's industrialisation. In addition to companies such as OCBC (Oversea-Chinese Banking Corporation), UOB (United Overseas Bank) and OUB (Overseas Union Bank), the island provided a base for a number of major French banks. The Banque de l'Indochine had had a presence since 1905, and was renamed Banque de l'Indosuez in 1974. The Banque Nationale de Paris (BNP) opened a representative office in 1968. In 1979, Crédit Lyonnais became the third French bank to be represented in Singapore. The same year, Société Générale, a commercial bank which assisted its clients in their dealings with France, opened its third Asian office here, after Hong Kong and Tokyo. Thirty years later, the banks' activities are now focused on investment. These banks have obtained either a Wholesale or Offshore licence, and two of them have even opened banking halls, enabling French expatriates to have a cheque book and an account with a French bank.

With few natural resources, Singapore looked to develop sectors which are less resource-dependent, such as tourism. In 1964, the government established the Singapore Tourist Promotion Board (renamed the Singapore Tourism Board in 1997). The symbol of the Merlion (a lion with the body of a fish) was adopted in the same year to represent the Lion City. The aim was to attract increasing numbers of tourists in order to boost foreign currency revenue. 1972 saw the establishment of Singapore Airlines. The company commissioned French couturier Pierre Balmain to design the uniform for its flight attendants. Balmain reprised the idea, already in use by Malaysia-Singapore Airlines, of using traditional Malay costumes, the *sarong* and *kebaya*, to outfit the female members of the crew. The uniform was created in four colours, which corresponded to different ranks and functions. The Singapore Girl became a brand image for the company, and the airline won the World's Best Cabin Crew Service award for 17 consecutive years.

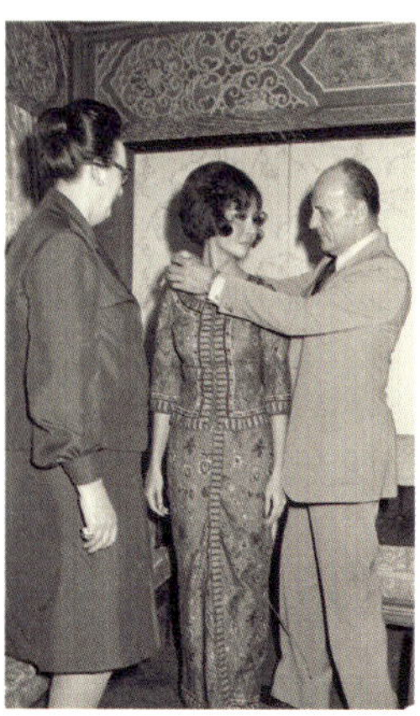

Two French airlines provided regular air services to the new nation. In June 1973, UTA made its inaugural flight to Singapore using a Douglas DC10-30 aeroplane, which could carry more than 250 passengers. From Paris, flights called at Athens, Colombo, Bangkok and Singapore, before continuing to Sydney, Nouméa, Nandi, Papeete and Los Angeles. In September 1989 UTA inaugurated direct Paris–Singapore flights.

OPPOSITE TOP: First bus from the Berliet Company, 1974.

OPPOSITE CENTRE: Advertisement for Banque Nationale de Paris, 1986.

OPPOSITE BOTTOM: In 1972, Pierre Balmain created history for Singapore's aviation industry by designing the uniform for the stewardesses of Singapore Airlines.

TOP LEFT: The back of the $20 bank note featuring the Concorde, 1979. The first president of the FBA, Claude Blangero from Banque Nationale de Paris, had convinced the Monetary Authority of Singapore to feature the Concorde on the note.

TOP: Advertisement for UTA, 1989.

Air France worked hard on its brand image, and in 1966 announced that on its long-range flights, such as Paris–Singapore, passengers would be able to watch films shown in colour on extra-large screens, as well as listen to classical and popular music programmes in stereo. Between 1977 and 1980, the Concorde supersonic airliner, built in partnership between Air France and British Airways, also operated a number of charter flights between Singapore and London.

Singapore's booming economy was sharply affected by the oil crisis of 1973. In October, during the Yom Kippur war, the Arab oil-producing countries placed an embargo on deliveries of oil to countries which supported Israel. Oil prices quadrupled in three months, and produced a hard shock in the USA and Europe. South Korea, Taiwan, Hong Kong and Singapore, the developing industrial economies which produced their goods at lower prices than their Western competitors, managed to absorb the oil price impact much more smoothly.

The French community in the young Republic of Singapore

The French community in Singapore quadrupled in size in the 1970s, reaching 818 in 1978. In November 1965, France's diplomatic representation in the young Republic of Singapore was designated an embassy. The Consul General, Edouard Hutte, became the first Chargé d'Affaires, and then, on 23 November 1968, the first Ambassador of France to Singapore. The embassy, which remained in the two "black-and-white" houses at Nos. 5 and 7, Gallop Road, employed not only French expatriate staff posted from Paris or recruited locally, but also Singaporeans, both for maintenance work as well as administrative tasks. From 1931 to 2006, two generations of the Pillay family, Singaporeans of Indian origin, worked for the French delegation—Subramania Pillay, from 1931 to 1973, and then his son, Chandran, from 1974 to 2006. Both worked as factotums, drivers and clerks in the consular section.

TOP: Ambassador of France to Singapore, Jacques Gasseau, at his desk at the French Embassy, 1974.

BOTTOM: Present-day logo of the French Embassy.

The French Embassy

The Embassy has very specific functions. Under the management of the Ambassador, the Consular section provides assistance to French nationals in difficulty and, among other things, provides the main administrative services of a town hall (for civil affairs) or a French prefecture (for passports). Since June 1975, the Consular section has also been responsible for organising certain electoral voting processes, mainly referendums and presidential elections. The Singaporean government approved the performance of such electoral functions on condition that these took place within the embassy compound and that no campaign materials were circulated.

In 1979, elections for the European Parliament were held for the first time. French citizens in Singapore could also cast their votes at the French Embassy for the first time. In his report to the Ministry of Foreign Affairs, the Ambassador, Mr Gasseau, wrote: "The European elections on 10 June 1979 took place under excellent conditions. The members of the French community (almost 800 people) turned out in relatively large numbers to vote or participate, or to help with the counting and announcement of the results, all of which occurred in an atmosphere which was both serious and playful." However, since April 2003, it has no longer been possible to vote in these elections in Singapore; voters must be registered in a commune in France and vote by proxy. When requested to participate in major national elections, such as presidential elections and referendums, the French community in Singapore is an eager participant at the voting booths.

In 1962, Malaysia (Malaya) and France signed an agreement which eliminated the need for a visa for stays of less than three months. This agreement became invalid in 1965 when Singapore became independent. In 1985 a mutual waiver of short-stay visas between France and Singapore was instituted with a new bilateral agreement.

The Embassy used the French community's media tools (*Lien, La Gazette*) to communicate with French nationals and Singaporeans.

The new French embassy comprises a number of sections. Today the Consul is responsible for French nationals, be they residents or merely passing through, and is in charge of the Consular section. The Diplomatic Chancery keeps abreast of events in Singapore on behalf of the French government, and facilitates communication with the local political authorities. The Department for Culture, Science and Education organizes scientific, cultural and educational events between France and Singapore. The Regional Economic Service represents French interests in relation to local and regional authorities, and the French Trade Commission–UBIFRANCE helps French exporters to identify and contact new customers and partners. The Defence Section is responsible for cooperation between the armed forces of France and Singapore, both in terms of armament

Ambassade de France à Singapour

Liberté • Égalité • Fraternité

RÉPUBLIQUE FRANÇAISE

OCCASIONALLY TENSE DIPLOMATIC RELATIONS

In 1961, Singapore extended a warm welcome to Algerian independence leader Ferhat Abbas. S. Rajaratnam, then-Minister of Culture, offered him a contribution of $25,000 for the "Aid to Algeria" fund. France did not appreciate Singapore's support for the movement, which it had been fighting since 1954.

In 1973, during the French nuclear tests in the Pacific, Singapore again disagreed with the French government. From 1966 to 1974, France performed a series of atmospheric nuclear tests in the Pacific Ocean, on the atoll of Mururoa. The international community was in uproar, including Singapore. On 22 June 1973, leaders of Singapore's National Trade Union Congress (NTUC), accompanied by 300 people, expressed their opposition to France's nuclear tests, and demonstrated in front of the Embassy of France. The delegation was received by the Ambassador, Marcel de Flory. Following this meeting, the demonstrators circulated a petition and called for a boycott of French products.

During the 28th General Assembly of the United Nations on 24 September 1973, S. Rajaratnam, then Singapore's Minister for Foreign Affairs, proclaimed: "The International Court of Justice met recently to decide upon the right of France to try out its nuclear weapons in the Pacific. The marine pollution from ships, the discharge of industrial waste and the underwater dumping of nuclear waste, in short the increasing tendency to consider the sea as the dustbin of humanity, are potential sources of conflict."

Demonstrators in Singapore gathered on 22 June 1973 to protest against France's nuclear tests.

French diplomats, under instruction from the French Foreign Ministry on the Quai d'Orsay, replied that these nuclear trials were necessary for France's defence during the Cold War. In 1975, the French government abandoned atmospheric testing and then began underground testing. These too were stopped in 1996.

as well as technological research. The Press and Communications Department, meanwhile, aims to raise awareness of France and to explain the positions of the country's government to the Singaporean media and public. The International Police Cooperation Unit promotes cooperation between France and Singapore with regards to international policing. Lastly, the general administration of the Embassy is managed by an integrated Administrative and Financial Section.

The French Embassy's economic mission

Over time, the Regional Economic Service has grown. It supports the commercial initiatives of exporting companies, through the publication of books, reports and brochures analysing the country's economic and financial situation. The Economic section also serves as a liaison point at the European Community and ASEAN level, promoting France in its host country.

To promote commerce, the diplomatic authorities took initiatives to showcase the image of France. Exhibitions, conferences, festivals and commercial events were organised to raise local awareness of France, its companies, know-how and products. A French Fortnight ran from 18 to 30 September 1967: the major department store Robinsons was completely re-decorated with a "Streets of Paris" theme, with an Eiffel Tower on its façade. Two employees wore Paris policemen's uniforms, while three shop assistants were dressed in regional costumes. The event was successful, and Robinsons reported that turnover during the promotion was 50% higher than average. The *Tour de France: Festival of French Food and Art* ran from 12 June to 14 July 1974, with the support of the Imperial-Oberoi hotel. Events open to the public included concerts, tastings and exhibitions.

From 16 March to 16 April 1977, the Singapore Hilton hotel, together with UTA, organised *Springtime in Paris*, with fashion parades and the revue show *Folies Pigalles*. The hotel created a truly French atmosphere for a month. In 1980, the event ran again, this time with the participation of the Shangri-La hotel and the shops Isetan and Fitzpatrick's.

Specialist events were also organised to help French entrepreneurs visit Singapore and the region. The first of these events, the *France Technical Exhibition*, took place from 7 to 16 March 1975 at the National Stadium, and attracted 209 French companies and no fewer than 600 participants from France. The Ambassador, Jacques Gasseau, stated: "This exhibition was organised to encourage French industrialists to assert themselves in this market. Marine industries, communications, computers, electrical and electronic products, chemical and nuclear apparatus were displayed in an area of 10,000 square metres. This exhibition featured banks and trading companies who looked after transport and tourism."

Building on this success, other specialist events took place in which numerous French companies participated: *Time Fair* organised by the Singapore Clock and Watch Trade Association in 1976, *International Machine Tool Exhibition* in 1977, an international toy fair, *Toycraft*, in 1978, and *Computa* in 1979 for information technology, as well as aviation trade fairs.

The embassy encouraged Singapore's media to report on France's technological achievements and French products. For Bastille Day in 1978, Ambassador Gasseau issued a press release which cited the economic links between the two countries, the increasing importance of the French language in Singapore, the scholarships provided to local students, the assignment of a young Singaporean soldier to the naval training ship *Jeanne d'Arc* for a year, and the first Singaporean enrollee in the Saint-Cyr military academy.

As Singapore's trade, educational systems and cultural scene developed, it became increasingly open to other cultures. More French language classes were offered, which helped Singaporeans to get jobs with French companies which were moving to the new country.

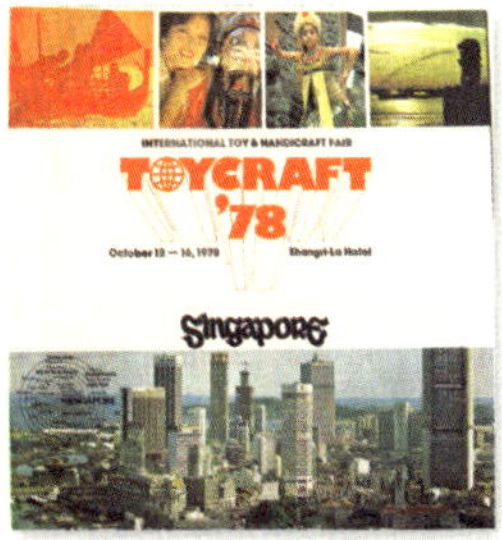

The rise of the Alliance Française in Singapore

Established in 1949, the Alliance Française was initially known for its recreational activities—its bar and its film screenings. In 1966, assistance from the French Ministry of Foreign Affairs enabled it to further develop its language courses. The appointment of a deputy director and trained teaching staff, and support from major French companies in Singapore, helped it to grow. During its first few years, its students were mainly European (particularly the wives of British military personnel), but the institution gradually inducted more Singaporeans. Fun activities were organized to attract students: games of pétanque and bridge; and cooking and painting courses. Like many French institutions in Singapore, the Alliance moved frequently before acquiring its own premises. After five years at No. 23, Chatsworth Road, the Alliance's Committee leased a large house with a garden at No. 34, Scotts Road in November 1965. Due to the lack of space, between 1975 and 1978, some of its courses took place in an annex located at the Golden Mile Shopping Centre on Beach Road. In January 1978, the staff and students inaugurated Flagstaff House, spacious new premises at No. 4, Draycott Park, on Stevens Road, close to the Tanglin Club—this accommodated 16 classrooms, with room for exhibitions in the building's hall.

Although it is primarily a language school, the Alliance Française played a permanent role in Singapore's cultural life. Each year, its management committee organised a ball or gala. From 1970 onwards, the annual award of the Runme Shaw Cup to the best student of the year (named after the Alliance's president from 1968 to 1983), also became a highlight of the institution's calendar. Since its founding, the Alliance Française has organised exhibitions (including, from 1951 onwards, the *French Sacred Art* exhibition at the Victoria Memorial Hall, showcasing almost 164 works of art). A French Film Week was started in 1974. Unfortunately, this festival became the French Film Weekend in 1979, because of the seven films which were planned for that year, only two were shown. The Singapore censorship board had wanted to trim scenes from five films; the director of the Alliance Française had refused, and thus only *Le grand escogriffe* and *Mais où est donc passé la septième compagnie?* could be shown. The five censored films were *Le Gifle; Cousin, cousine; Les petits câlins; Il était une fois un flic*; and *Kung Fu Wu Su*. Later that year, the director put on another festival in which the seven films were shown in their entirety.

In January 1975, Maurice Venet, the director of the Alliance, launched the first issue of *Lien*, a bilingual magazine in French and English. The institution also

OPPOSITE TOP: Brochure of the *French Fortnight* held from 18 to 30 September 1967.

OPPOSITE BOTTOM: Singapore's Minister for Finance, Hon Sui Sen, and the French Minister for foreign trade, Mr Segard (far right), officiating at the opening of the *France Technical Exhibition*, 1975.

TOP: Cover of the flyer for *Toycraft*, held from 12 to 16 October 1978, at the Shangri-La Hotel.

ABOVE: Cover of the flyer for *Computa*, held from 11 to 14 August 1979, at the World Trade Centre.

LIEN, THE ALLIANCE FRANÇAISE MAGAZINE

Jessie Quan, who had worked at the Alliance since its establishment, remembered the deliberation over the name of the magazine: "Bishop Van Melkebeke, thanks to his great erudition, suggested '*Lien*' with the Chinese character for 'link' [or 'joining together'], a character which is also used to signify Alliance."

From 1975 to 1997, the magazine was a source of valuable information for the French community. On the publication of the hundredth issue in April 1983, Philippe Greffet, the Secretary General of the Alliance Française in Paris, wrote: "I like *Lien*—it has its own personality, and it covers everything with the same level of dedication—be it the latest pétanque competition or the major cultural events of Asia. I love its vibrant pages in which students stand side by side with the Ambassador, bankers or teachers." Subsequent chief editors turned *Lien* into a magazine which was mainly dedicated to the activities of the Alliance.

Cover of the first issue of the *Lien* magazine, featuring the Alliance Française building.

TAN SWIE HIAN: A FRENCH-SPEAKING ARTIST

Born in 1943 to a family of very modest means, Tan Swie Hian took French classes at Nanyang University. He worked at the Embassy of France as press attaché from 1970 to 1994. Known for his writings (poems, translations and criticism), his calligraphy, paintings and lithography have been exhibited internationally. This Francophile Singaporean artist "who speaks English with a French accent" has received several awards from both France and Singapore.

In 1978, he was made a Knight of the Ordre des Arts et des Lettres. Seven years later, he received the Gold Medal of the Salon des Artistes Français. In October 1987, he became a member and official correspondent for Southeast Asia of the Institut de France à l'Académie des Beaux-Arts in Paris—the third Asian, after I.M. Pei and Kenzo Tange, to be thus honoured. In his presentation speech, Arnaud d'Hautrives, the president of the Académie, stated: "Tan Swie Hian is a Buddhist poet; a poet whose name is linked to the birth of modern Chinese poetry in Singapore, [and] a Buddhist following the discipline of the great Eastern philosophy. As a lover of French literature, he has translated French writings into Chinese, and has been a personal friend of our great poets Henri Michaux and Eugene Guillevic." The same year, he received the Cultural Medallion, the highest award which can be given to a Singaporean artist. In 1989, a new medal was pinned to his lapel—the Ordre national du Mérite. In 2006, he became an Officer of the Légion d'Honneur.

published books. In 1979, it published *L'Etranger* by Albert Camus, translated into Chinese by Miss Lynn Ma, and in November of the same year, *Les sceaux de Tan* by Tan Swie Hian, illustrated by poems in French by Michel Deverge, the cultural advisor to the Embassy de France.

The "Petite école française abroad"

As Singapore's economy developed through the 1960s and '70s, the French community grew slowly. Couples, who were generally young, moved there, and from 1963, the idea of a French school began to take root. Only in 1967 would a group of parents establish and manage a school of their own, however.

The project took off in 1968, thanks to the Cultural Attaché, Philippe Guillemin. Twenty or so children, from kindergarten to the last year of primary school, were welcomed by the school, as were the children of all French-speaking expatriates. In September 1968, Jean Navrot was posted for a two-year period as a VSNA (national service volunteer) to teach in this single-class school. A room on the premises of the Alliance Française, located on Scotts Road at the time, was used as a classroom. Tuition, in line with the French curriculum, was provided with support from the CNTE (a French organization which promotes distance learning). In 1973, at the request of the Ministry of Foreign Affairs, Jean Navrot returned to head the school. He taught lower secondary 1 and 2 classes. Two other teachers took care of the preparatory and elementary classes. A prefabricated building, consisting of a mere three classrooms, was expanded in 1974 to accommodate a nursery and a sixth form class.

On 14 September 1976, the Petite école became the Ecole Française, and was integrated into the French public education system. During the Christmas holidays in 1977, the Ecole Française moved with the Alliance Française to Draycott Park. There were fewer classrooms than classes to be taught, and the secondary classes were thus held in the same room. Jean Navrot left Singapore, and Mr Villarmé took over the management of the school in September 1978, while still teaching a primary school class. In 1980, Francis Bogner, a mathematics teacher, became the head of the Ecole Française, which had 150 students in very crammed premises.

Places for the French community to mingle

In the 1970s, the French, living on their own or with their families, formed a small community which loved to come together and mingle. Before the advent of condominiums with their leisure facilities, they would meet in clubs such as the Swiss Club or the Hollandse Club, to engage in sports or spend their weekends.

The garden of the Alliance Française at Draycott Park was a favourite spot for holding festivities. Thus, in 1979, the Bastille Day celebrations took place not at the Embassy, but in the gardens at Draycott Park instead, and featured an immense ice carving of the Arc de Triomphe.

THE CROCODILES INVITED THEMSELVES TO THE PETITE ECOLE

In 1970, the rainy season was particularly violent. The Alliance Française and the Petite école were submerged under a metre and a half of muddy water. Jessie Quan, a teacher at the Alliance, described her discovery as she tried to cross the garden: "When I reached the top step, which was still dry, I stopped to catch my breath, and ... what should I see between the piles of the Petite école, two steps away? You guessed it: crocodiles! I watched them, dumbfounded. Where could they have come from? The answer was given to me by two men armed with jute sacks wading in the mud trying to catch the escapees: our neighbours, unbeknown to anyone and particularly the authorities, were breeding crocodiles! Six of the reptiles were captured in the garden of the Alliance, and another four on Scotts Road. It is said that some went for a stroll as far as Newton Circus, and others to the market on Orchard Road."

In 1975, Jacques Berthod, the Chargé d'Affaires at the Embassy of France, proposed building a cultural complex which would house a school, the Alliance Française, an auditorium, the offices of the cultural department, a library and a cafeteria. However there were insufficient funds to realise this plan. Three years later, the management committee of the French Association of Singapore (AFS), which brought together the members of the French-speaking community, once again launched a project for a French Club, but this also met with no success. Ambassador Gasseau, in a report to the Ministry, stated: "The high professional level, the affluence of the community and the numerous distractions which the

city-state offers does not encourage them to meet and explains the lack of interest in establishing a Club."

The birth of the French Association of Singapore

In May 1948, a number of French nationals had founded the French Association of Malaya (AFM). In 1966, a year after Singapore's independence, the members of the AFM established the French Association of Malaysia and Singapore. In 1974, the Singapore division, under the direction of Robert Neuville, a director of the Société des Matières Premières Tropicales (SMPT), decided to form a more dynamic group. The French Association of Singapore (AFS) was officially born on 1 January 1975, and Neuville was returned as president. The slogan of the Union des Français à l'Etranger (UFE), "A Frenchman is never alone abroad", was taken up by the association in Singapore and became "A Frenchman is never alone in Singapore". Members focused on welcoming new arrivals and assisting with the integration of AFS members into life in Singapore.

The AFS was given its own page in the Alliance Française's magazine, *Lien*. In 1976, the AFS published *Le guide du Français de Singapour*, which at the time comprised around 30 pages of useful addresses and advice for French nationals settling in Singapore.

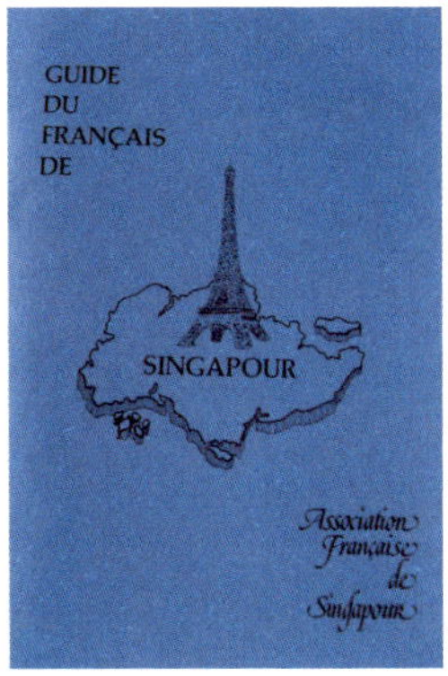

OPPOSITE BOTTOM: Pupils from "the Petite école", during playtime in the garden of the Alliance Française of Singapore, Scotts Road.

TOP: Cover of *Le guide du français de Singapour* booklet, 1976.

BELOW: Father Pierre Abrial (1922–1990).

BOTTOM: The church Our Lady Queen of Peace was founded in 1954 at 4 Sandy Lane.

The Missions Étrangères de Paris (MEP): the 1960s–1970s

From the 1960s, clergy of Singaporean or other nationality began to replace the French missionaries of the Missions Etrangères de Paris. In 1970, a census recorded 21 French MEP clergy in Singapore. In 1977, the leader of the Catholic community in Singapore, Bishop Michel Olçomendy of the MEP, was replaced by Bishop Gregory Yong, originally from Taiping, Malaysia. The main aims set forth by the MEP founding fathers, i.e., the construction of places of worship and welfare activities, continued in modern Singapore. In 1953, Father Albert Fortier, in charge of the community in Sembawang, built the Church of Our Lady Star of the Sea at the entrance to the British naval base. The church, designed by architect Ho Kok Hoe, was in the shape of a ship; it was moved to Yishun in 1992 by Father Louis Amiotte-Suchet. In 1954, Father Octave Dupoirieux built Our Lady Queen of Peace in Tanjong Katong. Shortly thereafter, the community of Serangoon Gardens also received its own place of worship. Father Pierre Abrial's Church of St Bernadette was consecrated in 1959—its floor plan in the shape of an aircraft wing was the work of architect Alfred Wong. In 1971, Father Abrial embarked on the construction of the Church of the Risen Christ in Toa Payoh, the first church to be fully air-conditioned.

In the field of social initiatives, the missionaries continued the works of their predecessors. In 1962, Bishop Olçomendy called upon the Frenchman René Delécluze, "a lay international social worker", to implement an "adult lay apostolate with a social orientation". The aim of this Catholic Family and Social Movement (CFSM) was to promote the Christian message in society in general.

From 1965 to 1970, Singapore strengthened its political institutions, and its economy developed unabated. Six years after the first oil crisis of 1973, the Iranian revolution and the Iran-Iraq war brought about a new hike in oil prices. Japan and the West, including France, were particularly affected by this second oil crisis; Singapore was only moderately affected. During these 15 years, the French community had grown. As of 1988, there were 1,486 members.

Building on business: Riding the Tiger economy (1980–1997)

During the 1980s and '90s, in spite of a number of crises, the Singaporean economy showed relatively strong economic growth. Its urban landscape evolved accordingly. The city centre saw little change on the side of the river formerly occupied by British institutions, but on the opposite side of the river, the Central Business District (CBD) developed in spectacular fashion. In 1986, the Overseas Union Bank Centre with its 66 floors was the world's highest skyscraper.

To keep pace with developments in the global economy, the government of Singapore constantly redefined its economic policies. France, multinationals and French entrepreneurs took a growing interest in Singapore, whose role as a gateway to Southeast Asia became increasingly important, especially with the signing of the ASEAN-EEC (EU) agreement in 1980. The French presence would grow as a result, and the community would expand from 819 in 1978 to almost 3,000 in 1997.

From 1979 onwards, a new economic policy was implemented by the government of Lee Kuan Yew. Key sectors—construction, shipyards and petrochemicals—made way for sectors that focused on advanced technologies as well as high value-added services. Singapore would encourage "development niches", leaving the production of energy and manufactured goods to its neighbours. At the same time, the National Wages Council decided to increase salaries by up to 20% to encourage businesses requiring a low-qualified labour force with low salaries to relocate elsewhere. Simultaneously, the government focused on improving productivity, providing a better education to its population and developing an ultramodern infrastructure to attract a greater number of multinational firms.

BELOW: Overseas Union Bank (OUB), was founded in 1947 in Singapore by Lien Ying Chow. The 1980s saw it grow into one of the "Big Four" local banks. The OUB Centre was opened in 1988.

Singapore continued to call on a foreign labour force to work on its building sites and in its factories. In contrast, thanks to their better training, qualified Singaporean staff were able to meet the needs of foreign companies wishing to establish a base in the city-state. As part of the new International Division of Labour, Singapore progressively specialised in high-end products and gradually positioned itself among developed countries with ever-increasing purchasing power. Lumped together with Taiwan, South Korea and Hong Kong and dubbed one of the "Asian Tigers" (or "Asian Dragons"), Singapore achieved its "second industrial revolution", focusing on advanced industries and the services sector.

Goh Chok Tong, who became Prime Minister in 1990, kept the Singaporean economy focused on services and high value-added manufactured products. However, as economist Manu Bhaskaran has noted, "There were considerable qualitative improvements. The manufacturing sector grew in sophistication with production moving up the value chain ... In the financial sector, the fund management industry took off rapidly, diversifying away from its previous substantial dependence on electronics productions." The 1991–6 period constituted a period of exceptional growth, with an average increase in GDP of 8.7% and an unemployment rate of 2.2%. It was during this period that the government began to take an interest in outsourcing its economy by signing partnership agreements with Indonesia (Batam and Bintan) and China. By introducing a value-added tax of 3% in 1994, the government also hoped to consolidate its revenues, while reducing the corporate tax rate in order to remain competitive at the international level. This period also saw a speculative bubble in the real estate sector, with a 201% increase in the cost of residential housing.

THE 1985 RECESSION

Since its independence in 1965, Singapore has undergone an unprecedented period of economic growth. In 1984–1985, however, this plummeted from 8.2% to -1.8%. In a few months, almost 96,000 jobs vanished, leading to an unemployment rate of 4.1%, of which 45% were below the age of 25. In a 1986 report, a committee of the Ministry of Trade and Industry, explained the causes of the recession and proposed potential solutions. The report explained that traditional growth sectors such as oil, construction, shipbuilding and the hotel industry had entered a period of recession. Increase in salaries and production costs had made Singapore less competitive on the international arena. The overvaluation of the dollar and lower oil prices had an effect on business passing through Singapore.

The February 1986 report also contained recommendations for pulling the country out of the crisis. The economist Philippe Régnier later summed these up: "There should be a reduction in the costs of production and corresponding efforts to improve productivity; a greater contribution from savings to boost local investment; a lessening of the tax burden on companies and individuals; active promotion of the tertiary sector, state-of-the-art technologies and research; a partial disengagement by the authorities from their control of the national economy (80 organisations and 450 commercial enterprises being under state management), giving priority instead to local businesses in private ownership, both local and foreign; and a programme of education and training for all ages and levels of ability." From 1986 onwards, Singapore achieved growth of 1.9%, and 8.8% in 1987, thanks in part to the government's measures and in part to global economic forces.

BELOW: Claude Blangero.

BOTTOM: Patrick Hays.

OPPOSITE TOP: Poster of the French Festival, 1993.

The flourishing economies of the neighbouring countries such as Malaysia and Thailand increasingly challenged Singapore for its position as a regional hub. Singapore had to redefine its economic policies again to face these challenges.

The French economic presence matures and grows

The favourable economic and political conditions of the 1980s and '90s encouraged French companies to establish operations in Singapore, with the support of the Embassy. Although the USA, Japan and the United Kingdom remained privileged trading partners, Singapore also wished to attract the European Community and especially French and German investors. In order to help these businesses, the Singaporean and French governments signed new cooperation agreements. The French business community in Singapore provided assistance to investors and entrepreneurs by establishing the French Business Association (FBA). France also aimed to promote its trading initiatives by encouraging the spread of the French language.

The founding of the French Business Association

The French Business Association (FBA) was founded in December 1979 under the guidance of four Frenchmen—André Utard (Banque de l'Indochine et de Suez), Claude Blangero (Banque Nationale de Paris), Pierre-Marc Bourgoin (Union des Assurances de Paris) and Patrick Hays (SMPT). Henri de Courtivron, one of the founding members, defined the association: "The French Business community has formed a national body to act as its voice. The FBA will provide a forum for French businessmen to identify and discuss common interests regarding economic, industrial and commercial objectives. Any French company or individual can apply to join. Membership is also open to Singapore firms which have dealings with France." From an initial 34 members at its founding in 1979, the association had grown 30 years later to include 330 members, of which a third were not French.

The main mission of the FBA is to assist French businesses to settle in Singapore and the surrounding region. The association provides its members with an extremely broad range of not-for-profit services. It is tasked with investigating the Singaporean market, providing information on setting up a company in Singapore, helping with local authority formalities, and encouraging corporate participation in specialist events in and near Singapore. Comprising a management committee of 20 people elected for two years, the FBA encourages the sharing of experience, provides concrete help to entrepreneurs, and provides information about economic events to its members on an ongoing basis.

In its early years, FBA's activities consisted mainly of organising lunches for businessmen, in which each would expound on their experience and ideas on

Singapore's commercial life. In the 1990s, it became much more active and developed closer links with the Embassy of France. It established committees which enabled members to discuss topics connected to a specific sector of activity, or to a regional zone. The Events and Gala Committee organised welcome dinners, an annual gala in June, and sporting competitions. The FBA newsletter, *News Brief from Singapore*, was launched in 1988. A 12-page bimonthly in English, this helped to introduce French companies to major economic role-players in Singapore and ASEAN.

The French economic partners also decided to organise PR events. From 22 May to 6 June 1993, the French community organised a series of events called *Singapore welcomes France* featuring a visit by one-man band Rémi Bricka, a *French Fashion* week, street performances and events to raise funds for the National Kidney Foundation.

Fifteen events were planned for the 15 days of a festival held in October 1995, including a pyrotechnics display on Clarke Quay by Pierre-Alain Hubert, street entertainment, and a collaboration between the Singapore Symphonic Orchestra and Jean-Claude Casadessus, conductor of the Orchestre National de Lille. The festival also hosted an exhibition at the Singapore Science Centre: *Technologies for the 21st Century made in France*. The French Festivals in 1993 and 1995 caught the attention of thousands of

THE FRENCH BUSINESS CENTRE

In January 1995, the French Business Centre opened its doors as a result of the joint efforts of the Embassy of France and FBA. Located on Neil Road, not far from Singapore's business district, it provided 2,500 square metres of office space for small- and medium-sized enterprises wanting to set up in Singapore and the region. In its eight years of existence, it helped around 20 companies annually, providing services such as the rental of fully equipped offices, assistance from legal and financial advisors and recruitment of —primarily French—staff. The French Business Centre closed its doors in 2003, as the services of the FBA, Embassy and Committee for External Trade became increasingly effective.

French Business Centre at Neil Road.

Singaporeans, with more than 20,000 spectators watching the opening show on the banks of the Singapore River in 1993.

The rise of French businesses

From 1979 to 1997, the number of French businesses based in Singapore doubled every five years on average. The new businesses were mainly subsidiaries, branches and representative offices of French companies in very diversified sectors. By 1991, more than 250 French companies in Singapore.

Some companies, such as Bachy Soletanche, Bouygues, Dragages and Bocotra, participated in the development of Singapore's road infrastructure such as the Central Express Way (CTE), and the Changi Airport in 1981. The capital goods sector, mechanical, steel and defence industries include names such as Alstom, Eurocopter, Snecma (Safran since 2005) and Thales. The energy, chemistry and materials sectors are represented by companies such as Air Liquide, Michelin, Rhodia and Total.

The French presence can also be found in the field of financial services and insurance. A dozen banks and insurance companies, including AXA and Groupama Transport, have bases in Singapore. In 1984, CIC (Crédit Industriel et Commercial) opened an office in the Central Business District, near the Singapore River. In 2001, its partner Banque Transatlantique also set up office here. Other banks such as Crédit du Nord, BFCE (Banque French du Commerce Extérieur) and CCF (Crédit Commercial de France) opened branches too. The Banque de l'Indochine, in Singapore for a century, underwent several mergers before being renamed Credit Agricole Corporate & Investment Bank in 2010.

Major French brands in the fashion, cosmetics and food industries were attracted to Singapore, because of its many tourists as well as a local population with a high disposable income. Mass distribution enabled notable brand names to gain a foothold on Singapore's streets for a number of years. These included Les Galeries Lafayette, which opened in Goldhill Square on Thomson Road on 3 December 1982, and Le Printemps, which opened the following

TOP: Logo of Banque Transatlantique, 2001.

RIGHT: Advertisements for Galeries Lafayette, 1991 and 1987.

ALSTOM

To take its economic development to progressively higher levels, Singapore needs to continually strengthen and modernize its infrastructure, and the French company Alstom has contributed to this task in several ways. Founded in 1928 by the merger of the Société Alsacienne de Constructions Mécaniques and Thomson-Houston, a French-American company, today Alstom is active in three sectors: transport, power and transmission grid. Alstom is present in all geographic markets, employing nearly 94,000 people and generating sales of 20 billion euros (as of 2010–2011).

Alstom has won several major urban transport contracts in Singapore. The Land Transport Authority (LTA) accepted Alstom's tender for the trains and signalling of the North-East Line. Inaugurated in August 2003, after seven years of construction, it was the first driverless line on the island, covering a distance of 20 km. In 2002, Alstom was awarded the construction of the Circle Line, a turnkey project for the longest automated line in the world, totalling 40 km. To maintain the rolling stock, Alstom, also the manufacturer of the French TGV (high-speed train), equipped Kim Chuan Depot at Upper Paya Lebar, the world's largest underground depot, equivalent to 17 football fields.

In the power sector, Alstom, the French world leader in turnkey electric power plants, maintains a long and strong relationship with all its customers. A customer since 2001, Sembcorp commissioned a 400MW gas fired combined cycle power plant (CCPP) in 2011, generating electricity and steam to numerous petrochemical companies. Keppel Merlimau Cogen Pte. Ltd. signed a contract in 2010 to build 2x400MW gas fired CCPP in addition to the first 500MW plant built by Alstom in 2007.

For over 40 years, Alstom has maintained its transmission grid business presence in Singapore, supplying many high voltage substations for the power grid and power plants. In the industries, Alstom has delivered the main high voltage power intake substations for the STMicroelectronics Semiconductor Wafer manufacturing complex, the Intel-Micron Wafer plant and the Exxon-Mobil's SPT mega petrochemical complex.

TOP RIGHT: Circle Line Metropolis train at depot. ABOVE: Keppel Merlimau Cogen power plant in Singapore.

year on Orchard Road, both advertising the arrival of French chic at affordable prices. In the food industry, Danone, the global healthy food brand, also established its Asia Pacific headquarters in Singapore.

TOP: Thales, at 21 Changi North Rise.

BOTTOM: Clean room production floor at the STMicroelectronics wafer fab in Ang Mo Kio, the company's single largest wafer production site by volume in the world.

OPPOSITE TOP: Artist's perspective of SDV Green Warehouse (more information on page 215–216).

OPPOSITE CENTRE: SDV brochure.

OPPOSITE BOTTOM: Special edition of a CashCard for the 15th anniversary of Gemplus Singapore 1989–2004.

As part of its development policy, Singapore encouraged the activities of companies in advanced technology sectors. Leaders in the French aerospace sector, such as Thales (formerly Thomson), Eurocopter and Aérospatiale, participated in the Asian Aerospace aviation trade fair. The show, held in Singapore between 1981 and 2006, has become one of the world's three major aviation events, and is a crucial showcase for the Groupement des Industries Françaises Aéronautiques et Spatiales (GIFAS).

In the electronics sector, STMicroelectronics (then SGS) established its first assembly plant in 1969 in the Toa Payoh industrial estate. In 1981, it opened a manufacturing plant in Ang Mo Kio to produce its first electronic circuit boards. The company was also responsible for setting up the first wafer fabrication plant and semiconductor design centre in Singapore, which took place in 1984. Today, ST's presence in Singapore spans the entire value chain of the semiconductor industry encompassing R&D, manufacturing, sales and marketing as well as supply chain management. It is one of the largest private sector employers in the country. The company was conferred the Business HQ status in 1994 and the Distinguished Partner in Progress award in 2000 by the Economic Development Board. For its exemplary practices in environmental protection and sustainability, the company was also conferred the President's Award for the Environment in 2009.

The year 1989 saw Gemplus Technologies Asia (Gemalto since 2006) open a plant here to develop smart cards. The company launched the first CashCards in 1995.

Taking advantage of Singapore's position as a global hub, the logistics sector continued to grow. Logistics manages the flow of materials by managing resources according to the customer's requirements, the economic conditions and a defined level of service, under defined safety and security conditions. In 1983, SDV Logistics (Scac Delmas Vieljeux), part of the Bolloré Group, opened offices on Upper Pickering Street. In 2011, the French company, with its Asia-Pacific regional office located in Fortune Centre on Middle Road and its Singapore head office located near Changi Airport (on Alps Avenue), employs almost 800 people. It manages nearly 100,000 square metres of warehousing across the island, and works with a wide range of companies, such as Clarins, LVMH, Sanofi Aventis and Singapore Airlines, which in 2010 entrusted it with the logistics management of all the parts and components for its fleet.

During this period, Singapore also continued to develop its tourism sector: the Singapore Tourist Promotion Board (STPB) opened its Paris promotion office on 1 February 1980, and the following year, the French version of its brochure, *Singapore—The Most Surprising Tropical Island on Earth* was awarded first prize during the Sixth World Tourist Guide Grand Prix.

After the 1985 recession, the Singaporean government took steps to protect its cultural heritage. To attract more tourists, it decided to showcase its ethnic districts and the city's architectural treasures. In 1986, Pamelia Lee, in charge of tourism product development at STPB, called upon Didier Repellin, the architect-in-chief of France's historic monuments, to draft a report on Singapore's architectural heritage. Repellin became a consultant to the Singaporean government for more than decade. Thanks to him, the Convent of the Holy Infant Jesus (CHIJ), which had been slated for demolition, was eventually restored. French craftsmen have worked on restoration projects around the city for several years. F. Bourgeois Restoration Consultant Asia Pte. Ltd. opened in 1988. With a wealth of experience in roofing, carpentry and sheet metal work, the company undertook all of the restoration work for the woodwork and the tiled roofs of CHIJ. Its craftsmen also worked on the Empress Place Museum, Victoria Memorial Hall, and Raffles Hotel. At the request of the URA, Hervé Nicolas, an expert in heritage conservation, offered courses in architectural restoration in 1989.

As part of its tourism development policy, the government transformed the island of Pulau Blakang Mati into an amusement park in 1972, changing its name to Sentosa. Recreation areas such as Fort Siloso and Underwater World attracted large numbers of tourists. In 1992, the yacht *Club Med II* dropped anchor off Sentosa. On board was Alexis Agnello, Club-Med Director for Asia-Pacific Indian

DIDIER REPELLIN AND THE RESTORATION OF THE CONVENT OF THE HOLY INFANT JESUS

Following the publication of Didier Repellin's report, the Urban Redevelopment Authority (URA) took the decision to preserve the CHIJ, built in the 19th century, and sell it to the private sector. A dual international competition was organised, with investors and promoters on the one side, and architects on the other. Mr. Repellin's company and the local architectural firm of Ong and Ong won the day, and the renovation work started in 1992. The site is complex and architecturally varied, and the challenge was to transform a religious school into a recreational facility (the present-day CHIJMES).

Repellin described the worksite: "We dismantled the clock tower and I brought in French master roofers, to whom I appointed local workers, Malays, Filipinos, Bengalis .... As for the stained-glass windows, after the war, large portions were missing, and these needed to be redone. There were superb draperies, stunning drawings ... and an amusing anecdote: in Asia, Saint Michael cannot kill a dragon, so he crushes invading armies instead! As for the sculptures, the bird motifs were in poor condition, and everything had to be demolished. The entire restoration was thus done manually. The column capitals were an encyclopaedia of the flora and fauna which had been discovered in Singapore in 1850, and were intended to educate the students."

Ocean, who announced his intention to transfer the company's offices from Hong Kong to Singapore. Club Med had opened its first Asian holiday resort in 1980, in Cherating in Malaysia.

In the same way as multinationals, small companies and independent entrepreneurs also benefited from the relocation assistance offered by the Singaporean government.

French entrepreneurs in the 20th century

In the tradition of the trader-adventurers of the 19th century, French entrepreneurs took advantage of Singapore's port facilities to develop their import-export activities. One such pioneer was Bernard Forey, who established CFA Investments in 1970 and the Boulangerie de Paris in 1982, in cooperation with the French group Lenôtre. Bread, pastries, cakes, sorbets and ice-cream were made in a workshop at No. 263, Pandan Loop. In 1983, the first Lenôtre shop opened on Robinson Road. A few years later, Forey sold the business to Les Grands Moulins de Paris, which teamed up with a Hong Kong investor. In 1988, the joint venture began to develop a concept for bakeries under the Délifrance brand.

More individuals were attracted by the open-door policy and set up base here. In May 1990, Jean-Jacques Bély, with the help of his father, Georges Bély, established the Franco-Asian Enterprises Singapore Pte. Ltd. (FAE). He engaged in the trading and brokering of foodstuffs, particularly palm oil. In 2010, FAE, which started off with a part-time secretary, employed more than 70 full-time staff.

The trade in wines and spirits, so lucrative for the earliest French traders, continued to flourish. In 1992, two cousins from Bordeaux, Hervé Aymond and Laurent Ducourneau, began to trade in Bordeaux wine, and mainly worked for a private clientele. The company Corndale Consultants was the first to import 'Bordeaux futures' to Singapore, and to specialise in the importation of Grands Crus Classés.

In the field of street lighting, Petitjean, which first started business in 1959 in the Aube region, won contracts in Singapore at the end of the 1970s, including from the Housing Development Board and the Public Utilities Board. In 1986, the company opened a representative office there, and by 1988, more than 10,000 Petitjean lamp posts provided lighting for the airport, MRT exits and highways. In 1993, Pascal Petitjean established Partex International Pte. Ltd. and together with

INTERNATIONAL SOS

Another unique business was established by Pascal Rey-Herme and Arnaud Vaissié: International SOS.

In the early 1980s, Pascal Rey-Herme, a French doctor who worked at the French Embassy in Jakarta, decided to establish a "local, pre-hospital, medical emergency service" for expatriates in Indonesia and Vietnam. Together with Arnaud Vaissié, they formed AEA International (Asia Emergency Assistance) in Singapore in 1985. At the time, they employed 15 staff. The company benefited from the island's location, as well as its hospital infrastructure and its company-friendly legislation. In 1987, the two associates appointed a Managing Director, Laurent Sabourin.

The company prides itself on using the latest medical equipment and on providing highly qualified doctors and nurses for emergencies and during evacuations. It was an immediate success with multinationals and soon the company opened branches in Hong Kong, Australia, Japan and China. In 1998, AEA International acquired SOS Assistance Inc., headquartered in Philadelphia and Geneva, and expanded to Russia and Eastern Europe. AEA International was renamed International SOS in 1999. Under this name, the company was incorporated under Singaporean law. Run under French-management and financed with French capital, it has become the global leader in its field.

In 2011 the Group is still run by its founding members and comprises almost 10,000 staff, who provide companies with tailored solutions for all issues relating to health and safety.

Singapore enabled International SOS to develop from a local to regional and now global scale.

In 2009 Arnaud Vaissié received the Ernst & Young Entrepreneur of the Year Award and in 2010 International SOS was named Enterprise of the Year at the Singapore Business Awards.

Arnaud Vaissié of the International SOS receiving the Ernst & Young Entrepreneur of the Year Award in 2009 in Singapore.

inventor Pierre Chabert, worked on the development of Airstar brand lighting balloons. These unique balloons have since become known worldwide, be it in Hollywood (where they provided lighting for the James Cameron's film, *Titanic*), in the 2000 Sydney Olympics, and during the Singapore Formula 1 Grand Prix. In 2010, the balloons were represented by 120 distributors in over 40 countries.

Thanks to relatively flexible local legislation, creative talents were also able to set up their own businesses. For example, in 1989, Jacky Deromedi established her company, Aprim Interior Design. The company initially focused on interior décor but soon began to specialise in shop-fitting for offices, shops, hotels and spas, with a mainly French and European clientele. From the day she arrived, Deromedi has been very involved in the French community, to which she provides active support. In 1990, she became the vice-president of the Alliance Française. In 1995 and 1996, she also held the presidency of the FCCS. In 2010, she was a member and president of the Conseil du Commerce Extérieur (CCE) in Singapore, as well as a member of the Comité National du Commerce Extérieur in Paris. These positions enabled her to provide French companies with the support they require during their start-up period. She also served as president of *European Season: Encore!*, which promoted European culture. Since 2005, she has also been an honorary consul of the Principality of Monaco. In this capacity, she has organised study tours by Singaporean ministers to the Principality, trips which were connected with the establishment of Singapore's Formula 1 Grand Prix and the two casinos.

In May 2011, she was made Officier de l'Ordre National du Mérite (Officer of the National Order of Merit), an award given by the President of the French republic. Working in the company since 1996, Jean-Marc Deromedi is the general manager of Aprim Interior Design. Under his care, the company has grown steadily. He is also actively involved in the French community, being an executive committee member of the Lycée Français (since September 2008), as well as a vice-president of the FCCS.

The French language: a policy of cooperation in the service of economic interests

To promote commerce between France and Singapore, the two governments agreed to strengthen the position of the French language in Singapore.

Georges Bidault, then Minister of Foreign Affairs, wrote in 1945: "At the moment, culture is our ace card in the field of French expansion. I believe that, particularly in the field of human exchanges (notably with the arrival of foreign scholarship holders in France), the decisions which we take will have a decisive influence, both in the near future and in the longer term, on the position of French culture in the world, and indirectly on France's political and commercial influence." This cultural dimension is peculiar to France and has been the main focus of France's policy of cooperation with foreign countries. The continuous promotion of culture is meant to deliver economic benefits: "Wherever one speaks French, one buys French." Through the cultural departments of the embassies and the network of Alliances Française, the French language has become a tool for technical cooperation, and cultural bodies were invited in the 1980s to strengthen their role as showcases for French technologies.

There are numerous players in Singapore's initiative to promote the French language, including French government agencies which are attached to the diplomatic mission. On the Singaporean side, the Ministry of Education Language Centre (MOELC) has offered its best students the chance to choose French as a third language since 1979. The "New Foreign Language Scheme" complements the activities of the Regional Language Centre (RELC), established in 1968 as part of ASEAN, and based in Singapore. The centre trains teachers and organises seminars which have for many years been financed by subsidies (French subsidies in particular), and have run in close collaboration with French partners based in Singapore.

In 1984 the French government launched a more aggressive policy to improve the country's image. The French staff of the Cultural section began to organise events in schools, competitions, and other such initiatives. From 1987 onwards, the Bureaux d'Action Linguistique (BAL) took over the teaching of French classes in Singaporean schools and worked in close cooperation with the cultural services of the French Embassy.

As part of this technical cooperation, the Franco-Singaporean Institute (FSI) opened its doors in 1983. The institute was set up to train engineers in French techniques. The future engineers were sent to the Ecole Supérieure d'Ingénieurs

OPPOSITE TOP: The Jellyfish balloon by the Airstar lighting balloons company, with Singapore's Central Business District in the background, 2010.

OPPOSITE CENTRE: Present-day logo of Aprim Interior Design.

OPPOSITE BOTTOM: Mrs Jacky Deromedi, 2011.

en Electronique et Electrotechnique (ESIEE) at Marne la Vallée, France to complete their studies. Initially, the FSI was located in Jurong, close to the Singapore Science Centre. In 1993, it moved to the Nanyang Polytechnic, together with the German-Singapore Institute and the Japan-Singapore Institute.

At the same time, in order to raise awareness among Singaporean youth, the BAL established the French Elective Programme at the Victoria Junior College. This provided around ten of its top students, who were often French government scholarship holders, the opportunity to study French and to prepare for examinations for the major universities.

To help the students learn more quickly, the Alliance Française, together with other institutions, organised language stays in partnership with French cities from the 1980s onwards: for example Vichy in 1980 and Bourges in 1990. The biennial Lyon-Singapore exchange, launched in 1982, is an example of long-term linguistic cooperation. Started by Alain Labat, a

DAVID MARSHALL AND HIS PASSION FOR FRANCE

David Saul Marshall was born in 1908 in Singapore, into a family of Baghdadi Jewish merchants. At the age of 17, he contracted tuberculosis and was sent to a sanatorium in Switzerland, where he learned French with a passion. In 1926, he returned to Singapore and worked for the Messageries Maritimes. After studies in London, Marshall began a distinguished career as a lawyer, and also became involved in politics, becoming Singapore's first Chief Minister in 1955, and Singapore's first ambassador to France in 1978. In an interview in 1984, Marshall explained that his aim was to build bridges between the two countries, to develop "a far warmer relationship and greater French presence in Singapore, and Singapore presence in Paris". His passion for French culture contributed to the success of numerous projects. In particular, he supported Alain Labat's school exchanges between Lyon and Singapore, and played a role in the creation of the Singapore Students Association of France in 1991. His contribution to the economic exchanges during this period was also vital. With an orchid in his buttonhole, Marshall worked his charm at countless Parisian social events. He remained in Paris for 15 years. At the age of 85, Marshall retired from his diplomatic career and returned to Singapore where he died in 1995.

Ambassador Gasseau (left) pinning the Knight of Honour award on Marshall, 1978.

THE "FRENCH ALUMNI" OR ASSOCIATION DES ANCIENS ÉTUDIANTS SINGAPOURIENS EN FRANCE

The association of Singaporeans who once studied in France was founded in 1981, with around 50 members. The association has multiple aims. It enables former students to meet up, in a social setting if possible, in order to share experiences, and thus create a network of relationships. Evening activities are regularly organised by its very active members, one of whom is Mrs Angeline Ng. The French Alumni association also aims to promote the French language and culture in Singapore. It organises shows brought over from France, such as in June 1981, when the Claude Beauclair theatre company performed Sartre's *Huis Clos*. It also brought over the Ballets de Lyon on their tenth anniversary. In 1992, the association awarded the first French Alumni French Language Award to the best French students. Over time, the association has forged links with other French organizations in Singapore. In 1988 members of the association were officially received by the Ambassador of France, Frédéric Grasset. The following year, the association, led by the energetic Dr Eric Teo, organised a dinner and dance together with the French Association of Singapore to mark the bicentennial of the French Revolution. From the 1990s onwards, the French Alumni also developed links with French companies and offered conferences and seminars. In 2009, the association became a member of the French Chamber of Commerce in Singapore (FCCS). Today with around 350 members, including a number of French nationals (both privately and through their companies), the French Alumni is a successful example of the policy of cooperation between France and Singapore.

Chinese-language teacher in Lyon, the exchange received the support of David Marshall, the then-Singaporean ambassador to Paris, as well as the City of Lyon. Each year, around 15 French students come to Singapore for a month to perfect their Mandarin. These exchanges were initially supported by French companies based in Singapore, and later by government institutions. A reciprocal arrangement was put in place for Singaporean students. Since 1982, almost 500 students have taken advantage of this language exchange between "the Little Dragon and Grand Lyon". The programme stopped in 2008.

In 1980, a few Singaporeans who had studied in France decided to establish the Association of Former Students in France, now better known as the French Alumni. Francophile Singaporeans formed clubs to encourage students to discover French culture. These include the Hexagone French club at the Nanyang Polytechnic, established in 1996, and the French Society at the Nanyang Technological University (NTU), set up in 2004. There are also a number of professional associations such as the Association des Juristes Francophones à Singapore (Association of French-speaking Lawyers).

In France, the Singapore Club France was established in 1985 to enable Singaporeans living in France to meet up. In 2010, it had over 100 members, who meet regularly during holidays. In 1991, another association, the Association des

OPPOSITE TOP: Drawing of the building of the Institut Franco-Singapourien d'Electro-Technologie, *Lien*, December 1980 issue.

Étudiants Singapouriens en France, was established in Paris, with a membership of 52 Singaporean students at the time.

The French community grows and forms societies and organizations

During the 1980s and '90s, the French community expanded as new multinational companies established themselves in Singapore. Popular places to relax were still the Hollandse Club because of its many activities for children, and the Swiss Club. Restaurants offering high quality French cuisine were still few and far between. Some expats remember La Brasserie at the Marco Polo Hotel, at the corner of Tanglin Road and Grange Road, the Grill at the Hilton, and the restaurants run by Boniface Bidou, while others mention La Jonque on Collyer Quay or the first al fresco brasserie beside Centrepoint: Saxophone.

Institutions such as the Alliance Française in Singapore, the French Association of Singapore (AFS) and the French Business Association (FBA) continue to be very active and bring together the many members of the French community. The French School, which in 1985 moved to its Bukit Tinggi site, not far from the Swiss Club, is also a venue for popular annual get-togethers such as carnivals, fairs and the Asian Games.

The influence of the Alliance Française

For the French community in Singapore, France's policy of cultural cooperation has many benefits. Even though the initiatives taken to promote the French language are not directed towards the French community, the cultural events are often much appreciated by the expats. During the 1980s and '90s, the Alliance

VISITORS TO THE ALLIANCE FRANÇAISE IN SINGAPORE

Numerous luminaries have visited the Alliance Française to meet its students and members. In chronological order, they include: Jules Romain in 1953, Somerset Maugham in 1959, Lee Kuan Yew in 1962, Paul Vialar in 1976, Les Charlots in July 1981, Rufus and Valéry Giscard d'Estaing in 1982, Charlelie Couture and Charlotte de Turkheim in 1986, Claude Lelouch and the mime Marcel Marceau in 1988, Prime Minister Michel Rocard in 1990, President Jacques Chirac in 1996, Plantu and Julien Clerc in 1999, 2be3 in 2001 (at the time, their song *Excuse my French* ranked fifth in the Singaporean music charts), Yannick Noah, Henri Leconte and Claude Nougaro in 2001, the illustrator Jacques Ferrandez in 2003, Alain Robbe-Grillet in 2004, and Pierre Schoendoerffer and the then President of Singapore S R Nathan in 2005.

Mime artist Marcel Marceau and Shaw Vee Meng, in the Alliance Française's garden, 1988.

CHEZ BIDOU

Boniface Bidou, a Corsican by origin, visited Singapore for the first time in 1975, during a promotional campaign for French cuisine. In 1979, he shut down his restaurant in Nice to open Chez Bidou on the premises of the Ming Court Hotel, on Tanglin Road; it offered Provençal cuisine. A very colourful figure, Bidou loved to sing his favourite songs while his customers tucked into a bouillabaisse of local fish. In 1987, he opened Le Pescadou in a hotel of the French Novotel chain, the Orchard Inn, on Dunearn Road. Boniface Bidou, after hosting countless dinners which were popular get-togethers for the French-speaking community, left Singapore a few years later.

Française in Singapore played a very important role, building on the hard work done in previous decades with the support of the Union des Assurances de Paris (UAP) and BNP and other companies.

As early as 1963, when it obtained its first projector, the Alliance Française organised weekly French film screenings. Under the presidency of Shaw Vee Meng, who succeeded his father Tan Sri Runme Shaw in 1983, the Alliance Française decided to re-launch the French Film Week which became the French Film Festival the following year. This also formed part of the European Community Cinema Festival during that period. From 1988 onwards, the Alliance also rented French videos and audio cassettes to its members.

Theatre was also a major activity for the Alliance Française. In its early years, it brought theatre troupes over from France. It also encouraged local productions and artistes, both Singaporean (such as Kumar in March 1997) and French. Teachers at the Alliance Française regularly ran theatre workshops which culminated in productions. One of these ventures was the Alliance Française's first troupe, Le Théâtre de Poche, led by Didier Baumlé, which performed its first play in June 1982: *Le Bébé Bleu* by Victor Lanoux. This was repeated in May 1983, with the J.J. Bricaire and M. Lasaygue play, *Les deux vierges* (A Tale of Two Horoscopes), which the budding comedians performed on the Alliance Française stage at Draycott Park. The Alliance Française was also a social venue for the French community. From 1976 to 1980, a football team of French and Singaporean players, including the Alliance Française security guard, Krishnan, played regularly in tournaments against expatriate teams. With around 30 matches per season, the team played in every stadium in Singapore, as well as in Indonesia, Malaysia, and Thailand. The French team was also involved in the Cosmopolitan League, which brought together around ten teams from various expatriate communities. In 1980, at the initiative of its director, Roland Drivon, an Alliance Française French Cup became a regular game trophy, also known as the Krishnan Cup.

The French Film Festival,1988 was featured on the cover of *Lien*, October 1988 issue.

THE ALLIANCE FRANÇAISE: A "NURSERY FOR HUSBANDS"!

In 1980, journalist Violet Oon wrote in *Her World* magazine that "The world is full of unmarried men", before proceeding to explain to her readers where the men were to be found in Singapore. One such promising location was the Alliance Française, "a nursery for husbands". She added: "the majority of the gentlemen learning French are young, ambitious executives—and also bachelors".

In the same vein, on 17 October 2003, the Alliance organised a speed dating event in its cafeteria. The Singaporeans were required to speak French, while the French had to express themselves in English.

In the 1970s, pétanque was already widely played by the French community in the gardens at Draycott Park. In 1985, the Singapore Sports Council decided to promote this activity, and during festivities to mark Singapore's National Day in 1986, held sport demonstration sessions on how to play pétanque at Marine Parade. These sessions were organised with the Alliance Française. Three years later, the Singaporean Pétanque Federation was established and participated for the first time in the game's world championship in October 1991.

In the field of education, France's policy of cooperation with Singapore has borne fruit. The Alliance Française welcomes ever increasing numbers of Singaporeans. The number of students more than tripled in only a few years—it reached 3,000 students in 1983. In the 1990s, the Alliance acquired a plot of land on which to build a larger building, and its new home, located on Sarkies Road, was inaugurated in October 1995. Since the move, and thanks to the patronage of the Société Générale, Singaporean and French painters, photographers and sculptors have held exhibitions of their work in the Société Générale Private Banking Gallery.

The French Embassy

The Embassy's various diplomatic services organised regular events to educate Singaporeans about France. This was often done with the help of the FBA and the Alliance Française. During these years, the Embassy continued to rent the colonial-style houses at Nos. 5 and 7, Gallop Road from the Straits Trading Company Ltd. However, a dispute arose between them: in 1983, the Embassy paid a monthly rent of $1,000 which was protected under the 1947 Rent Control Act; the Straits Trading Company Ltd. however wanted more than $20,000. In July 1990, the Singaporean government announced the requisition of the premises under the Land Acquisition Act, and the Embassy had to vacate the buildings.

A competition was organised by the French Ministry of Foreign Affairs to select a design for the future embassy, and in October 1999 the diplomatic and consular departments moved to a new building at Cluny Park Road. The Embassy building was designed by the French architectural firm Dubus-Richez together with its Singaporean counterpart, TSP Architects & Planners Pte. Ltd. The French Residence on Cluny Park Road, where the Ambassador lived, was only a few hundred metres away. This was a "black-and-white" house built in 1923 to a design by architect Frank Brewer.

Award ceremony receptions and Bastille Day festivities took place at the Ambassador's Residence, as did visits by dignitaries. Following Georges Clemenceau's visit in 1920, Singapore would have to wait until 1985 for the next visit by the head of the French government: then-Prime Minister Laurent Fabius, who, to use his own words, had come to "bathe in Singapore's modernity". Other political figures have visited the city-state, such as former President of the Republic Valéry Giscard d'Estaing in December 1982, and then-Prime Minister Michel Rocard in December 1990.

However, it was the official visit by the President of the French Republic Jacques Chirac on 28 and 29 February 1996 which made the biggest impression on the French community. Numerous French dignitaries, business leaders, parliamentarians, and leading figures in the entertainment, literary and scientific worlds have also visited.

French naval vessels regularly call in Singapore to refuel. The diplomatic mission organises visits and receptions to enable the French community to meet.

OPPOSITE TOP: Pétanque players in the Alliance Française garden, 1981.

OPPOSITE BOTTOM: Opening of the Société Générale Private Banking gallery at the Alliance Française at Sarkies Road, by Daniel Truchi, CEO of the bank.

LEFT: The French Embassy building, at Cluny Road.

When the *Var* visited from 2 December 1985 to 2 January 1986, 200 sailors were invited to celebrate the New Year with French families. At the beginning of 1994, during a visit by the training vessel *Jeanne d'Arc*, the Embassy, with the help of the French Association of Singapore, organised a reception for almost 300 French expats and 150 students and officers.

The French Business Association

In addition to its economic services, the FBA also played a political role at the beginning of the 1980s. In 1981, when communist ministers were appointed to the French cabinet by President François Mitterrand, the Singaporean government preferred to talk to the FBA rather than the Embassy, especially when discussing the issue of the Vietnamese refugees in transit in Singapore. Anthony Bouthelier, the president of the FBA from 1984 to 1987, described this period: "In the context of the spread of communism in Asia, Singaporeans, inclined to privilege the economic rather than the political aspect, propelled the FBA to the first rank of their French interlocutors. For example, when the Vietnamese refugees picked up by the French boats in transit in Singapore refused to be dispatched to our country, which they described as Socialist, synonymous of a terrifying oppression. The Ambassador of France, Mr Chollet, not having much credit in this circumstances, [thus] it was the President of the FBA, Mr Blangero, whom the Singaporeans gave the responsibility to convince the Vietnamese that the 'rose' was not the emblem of the gulag."

The FBA also invited an assortment of dignitaries to Singapore. It welcomed Edith Cresson in 1984, at the time Minister of Foreign Trade and Tourism of the Mauroy government, followed by the French Prime Minister, Laurent Fabius, in 1985, Raymond Barre in November 1987, Edouard Balladur in October 1990, and Prime Minister Michel Rocard in November 1990, among others. The Association also participated in visits by scientists: in October 1989, it organised a conference called *The New Frontiers of France*, with astronaut Patrick Baudry and medical professor Léon Schwarzenberg. The event showed Singapore's economic elite that France is also a significant player in terms of science and technology.

The FBA, and in particular its founding member and representative Patrick Hays, who worked for SMPT, played a pivotal role in the development of the Lycée Français. By 1980 it was actively involved in the acquisition of land and in the construction of a school. French entrepreneurs had understood that a good school for employees' children was an important factor when companies were deciding whether to set up shop in Singapore.

A little school becomes a real Lycée in Bukit Tinggi

The school was managed by parents who were expatriates and who mainly worked for major French companies. In the 1980s, the growing community came to the realisation that the school needed to expand, but funds had to be raised. Patrick Hays took on the project and collected $3 million in donations. In 1982, work started on the plot of land in Bukit Tinggi. During the three years of construction, the school, under the headmastership of Francis Bogner, found a temporary home in the buildings of the former Pei Hwa School in Yio Chu Kang. At the start of the 1985 school year, the new headmaster, Roger Pinsard, inaugurated the new facilities. Enrolments increased more quickly than expected, from 150 in 1980 to 375 in 1989, and the school soon filled its new premises.

The first students took their baccalaureate in 1986. In 1987, the school was visited by the famous French football player, Michel Platini. In September 1989, the school changed its name, becoming the Lycée Français de Singapore (LFS)—a company under Singaporean law managed by an Executive Committee, which was comprised of parents. When Robert Brandt took over the headmastership in September 1990, the student body was still increasing, particularly in the lower level classes. In 1992, the primary school, which had become too small, moved to Thomson Road, to a disused school rented from the government. The end of the school year was marked by drama when Brandt suffered a heart attack on 17 June 1994, while in his office. In 1994, Mrs Annick Bouvier-Feuillade took over the headmastership of the Lycée Français, with the mission of building a larger school.

OPPOSITE: Ecole Française de Singapour, at Bukit Tinggi, 1985. The school was modern, spacious, situated in a nice area and could accommodate up to 500 students. If crocodiles went to the Petite école, monkeys and snakes visited the French pupils in Bukit Tinggi!

ABOVE: The soccer player Michel Platini during his visit to the French school on 19 November 1987.

THE AFS AND HUMANITARIAN ACTIVITIES

Since its establishment, AFS members have contributed to humanitarian initiatives. In February 1975, the association organised a fund-raising drive to provide assistance to a French national hospitalised in the Tan Tock Seng Hospital. At the end of the 1980s, advertisements in the *Gazette* asked members to donate blood. For many years it has canvassed for volunteers to create welcome groups, as well as to visit French nationals in the city's hospitals, an initiative which now includes visits to prisoners. The AFS is also active in humanitarian aid on a larger scale. In the 1980s, the community came together on behalf of the Vietnamese boat people, who had been sequestered in the camp at Galang in Indonesia. The association also organises annual charity bazaars. The Christmas market is a highlight of its calendar, and features stands where charities sell gifts and other items to raise funds.

The French Association of Singapore expands

The AFS continued its activities. In the mid 1980s, it published a monthly newsletter, the *Lettre mensuelle de l'AFS*, of around 10 pages. By 1987, the French community was much larger, and volunteers embarked on producing a bigger magazine. Spurred on by Annig Huchet, Denise Dutrillau and Béatrice Léon-Duffour, the inaugural issue of *Singapore Gazette*, around 30 pages long, was published in October 1987. In 2002, it became simply the *Gazette*—and in 2006 went from monthly to quarterly.

In terms of its contents, the *Gazette* contained the usual fare, such as Chinese astrology, articles on the various religious festivals celebrated in Singapore, a description of the AFS-UFE, and reports on trips and visits. Also included were articles on the school curriculum, student essays on, for example, the Spice Route, tips on where to bring family members who are visiting Singapore for the first time, comic strips poking fun at the French community in Singapore, portraits of members of the community, interviews with prominent French and Singaporean figures, all which were illustrated with numerous photographs. In 1996, the management committee published its first *Carnet d'adresses de l'AFS*. This is a directory of shops and services which might be needed by or be of interest to expatriates, particularly those who had just arrived. The AFS also organised car rallies from 1982 to 1991 (and once again in 2003) to enable the French community to discover Singapore.

ADVERTISING CAMPAIGNS TO PROMOTE FRANCE

The French Business Association has helped to shape the image of France in Singapore. In 1985, the FBA and the French Embassy commissioned research into how Singaporeans viewed France. The results were unsurprising: for most Singaporeans, France meant luxury, fashion, gastronomy and wines and spirits. To modify this image, two 30-second advertising "spots" were repeatedly broadcast in 1988 and 1989, highlighting French technological successes such as Ariane rockets, the TGV (high-speed trains) and helicopters. In 1993, the *Aujourd'hui en France* (Today in France) TV programme was first aired on SBC 12. This was a series of 30-minute broadcasts, transmitted every Saturday evening at 7pm. It was produced by the Cultural section of the Embassy and the Yarras Films production company, in collaboration with the Singapore French Business Association. The sponsors hoped to show Singaporeans a different view of France than the usual clichés. Each week, viewers could take part in a game and win a range of prizes, such as an Air France flight, a stay at Disneyland Paris or a cruise on the *Club Med II*.

Advertisement for the TV programme *Aujourd'hui en France* (Today in France).

SINGAPORE AS A SOURCE OF INSPIRATION

Singapore continues to fascinate and inspire artists and photographers, whether they live there, pass through, or only hear about it. One of them was Gilles Massot, who exhibited his photographs in 1985 in the Lucina Talib gallery. A photographer as well as a dancer, he designed and produced the *Yin Yang Festival* with the National University of Singapore. In 1986, he danced in the Singapore Festival of Arts Fringe, followed by a series of photographic exhibitions. He taught courses and held seminars at universities and at the LASALLE College of the Arts. One of his photographs, printed on glass, was exhibited in the Buona Vista MRT station.

Writers passing through sometimes described their impressions. In *L'Antivoyage*, published in 1976, Muriel Cerf dedicated a chapter to Singapore, which she named "the citadel of dollars". She discovered the joys of consumption—and love. "This country keeps me in a state of amorous bulimia," she wrote. She was also touched by the magic of its streets: "That's where you need to go—those streets which shine like diamond necklaces where you eat in the open air on wooden chairs."

In 1986, Jean Echenoz, in *L'Équipée malaise*, celebrated the nation's tailors: "In Singapore, as Pons had attempted to convince Charles of the benefits of new clothes, Illinois gave them the address of a speedy tailor where, in this tropical climate, all kinds of suits would bloom at lightning speed."

Since the 1930s, Singapore has also inspired writers of thrillers and pulp fiction. From the 1930s onwards, the city stimulated the imagination of novel writers in search of shady, exotic backdrops. In 1936, Louis-Charles Roye wrote *La Danseuse de Singapour* (*The Dancer of Singapore*). In 1941, Jean Le Hire published *Les Pirates de Singapour*. These opened the door to a plethora of suggestively entitled works: *Singapour où es-tu mon Amour* (*Singapore Where are You, My Love?*) by Hélène Roudaud in 1960, *Mission à Singapour* (*Mission in Singapore*) by André Montiac in 1965, *Cinq Gars à Singapour* (*Five Young Men in Singapore*) by Jean Bruce in 1967, *Prisca à Singapour* (*Prisca in Singapore*) by Jean Dominique in 1970, *Le Général à Singapour* (*The General in Singapore*) by Pierre Nemours in 1974, *Le Disparu de Singapour* (*The Disappearance of Singapore*) by Gérard de Villiers in 1976, *Le Marin de Singapour* (*The Sailor of Singapore*) by Paule Alban in 1981, *Les Scandaleuses de Singapour* (*Scandals of Singapore*) by Pierre Lucas in 1982, *Les Amants de Singapour* (*The Lovers of Singapore*) by Michel Brice in 1983, and, in the same year, *L'Orchidée de Singapour* (*The Orchid of Singapore*) by Stéphane Ardant. Even comic strip artists found Singapore colourful and exotic. In 1984, the Dargaud company published *La Dame de Singapour* by Francis Lambert and Al Coutelis. The second volume of *Les Tigres Volants* by Nolane and Molarini was called *Mission à Singapour.* This told the story of ten American pilots who fought the Japanese air force during the Second World War.

The French-speaking media

Despite being thousands of miles away, the French community of Singapore remains in constant touch with France thanks to the plethora of means of communication, including the mass media and Minitel (an online information service provided by France's national phone company).

In line with the French government's cultural policies, the media were expected to promote the use of the French language. In 1983, the French government decided to develop Radio France Internationale (RFI). Singapore

was able to receive this radio frequency from October 1988 onwards. Ten years later a radio station was launched by the Singaporean MediaCorp group, targeting the expatriate community. In 2008, this was renamed XFM 96.3, and broadcast programmes in five languages: French (provided by RFI), German, Japanese, Hindi and Korean.

In 1984, five French television channels came together to launch TV5, but it was only in 1997 that the channel could be viewed in Singapore. This provided daily news programmes, documentaries, games, and TV films. In 1989, another French-language television channel was founded in France: Canal France International (CFI). During the 1990s, CFI established itself in Southeast Asia, but not in Singapore. In recent years, CFI (now a subsidiary of France Télévisions and Arte France) has signed agreements with Singapore's MDA (Media Development Authority) to enable joint French-Singaporean productions.

Access to the French press has also become easier. The opening of specialist departments in the major department stores such as the Galeries Lafayette and Le Printemps and in bookshops such as Kinokuniya have broadened the circulation of French titles. Some French community organizations also launched publications aimed at Singapore's French community: the Alliance Française's *Lien* magazine (1975) and the AFS's *Gazette* (1987).

In 1988, the Embassy's Cultural, Scientific and Technical Cooperation departments adopted the Minitel service to promote French technology and to create a local network. The École Française de Singapore, RELC language centre, FSI, French Business Association and Embassy all made a number of units available, often free of charge. French companies established in Singapore such as UAP, L'Oréal and Total also made use of this videotext technology. The Bureau

TOP: Covers of *La Gazette Française*, the magazine of the AFS (October 1987, November 1990 and March–April 1997 issues).

ABOVE: Logos of RFI (Radio France Internationale) and TV5 Monde.

d'Action Linguistique also put exercises and tips for learning French online. Two Minitel terminals were installed at the Galeries Lafayette in 1989, as well as another ten units in the *Informatic's 89* exhibition hall at the World Trade Centre.

Diverse and motivated: The new French Community in Singapore (1997–2010)

In recent years, Singapore's urban landscape has changed dramatically due to many building projects as well as land reclamation along its coastline. The airport at Changi has become an international hub with three ultra-modern terminals. Singapore's high-technology port infrastructure earns it a place among the world's leading cargo hubs. Its tourist facilities such as Sentosa and Marina Bay, and cultural venues such as the Esplanade—Theatres on the Bay have all played a role in the country's growth .

Under the Prime Ministership of Goh Chok Tong from 1990 to 2004, and Lee Hsien Loong since 2004, Singapore has strengthened its position as a global city. The French presence has grown from almost 3,000 people in 1997, to more than 9,000 in 2011, forming an important community in this cosmopolitan nation.

During the Asian financial crisis in 1997, Prime Minister Goh took steps to reduce its impact on the country. New policies were implemented, in particular the opening up of financial institutions to foreign capital. Singapore reacted to the crisis rapidly by accelerating the liberalisation process in its main service sectors, including financial and telecommunication services, and planned to implement the same policy in the energy sector. More emphasis was placed on infrastructure, education and culture. From 1999, Singapore would benefit from the growth in the information technology sector and would become more involved in the development of its pharmaceutical, biotechnology and education sectors. Singapore is also the world's third-leading oil refinery centre, processing fuel into derivate products for export markets. The country has become a largely

THE 1997 ASIAN FINANCIAL CRISIS

The crisis began on 2 July 1997 with a drop in the value of Thai baht caused by over-investment and excessive levels of debt. Within the space of a few weeks, the loss of confidence had spread across the region. The Indonesian rupiah, the Philippine peso and the Malaysian ringgit all fell one by one. In the autumn, Korea, Hong Kong, Taiwan and Singapore were also affected, albeit to a lesser degree. Banks and companies in these countries, which were massively in debt, were no longer able to honour their debts. The entire banking system was affected. The flight of foreign capital caused a brutal drop in stock indices. And given the deep involvement of the countries of the region in the global economy, stock exchanges around the world in turn suffered a number of panics.

RIGHT: French President Nicolas Sarkozy welcoming Singapore's Prime Minister Lee Hsien Loong to the Elysée Palace, 2008.

OPPOSITE TOP: Logo of *Voilah!* Festival.

OPPOSITE BOTTOM: Logo of *Encore!* Festival.

profit-making trading platform and is very interested in free-trade agreements. By 2006, besides the ASEAN Free Trade Agreement, Singapore had signed bilateral trade agreements with Australia, Japan, Korea, the USA, Europe (the European Free Trade Association) and China. The country also remained very open to direct foreign investment from 2001 to 2006. This was hindered by the Asian crisis in 1997 and by unfavourable international conditions with the terrorist attacks of 11 September 2001, Bali in October 2002, the occurrence of the Severe Acute Respiratory Syndrome (SARS) in 2002, and finally the Iraq war in March 2003.

Since the year 2000, French economic partners based in Singapore have continued their campaign to promote French products. In October and November 2005, for example, the Embassy of France, the FCCS and the Alliance Française

FRANCO-SINGAPOREAN CULTURAL EXCHANGES

Internationally renowned French artists have often taken part in Singaporean events, such as the *Singapore Arts Festival*, *Mosaic Music Festival* and *Photography Month*. The *French Film Festival* at the Cathay cineplexes and Alliance Française has been an annual cultural highlight since 1984. Museums in Singapore and Paris have established fruitful partnerships: The Louvre, the Musée d'Orsay and the National Museum of Singapore; the Asian Civilisations Museum (ACM) and the Musée du Quai Branly; the Singapore Art Museum and Centre Pompidou all worked together to present exhibitions, such as the *Baba Bling* exhibition of Peranakan culture, held in 2010 at the Musée du Quai Branly. During the same period, ACM also hosted *Congo River*, in which the majority of exhibits were from the Musée du Quai Branly.

Cover of the exhibition guide for the *Baba Bling* exhibition.

"WE'RE CLOSETED FRANCOPHILES"

This was how journalist Gwendolyn Ng from *The Straits Times* referred to Singaporeans in a special report written to celebrate the 45th anniversary of the birth of the nation in 2010. "When we want to add a bit of continental *elan* to our names, the accent here is very much French." Very often, a French word or a 'de' or 'la' gives a French touch to a beauty parlour or hairdressing salon. Condominiums have been christened Le Rêve, Côte d'Azur, Palais Renaissance and Versailles. Francis Doumecq, the Convenor for the French Language Programme at the Centre for Language Studies at the National University of Singapore (NUS), also notes that "the names forged are often funny or puzzling for French people". Many have a pleasant sounding ring, as well as a "chic" connotation, for example Le Champagne, Chantilly Rise and Chez Bright apartments.

came together to organise the French Affair with Singapore salon, an event highlighting French culture and know-how. Stands were set up on Orchard Road so that French companies could present their products; fashion houses such as Jean-Paul Gaultier, Kenzo and Givenchy also put on fashion shows.

Besides the economic and commercial support which it provided through Ubifrance and the Regional Economic Section, the Embassy of France worked towards ever more intense cultural cooperation between the two countries. Singapore had become a hub for cultural activity in Asia and the Embassy contributed to the diffusion of French thought, literature and art, by organizing exhibitions and events, and by attracting visiting artists.

The Cultural Section of the Embassy of France has also continued its efforts to promote the French language in Singapore. The Association des Professeurs de Français de Singapour (Association of French Language Teachers in Singapore) was established in 2005. Its members have the common aim of teaching the French language as well as the promoting the spread of French and French-language culture. In 2010, the APFS comprised around 60 teachers, of whom the majority were French, as well as Singaporeans and around 15 teachers from other countries, such as Belgium, Switzerland and Morocco. Each year, the association organises a range of activities such as the Jeux de la Francophonie and training courses for teachers. The French and Singaporean governments have also established a French corner at Singapore's National Library (NLB). This space, inaugurated in March 2008, comprises approximately 1,000 books by French authors, translated into one of Singapore's four official languages.

Various French institutions, such as the Embassy of France and the FCCS, have decided to promote economic sectors like gastronomy and fashion in Singapore by organising cultural events. The year 2007 saw the launch of a French festival called "*Voilah!*"—a name formed from the French word *voilà* and the Singaporean colloquial "*lah*". This is organised on a yearly basis by the French Embassy and the French Chamber of Commerce in Singapore (the FBA's new name since 2003).

In 2008, "*Encore!*", a European version of the festival, was launched. Spanning a year, the programme presents cultural, technological and economic events organised by the nations of the European Union. The two festivals continue to evolve, but retain their original aim: to promote France and Europe.

Besides the French Embassy, the other key player in French economic life in Singapore is the French Business Association (FBA), which in 2003 changed its articles of association to become a fully independent chamber of commerce. During the gala dinner organised to celebrate its 25th birthday, the new logo of the FCCS (French Chamber of Commerce in Singapore) was unveiled.

In 2000 the FBA launched a quarterly magazine, *FOCUS*. With a print run of 4,000 copies, the magazine covers topics relating to the French economic presence in Singapore and Asia. FBA members can also receive the *Weekly Link* newsletter and *Singapour Actualités* in digital form. In addition, more than 1,500 copies of the *Members Directory* are published each year.

Growth and diversity of the French economic community in the 21st century

TOP: The Republic of Singapore Navy frigate RSS *Steadfast*, a transfer of technology by the French company DCNS.

OPPOSITE: The Michelin guidebook to Singapore (2009 edition).

In 2010, more than 450 French companies were listed in Singapore. The majority were active in the electronics industry and financial services and they employed more than 27,000 people, or about 1% of Singapore's workforce (according to the FCCS). In terms of business turnover, more than 25 of these companies are listed among Singapore's 1,000 most important companies. About 40 of them were also founded locally, including many restaurants and wine and spirits traders.

French high-tech industries in the electronics, IT, pharmaceuticals and chemicals sectors, as well as those engaged in research, contributed to the growth of technology parks such as Biopolis and Fusionopolis, both founded by A*STAR, a statutory board under the Ministry of Trade and Industry of Singapore.

DCN (Direction des Constructions Navales) is a French naval defence company. The group designs, builds and supports surface combatants, submarines, systems and equipment. In 2007, the company and Thales joined forces and changed its name to DCNS. In the mid 1990s, the Republic of Singapore Navy (RSN) decided to replace its missile gunboats, acquired in the 70's. The Singapore government's aim was to acquire state-of-the-art technology. In March 2000, the Singapore Ministry of Defence (MINDEF) signed a contract with DCNS for the construction of six frigates, including technology transfer through Singapore Technologies Marine (ST Marine). The design of the Singapore Formidable class frigates is based on the French Navy's *La Fayette* class frigate. The first frigate was built in France while the others were built in Singapore.

Since 2000, Singapore's tourism sector has continued to grow. The opening of casinos connected to hotels and shopping malls, the annual Formula 1 Grand Prix and various attractions have all increased tourist numbers. The Singapore Tourism Board tallied up approximately 11.6 million visitors in 2010, mainly from Indonesia, China, Malaysia, Australia and India. These included almost 120,000 French nationals. Michelin published a guidebook to Singapore in 2008. Three years later, Le Petit Futé followed suit. The average tourist spends four days in Singapore and visits at least one of the 250 shopping malls, where there are shops offering quality, luxury products that form part of France's image abroad.

With the establishment of the National Environment Agency in 2002, and the launch of the Singapore Green Plan 2012, Singapore aims to position itself as a responsible country embarked on a voluntary policy of sustainable development. In 2010, with a population of 5 million inhabitants, clean water and waste treatment are key issues in the country. The French company Veolia, which specialises in environmental services, has won a major waste treatment contract.

An increasing number of Singaporean businesses as well as multinationals hope to play a major role in preserving economic growth without destroying the planet. Corporate social responsibility (CSR) is a big priority for a French company which forms part of the Bolloré Group: SDV Logistics. Its management encourages employee participation in local voluntary organizations, such as the Spastic Children's Association of Singapore. The company's latest major project has been to build the first logistics platform in the Asia-Pacific region which complies with the criteria defined by the US Green Building Council. In August 2012, SDV Logistics will complete a building of 42,400 square metres near the Jurong Bird

Park. This building will be the first certified Greenmark Platinum Warehouse in Singapore and one of the very few Leed Gold Warehouses in Asia Pacific. It will be able to recover and recycle rain water, and minimise the use of air-conditioning (the 4th floor will not be air-conditioned). The company is also creating a forest nearby. The entire logistics platform will, among other things, house SDV Logistics' French luxury "hub", which will be a regional distribution platform for high-end and luxury-goods clients, offering services such as the labelling, kitting and late customisation for the duty-free and retail industries.

During Singapore's real estate boom, a number of developers called on world-famous architects, including winners of the Pritzker prize (often referred to as "architecture's Nobel"). For example, Wing Tai Holdings commissioned French architect Jean Nouvel to build a new condominium. His design was inspired by Rubik's cube, and the new building was named after him: the Nouvel Ardmore. The interior designer Christian Liaigre worked with architect Chan Soo Khian on the luxury residential project at Nassim Park Residences in 2008. French designer Philippe Starck designed the interiors of the iLiv@Grange luxury building, expected to open in 2013.

The spirit of individual entrepreneurship, which had been present since the 19th century, continues to be strong in the 21st century. Every sector of activity is represented, be it consulting, electronics, retail trade, or the hospitality industry. This is equally true of the arts, for example with the establishment of the Sing'theatre company in 2006.

One of the current ambitions of the Economic Development Board is to turn Singapore into the "Boston of Asia", to rival the home of Harvard and MIT. The government body aims to attract companies specialising in research and to bring in multinationals who can recruit from its talent pool. In 2005, Singapore welcomed 72,000 foreign students into its schools and universities, which have achieved

SING'THEATRE: A FRENCH-LANGUAGE CULTURAL VENTURE

Nathalie Ribette, who arrived in Singapore in 1996, appeared on stage in about 20 different roles before establishing her own company, Sing'theatre, in December 2006. Its aim is to develop cultural links between France and Singapore. Before establishing her own business, she had produced numerous shows such as *Notre-Dame de Paris* (2002) and *No Regrets, A Tribute to Edith Piaf* (2004, re-staged in 2007 and 2010). With Sing'Theatre, she then produced *Jacques Brel is Alive and Well and Living in Paris* (2008), *Members Only* (2009) and *A Singaporean in Paris* (2010). Her productions are bilingual (French and English), and she works with both French-speaking and Singaporean artists.

FRENCH TERTIARY EDUCATION IN SINGAPORE

INSEAD

INSEAD was founded in Fontainebleau in 1957. The Institut Européen d'Administration des Affaires set itself the task of training business executives on an international scale. Located in France not far from the NATO headquarters (at that time), and initially focused on instruction in French leading to French qualifications, the institute gradually developed a more international outlook. Through its presence in Asia as part of the activities of the Euro-Asia Centre from the 1980s onwards, the ambition to open an Asian campus was finally realised: in 2000, Singapore was chosen from about a dozen shortlisted locations. The French companies which supported the establishment of the institute included International SOS. With a presence in France, Singapore, the United Arab Emirates and Israel, INSEAD has more than 7,000 participants in its various programmes.

ESSEC-Asia Pacific

The Ecole Supérieure des Sciences Economiques and Commerciales was founded in 1907. The institution trains large numbers of business executives, both at a national and international level. Attracted by the Singaporean government's programme, which aimed to turn Singapore into a global education hub, the ESSEC authorities decided to rent premises at the National Library Board building, on Victoria Street. Since its inauguration in 2006, the campus and its research centre have developed partnerships with international education centres such as the Indian Institute of Management and Seoul National University.

Grenoble Graduate School of Business (GGSB)

Founded in 1984, the Ecole de Management de Grenoble is one of very few French business schools to obtain triple accreditation from the Association of MBAs (AMBA), the Association to Advance Collegiate Schools of Business (AACSB) and the European Quality Improvement System (EQUIS). After initially focusing on Europe, the GGSB established partnerships on other continents. In Singapore, it partnered the Management Development Institute of Singapore (MDIS) to launch a Master in International Business (MIB).

Campus France

The EduFrance agency, which would later become Campus France, was established in 1998 by the French Ministry of Foreign Affairs with the aim of promoting and developing international exchanges and French culture around the world. It opened an office in Singapore in 2002 to promote France's universities and Grandes Ecoles to Singaporean students.

international recognition—it expects almost 150,000 in 2015. Against this backdrop, agreements were signed to establish the French-NUS Double Degree Programme. This offers Singaporean students the opportunity to complete their master's degree in one of France's Grandes Ecoles, and French students the opportunity to complete theirs at NUS. Similar agreements have also been signed between the Singapore Management University (SMU) and HEC (Hautes Etudes Commerciales), and the Nanyang Technological University (NTU) and the Ecole Supérieure d'Ingénieurs en Electronique and Electrotechnique (ESIEE). Other French higher education institutions have come to set up campuses in Singapore, attracted by its position as an Asian crossroads and the comfortable living conditions.

The French community in the 21st-century global city of Singapore

In 2011, more than 9,000 French nationals were officially registered with the French Consulate. This constitutes a sizeable proportion of European Union citizens in Singapore. In 2009, the French Consul wrote in his annual report: "Our Swiss and Dutch colleagues have registered approximately 2,000 residents. The Italians, Swedes, Norwegians, Danes and Russians have between 1,000 and 1,500, the Belgians 800 and the Spanish 600 (...) The European embassies are all noticing the same phenomenon: a steady growth in their communities and a dynamic birth rate."

The youthfulness of French nationals is a core characteristic of the community. In 2006, 35% of those listed were minors, of which 42% were less than six years old. Young adults (aged 25–44 years) in 2009 constituted the backbone of the community, making up 44% of the total registered. The workforce, mostly male, was particularly active in the services sector (70%) and often held business management positions. Most of the French stay in Singapore for a defined period of time. According to Lycée Français de Singapore statistics, the average student enrols for three school years.

OPPOSITE: Views of the Lycée Français de Singapour at Ang Mo Kio Avenue 3. This project was specially designed by Mr Wee, of Kumpulan Architect, to block out traffic noise from the avenue. The white metallic roof is in the shape of a huge plane wing and serves as a screen. The campus is comprised of three parts, alluding to the story of *The Three Little Pigs*—all of the construction materials were made with reinforced concrete. But the material for the façades of different sections of the school varies: the kindergarten façade is made of wood, the primary school with bricks, and the secondary school with concrete and glass. The French company Dragages participated in the project. This original architecture is now upheld as a model for other campuses in Singapore.

The LFS: From Bukit Tinggi to Ang Mo Kio

During the years 1989–1997, the number of students at the Ecole Française more than doubled, from 375 students to more than 800, and the school needed larger premises. In 1997, the Ambassador, Mr de Montferrand, acquired a 2.4-hectare plot of land in Ang Mo Kio, a satellite town in the centre of the island, for a period of 30 years. In May 1999, 14 months after the start of construction, the new Lycée moved into No. 3000, Ang Mo Kio Avenue 3. The modern, futuristic buildings could accommodate all classes.

At the start of the next school year, Patrick Ténèze became principal. The school's activities continued to expand: the "Un Lycée pour l'Espoir" humanitarian

association organised its first Walkathon; and major sporting events such as the international climbing championships, and swimming and rugby competitions have been held. Extra-curricular activities (such as trips and cultural activities) and particularly the quality of teaching have made the school an essential resource for the entire French community.

At the start of the millennium, student numbers levelled off. From 2005, Singapore underwent an economic recovery, and French companies began to arrive in force. The Lycée was able to accommodate 1,000 pupils, but in order to house its continuously expanding student population, expansion work was needed every year. In 2008, the kindergarten and a part of the junior school were temporarily moved to an adjacent school, the former Serangoon Gardens School, to allow construction of a new building. The school's capacity almost doubled: in September 2010, it was able to accommodate 1,800 students. The school's Executive Board is making plans to accommodate more than 3,500 students.

A French rendezvous in Singapore

The Alliance Française, with its multimedia library, cinema club and theatre, remains a venue for cultural events. It encourages the staging of local productions, be they Singaporean or French—such as *Starmania* in 1998, *Cuisines et dépendances* in 2000, and *Huit femmes* in 2009.

In 2010, the Association Française de Singapore (AFS), with its 2,220 members from 37 nations, had the largest French and French-speaking membership. It continues to represent the Union of French Citizens Abroad, which protects the rights and interests of French nationals abroad and helps expatriates to plan their return to France. Besides free activities, the AFS offers paid-for activities such as cultural tours, language courses, and hands-on activities. A football team, the

ETOILE FC: A FRENCH FOOTBALL TEAM IN THE SINGAPORE LEAGUE

In January 2010, the Etoile Football Club (Etoile FC) became the first exclusively French European football team to take part in the Singapore League, Singapore's own football championship. The club's manager, Johan Gouttefangeas, hopes to develop football à la Française. Etoile FC is based in the Queenstown Clubhouse. Its first match in the Singapore League took place at Jalan Besar Stadium against the Chinese team in the S-League, Beijing Guan, in February 2010. The final score was 1–0 to Etoile FC. The club has great ambition, and hopes to open an Academy for youngsters aged 10 to 16 years, which will also house a bar and French restaurant, as well as a gym and bowling alley. In November 2010, Etoile FC won the Great Eastern-YEO's S-League championship.

Etoile Football Club, has been a participant in the Singaporean S-League championship since January 2010.

Singapore offers its French residents a wide choice of organised religious activity. Father René Nicolas was the first priest assigned to minister specifically to the French-speaking Catholic community. He was succeeded by Father Loiseau, and then by Father Paul Ngo Thanh Phong of the Missions Etrangères de Paris in 2008. The organisation, which promoted Catholicism in Singapore throughout the 19th and 20th centuries, in 2008 comprised nine resident priests, out of 379 practising in Asia. In the *Official Catholic Church Directory and Ordo* for 2010, four Fathers belonging to the MEP still perform parish activities. Others hold administrative positions, such as Father René Nicolas, who is archivist in charge of MEP procurement, located in Siglap. The Association Catholique Francophone de Singapour in 2010 included almost 300 families, most of them French. It also leads prayer groups, charity work and Sunday mass in French in the chapel of the Sisters of the Good Shepherd in Marymount Convent. A number of French nationals are also active in the Jewish, Protestant and Muslim communities of Singapore.

Social spaces which cater to the French include a number of clubs, the Lycée Français and the Alliance Française. The French also continue to meet socially—though these days gatherings are more likely to take place next to condominium swimming pools rather than in the gardens of colonial houses. A French show at the Esplanade, a Beaujolais soirée in a French restaurant, or an AFS event are also opportunities to meet up. Since the mid-2000s, even more networks have come into being, thanks to the internet. In February 2004, the French Connection network appeared with the creation of an electronic mailing list, and through word of mouth, approximately 30 people replied to its first invitation. By 2009, 400 members would meet once a month in vibrant venues. As Emmy Tellier, who manages the mailing list with Guillaume de Penanster, explains, this "allows expatriates to come out of their cocoon and new arrivals to kick off their social life in a new country, all in a friendly atmosphere. There are no application forms, no pre-registrations for parties: the only formality is to register on the mailing list." In December 2005, Emilie Jouno created the Singafrog site, which she describes as: "an internet-based network which offers soirées and a forum which enables members to chat."

Little France in Singapore

Like all expatriate communities, the French are keen to retain their way of life. Their purchasing power is generally high, and a market has developed to meet their needs. As a result, the number of businesses offering French products continues to grow, incorporating hairdressing salons, bakeries, bookshops and restaurants—the Carrefour supermarket even offers traditional foods from the various regions of France. More and more French nationals in arts and science professions are moving to Singapore: doctors, psychologists, physiotherapists, sports instructors, lawyers, architects, designers, publicists and translators. It is even possible to take painting or music lessons given by French teachers.

However, in cosmopolitan Singapore, "Little France" does not spend its life turned in on itself, and there is no French district to speak of. Businesses have settled everywhere, and although Ang Mo Kio and Serangoon Gardens are becoming slightly more popular residential districts because of the proximity of the Lycée Français, Orchard Road and Bukit Timah also remain popular with the French community.

Over the last two centuries, the French community, which is currently growing rapidly, has played an active role in the development of Singapore. A transit point for the majority of French citizens travelling to Indochina, colonial Singapore became an El Dorado for a handful of them—individuals who can be rightly called adventurers. Today, in this globalised age in which *kampongs* have given way to a "global city", the French have made a notable imprint, be it at a cultural, linguistic, architectural or technological level.

A promising future

Today, in the age of globalisation, when the *kampong* of "Sincapour" has given way to a first-class "world city", the French footprint, although modest, nonetheless has an impact on the city's cultural and technological activities. Strolling through the streets of Singapore one detects the French presence through the architectural heritage, the names on street signs, and the presence of French brands and products. And the French institutions of Singapore are busy with many new projects that will ensure strong and lasting ties between the two countries.

Appendix A:
FRENCH AND SINGAPOREAN AMBASSADORS

French Ambassadors in Singapore

	Date of Appointment
M. Hutte, chargé d'affaires	9 August 1965
M. Hutte, Ambassador	16 November 1968
M. de Flory, Ambassador	13 June 1969
M. Gasseau, Ambassador	20 March 1974
M. Chollet, Ambassador	13 July 1979
M. Marandet, Ambassador	14 May 1982
M. Bernière, Ambassador	17 July 1984
M. Grasset, Amabassador	27 October 1986
M. de Faubournet de Montferrand, Ambassador	23 May 1989
M. Coste, Ambassador	28 July 1993
M. Barry Martin-Delongchamps, Ambassador	16 November 1995
M. Filhol, Ambassador	3 May 1999
M. Réau, Ambassador	14 October 2003
M. Buhler, Ambassador	10 September 2006
M. Caron, Ambassador	9 September 2009

Singaporean Ambassadors in France

M. Abdul Aziz Bin Mahmood, chargé d'affaires	1974–1978
M. David Marshall, Ambassador	1978–1993
M. Foo Meng Tong, Ambassador	1993–1997
M. T. Jasudasen, Ambassador	1997–2004
M. Chew Tai Soo, Ambassador	2004–2007
M. Burhan Gafoor, Ambassador	2007–2010
M. Tan York Chor, Ambassador	2011–present

Appendix B:
PRESIDENTS AND DIRECTORS OF THE ALLIANCE FRANÇAISE

Presidents

M. Paul Clerc	1949–1953
Sir Percy McNeice	1955–1957
M. Appajee	1961–
Tan Sri Runme Shaw	1968–1983
M. Shaw Vee Meng	1983–present

Directors

M. Jacques le Mercier	1953–1955
M. Jean-Michel de Kermadec	1955–1960
M. Jean Caudmont	1960–1962
M. Xavier Leclercq	1962–1965
M. Jean-Pierre Técourt	1966–1968
M. Guy Léo	1968–1972
M. Jean-Claude Rolland	1972–1974
M. Maurice Venet	1974–1978
M. Roland Drivon	1978–1983
M. Gilbert Faulques	1983–1990
M. Daniel Soha	1990–1996
M. Claude d'Anthenaise	1996–1998
M. Sidney Peyroles	1998–2002
M. Pascale Fabre	2002–2005
M. Pierre-Emmanuel Jacob	2005–2010
M. Yves Corbel	2010–present

Appendix C:
PRINCIPALS OF THE FRENCH SCHOOL

Petite Ecole Française

M. Jean Navrot	September 1968–June 1970
Unknown	September 1970–June 1973
M. Jean Navrot	September 1973–June 1978

Ecole Française de Singapour

M. Villarmé	September 1978–June 1980
M. Francis Bogner	September 1980–June 1985
M. Roger Pinsar	September 1985–June 1989

Lycée Français de Singapour

M. Roger Pinsar	September 1989–June 1990
M. Robert Brandt	September 1990–June 1994
Mme Annick Bouvier-Feuillade	September 1994–June 2000
M. Patrick Ténèze	September 2000–June 2003
M. Pierre Mondoloni	September 2003–June 2008
M. Patrick Sucur	September 2008–present

Appendix D:

CENSUS STATISTICS OF THE FRENCH COMMUNITY IN SINGAPORE (1819–JUNE 2011)

Year	Europeans (total)	French			Total Population
		Men	*Women*	*Total*	
1819	0				150
1821	29				4,727
1824	179				10,683
1825	216				11,851
1826	317				12,905
1827	275				13,732
1828	301				14,885
1829	394				17,764
1830	526				16,634
1832	525				19,715
1833	419				20,978
1834	464				26,329
1836	765				29,984
1840	900				35,389
1849	1,580				52,891
1860	2,385				81,734
1871	3,790	28	23	51	96,087
1881	5,558	43	21	64	137,755
1891	7,227	56	27	83	181,602
1901	9,768	58	41	99	226,842
1911	14,183	76	52	128	303,321
1921	17,298	79	75	154	418,358
1931#				104^	557,745
1947	9,279				938,144
1957				Approx. 150	1,445,929
1965				200–300	1,860,000
1967				225	1,955,000
1968				194	2,012,000
1969				313	2,042,500
1970	38,093			341	2,074,507
1971				412	2,110,400

(cont'd)

Year	Europeans (total)	French			Total Population
		Men	*Women*	*Total*	
1972				452	2,152,400
1973				508	2,193,000
1974				566	2,229,800
1975				762	2,262,600
1976				738	2,293,300
1978				819	2,353,600
1988				1,486	2,846,100
1989				1,434	2,930,900
1990	126,200			1,637	3,047,132
1991				1,836	3,135,800
1992*		1,031	844	2,025	3,232,100
1993		1,067	877	2,144	3,315,400
1994		1,338	1,099	2,637	3,421,100
1995				2,658	3,525,600
1996				2,666	3,670,400
1997				2,957	3,793,700
1998		1,688	1,355	3,343	3,922,000
1999		1,843	1,449	3,592	3,950,900
2000		1,707	1,373	3,580	4,017,733
2001		1,832	1,428	3,560	4,131,200
2002		1,877	1,413	3,590	4,171,300
2003		2,020	1,492	3,812	4,185,200
2004				3,934	4,240,300
2005				4,627	4,351,400
2006		2,900	2,076	5,276	4,483,900
2007				5,676	4,588,600
2008				6,933	4,839,400
2009				7,514	4,999,000
2010				8,000	5,076,000
June 2011				9,106	5,180,000

From 1931, Europeans were not identified separately in the census.

^ in the Federated Malay States.

* From 1992, the total French population includes an estimation of citizens not registered with the Consulate.

Appendix E:
SOME CHURCHES BUILT BY FRENCH MISSIONARIES*

Church	Founder	Year
Cathedral of the Good Shepherd	Father J.M Beurel	1847
St Joseph Church (Bukit Timah)	Father A. Mauduit	1853
Church of Sts Peter and Paul	Father P. Paris	1869
Church of Our Lady of Lourdes	Father J.A Meneuvrier	1888
Church of the Nativity of the Blessed Virgin Mary	Father C. Saleilles	1901
Church of the Sacred Heart	Father V. Gazeau	1910
Church of St Teresa	Father E. Mariette and Father Lee	1929
Church of the Holy Family	Father P. Ruaudel	1932
Church of Our Lady Star of the Sea	Father A. Fortier	1954
Church of the Immaculate Heart of Mary	Father M. Bonamy	1954
Church of Our Lady Queen of Peace	Father O. Dupoirieux	1954
Church of St Francis Xavier	Father P. Meissonnier	1959
Church of St Bernadette	Father P. Abrial	1959
Church of Our Lady of Perpetual Succour	Father P. Munier	1961
St Anne's Church	Father H. Berthold	1963
Church of St Vincent de Paul	Father H. Saussard	1964
Church of the Risen Christ	Father P. Abrial	1971
Church of the Holy Cross	Father P. Munier	1980

* E. Wijeysingha, and René Nicolas, *Going Forth...The Catholic Church in Singapore 1819–2004*, KHL Printing, 2006, pp 312-313.

SELECTED BIBLIOGRAPHY

The authors consulted and referred to various materials in the course of researching and writing this book. The primary sources that they had access to were the National Archives of Singapore, National Archives of London, the French Diplomatic and Consular Archives of Paris and Nantes and The National Library in Paris (BnF). The authors also referred to the local newspapers such as *The Straits Times* from 1845 to 2010, *The Syonan Times* and *The Singapore Free Press*, and the archives of the Foreign Missions of Paris (MEP) of Singapore. Thanks to the help of local French organizations, they obtained some information from *Le Lien* (Alliance Francaise de Singapour), *La Gazette* (Association Française de Singapour) and the magazine *Focus* from the *FCCS* (French Chamber of Commerce of Singapore). The authors also used the internet to access governmental and NGOs' websites.

Allan, Sheila. *Diary of a Girl in Changi 1941–1945*, 3rd Edition. Australia: Griffin Press, 2004. (first published in 1994)

Ban Kah Choon. *Absent History: The Untold History of Special Branch Operation in Singapore, 1915–1942*. Singapore: SNP Media, 2001.

Beamish, Jane; Fergusson, Jane. *A History of Singapore Architect: The Making of a City*. Singapore: Graham Brash, 1985.

Bellessort, André. *Une promenade à Ceylan Singapour Saigon Hong Kong Macao Canton.Une semaine aux Philippines*. Paris : Librairie académique Didier/Perrin et Cie, 1900.

Bieder, Joan. *The Jews of Singapore*. Singapore: Suntree Media Pte Ltd, 2007.

Boulger, Demetrius Charles. *The Life of Sir Stamford Raffles*. Amsterdam: Pepin Press, 1999. (Originally published in 1897)

Boulle, Pierre. *Romans héroïques*. Paris: Omnibus, 2005.

Braga-Blake, Myrna. *Singapore Eurasians: Memories and Hopes*. Singapore: Times Editions, 1992.

Brazil, David. *Insider's Singapore*. Singapore: Marshall Cavendish Editions, 2007.

Brown, Francis. *Memories of SJI : Reminiscences of Old Boys and Past Teachers of Saint Joseph Institution Singapore*. Singapore: The Institution, 1987.

Bruce, Jean. *5 gars pour Singapour*. Paris: Presse de la Cité, 1959.

Buckley, Charles Burton. *An Anectodal History of Old Times in Singapore 1819–1867*. Singapore: Oxford University Press, 1984, originally published in 1902.

Caubert, Léon. *Souvenirs chinois*. Paris: Librairie des bibliophiles, 1941.

Cheah Jin Seng. *Singapore 500 Early Postcards*. Singapore: Editions Didier Millet, 2006.

Church, Peter. *A short story of South-East Asia*. Singapore: John Wiley & Sons, 2006.

Cluny, Claude Michel. *Singapour, ville du lion*. Monaco: Editions du Rocher, 2007.

Coates, Austin. *The commerce in rubber. The first 250 years*. Singapore: Oxford University Press, 1987.

Combanaire, Adolphe. *Au pays des coupeurs de têtes. A travers Bornéo*. Paris: Pagodes, 1993.

Corfield, Justin. *Encyclopedia of Singapore*. Singapore: Talisman Publication, 2006.

Dobbs, Stephen. *The Singapore river : A social history 1819–2002*. Singapore: Singapore University Press, 2003.

Duncan, Maisie. *A cloistered War. Behind the Convent Walls during the Japanese Occupation*. Singapore: Times Editions, 2004.

Earman, B. *Voyage around the World on the Corvette la Favorite*. Singapore: Antiques of Orient , 1991.

Farrell, Brian. *The Defence and Fall of Singapore 1940–1942*. Stroud: Tempus, 2005.

Fontanier, Victor. *Voyages en Orient entrepris par ordre du gouvernement français de l'année 1821 à l'année 1829*. Paris: Librairie universelle de P. Mongie Ainé 1829

Frost, Mark Ravinder; Balasingamchow, Yu-Mei. *Singapore: A Biography*. Singapore: Editions Didier Millet, 2009.

Grandjean, Philippe. *L'indochine face au Japon: 1940–1945 Decoux-de Gaulle un malentendu fatal*. Paris: L'Harmattan, 2004.

Harper, R.W.E. and Miller, Harry. *Singapore Mutiny*. Singapore: Oxford University Press, 1984.

Haudrere, Philippe. *Les Compagnies des Indes Orientales. Trois siècles de rencontre entre Orientaux et Occidentaux 1600–1858*. Paris: Editions Desjonquères, 2006.

Haussmann, Auguste. *Voyage en Chine, Cochinchine, Inde et Malaisie*. Paris: Sagnier et Bray Libraires, 1848.

Hedwig, Alfred. *Living the Mission: the SJI story, 1852-2002*. Singapore: Archipelago Press, 2002.

Itier, Jules. *Journal d'un voyage en Chine en 1843,1844, 1845, 1846*. Paris: Dauvin et Fontaine, 1853.

Jaunay, Andrée. *Exploration dans la presqu'île malaise par Jacques de Morgan 1884*. Paris: CNRS Editions, 2003.

Kitching, Thomas. *Life and Death in Changi. The War and Internment Diary of Thomas Kitching 1942–1944*. Singapore: Landmark Books Pte Ltd, 2002.

Koh, Tommy; Auger, Thimothy; Yap, Jimmy; Ng Wei Chian (eds). *Singapore: The Encyclopedia*. Singapore: Editions Didier Millet and the National Heritage Board, 2006.

Kwa Chong Guan, D. Heng, Tan T. Y. *Singapore, a 700-year History: From Early Emporium to World City*. Singapore: NAS, 2009.

La Grandière, Auguste Benoist, de . *Souvenirs de Campagne 1858-1860 Les ports de l'Extrême-Orient.* Paris: Société Française d'Histoire d'Outre-mer, 1994.

Lal Brij V. (ed) *The Encyclopedia of the Indian Diaspora.* Singapore: Editions Didier Millet and the National University of Singapore, 2006.

Lee Geok Boi. *The Syonan Years, Singapore under Japanese rule 1942–1945.* Singapore: National Archives of Singapore, 2005.

Lee Kuan Yew. *From Third world to First: The Singapore Story, 1965–2000.* Singapore: Times Editions, 2000.

Lee Kuan Yew. *The Singapore Story: Memoirs of Lee Kuan Yew.* Singapore: Federal Publications, 2000.

Low N. I. *When Singapore was Syonan-To.* Singapore: Times Editions, 2004. First published in 1973.

Makepiece,Walter; Brooke,Gilbert E.; Bradell, Roland St (eds), One Hundred Years in Singapore, 2 VOL. Singapore: Oxford University Press, 1921.

Margolin, Jean-Louis; Hack, Karl; Delaye, Karine. Singapore from Temasek to the 21st Century: Reinventing the Global City. Singapore: NUS Press, 2010.

Maureen K. C. Chew, I.J. *The Journey of the Catholic Church in Malaysia 1511–1996.* Malaysia: Catholic Research Centre, Kuala Lumpur, 2000.

Metzger, Laurent. *Joseph Ducroux, a French Agent of the Comintern in Singapore (1931–1932).* Malaysia: MBRAS Vol LXIX, part 1, 1996.

Meuleau, Marc. *Des pionniers en Extrême-Orient. Histoire de la Banque de l'Indochine 1875-1975.* Paris: Fayard, 1990.

Meyers, Elaine. *Convent of the Holy Infant Jesus. 150 Years in Singapore.* Penang: The Lady Superior of Convent of the Holy Infant Jesus, 2004.

Miksic, John N. and Low, Cheryl-Ann Mei Gek (eds). *Early Singapore, 1300–1819: Evidence in Maps, Text and Artefacts.* Singapore: Singapore History Museum, 2004.

Millet, Raphaël. *Singapore Cinema.* Singapore: Editions Didier Millet, 2006.

Moore, Donald and Moore Joanna. *The First 150 years of Singapore.* Singapore: Donald Moore Press, 1969.

Mosbergen, Rudy. *In the Grip of a Crisis. The Experience of a Teenager During the Japanese Occupation of Singapore 1942-1945.* Singapore: Seng City Trading, 2007.

Munoz, Paul Michel. *Early Kingdoms of the Indonesian Archipelago and the Malay Peninsula.* Singapore: Editions Didier Millet, 2006.

O'Donavan, Patricius (Brother). *War-time in Bahau. Jungles are never Neutral.* Ipoh: Media Master Publishing, 2008.

Onraet, René. *Singapore: A Police Background.* London: Dorothy Crisp and Company, 1947.

Osborne, Milton. *Southeast Asia: An Introductory History.* Allen & Unwin, 2005.

Périé, Augustin. *Souvenirs de Malaisie. Onze ans sous l'équateur.* Paris: 1885.

Raffles, Sophia. *Memoir of the Life and Public Services of Sir Thomas Stamford Raffles.* Singapore: Oxford Press University, 1991.

Saw Swee Hock. *The population of Singapore.* 2nd Edition. Singapore: ISEAS, 2007.

Savage, Victor R.; Yeoh, Brenda S.A. *Toponymics: A Study of Singapore Street Names.* Singapore: Eastern Universities Press, 2003.

Shinozaki Mamoru. *Syonan, My Story: The Japanese Occupation of Singapore.* Singapore: Times Books International, 1992.

Slater, Ben. *Kinda Hot: The Making of Saint Jack in Singapore.* Marshall Cavendish Editions, 2006.

Tan Kevin Y L. *Marshall of Singapore, a Biography.* Singapore: ISEAS, 2008.

Tate, D.J.M. *The RGA History of the Plantation Industry in the Malay Peninsula.* Kuala Lumpur: Oxford University Press, 1996.

Toh, Jason. *Singapore through 19th century photographs.* Singapore: EDM, 2009.

Turnbull, C.M. *A History of Singapore, 1819–2005.* Singapore: NUS Press, 2009.

Turnbull, C.M. *The Straits Settlements 1826–1867.* London: The Athlone Press, 1972.

Tyers, Ray. *Singapore then and now.* Singapore: Landmarks Books, 1993.

Uhde, Jan; Uhde, Yvonn Ng. *Latent Images.* Singapore: Ridge Books, 2010.

Warren, James Francis. *Ah Ku and Karayuki San: Prostitution in Singapore, 1880–1940.* Singapore: Oxford University Press, 1993.

Wijeysingha, E.; Fr Nicolas R. *Going Forth...The Catholic Church in Singapore 1819–2004.* Singapore: Nicholas Chia, Archbishop of Singapore, 2006.

Wise, Michael. *Travellers' Tales of old Singapore.* Singapore: Times Books International, 1985.

Wong Hong Suen; Waterson, Roxana. *Singapore through 19th century prints & paintings.* Singapore: EDM, 2009.

Wurtzburg, C.E. *Raffles of the Eastern Iles.* Singapore: Oxford University Press, 1984 (originally published in 1954).

Yong, C.F. *Chinese Leadership and Power in Colonial Singapore.* Singapore: Times Academic Press, 1953.

AUTHORS' ACKNOWLEDGMENTS

We would like to thank everyone who supported us in this venture, particularly the numerous Singaporean, French and British organizations and associations, the editorial team of Editions Didier Millet, our colleagues and this book's sponsors. We also thank those who helped and supported us: Yves Azemar (Indosiam), Pauline Bocquillon, Caroline Chomienne, Diana Chua, Anne Combes, Aurélia de Vathaire, Françoise Frontisi-Ducroux, François Drémeaux, Roland Fauconnier, John Fung, Mme Houget, Ho Weng Hin, Annig and Patrick Huchet, Serge Jardin, Agnès Le Meur, Dr Jon Lim, Géraldine Lowe, Jean Marshall, Laurent Metzger, Jean-Pierre Mialaret, Martine Mondié, Geoffrey Morris, Rudy Mosbergen, Jean Navrot, Father René Nicolas, Chandran Pillay, Denise Plancon, Azizah Sidek, Matthieu Séguéla, Dr Kevin Y L Tan, and Mr Wee Chwee Heng.

These acknowledgments would be incomplete if we did not mention our respective friends, especially Dinesh Naidu and Cheng Heng Lim.

The authors and publisher wish to thank Pierre Buhler, French ambassador in Singapore from 2006 to 2009, and Ambassador Olivier Caron for their enthusiastic support for this book project.

The publisher also thanks Cofely (GDF-SUEZ), Denis Group, Dragages Singapore, the French Chamber of Commerce in Singapore, Partex International, and Thales Solutions Asia for their support.

PICTURE CREDITS

Every effort has been made to trace copyright holders for images used. In the event of errors or omissions, appropriate credit will be made in future printings of this work.

AFS, Association des Francais de Singapour Cover (pic 31); 210 (top)

Air France Cover (pic 3); 179 (top right)

Air Liquide 126 (bottom); 174 (bottom)

Airstar Asia 198 (top)

Alliance Française Cover (pic 32); 170; 171; 176 (top); 184 (top); 200 (top); 202; 203 (bottom); 207

Alstom Cover (pic 29); 193 (top); 193 (bottom)

Aprim Interior Design/Jacky Deromedi Cover (pic 27); 198 (centre; bottom)

Argus Newspaper Collection of Photos, State Library of Victoria 147

Ayam Brand collection Cover (pic 4; 14; 18); 88 (top); 88 (bottom); 162 (bottom)

Bridgeman Art Library 13 (bottom)

Campus France 217 (Campus France)

Central Press/Getty 166 (bottom)

Cheah Jin Seng Cover (pic 6); 5; 74 (bottom); 80 (top right); 91; 112 (top); 117; 120; 133; 163

CIC+Banque Transatlantique 192 (top)

Consular Archives, Nantes Cover (pic 13); 182 (top); 187 (top)

Convent of the Holy Infant Jesus 57; 108; 109 (bottom)

Marion Cordonnier Cover (pic 2); 24; 29; 66; 76; 82–83; 87 (bottom)

Credit Agricole Corporate and Investment Bank 98 (top); 125 (bottom)

Richard Curtis (private collection) 10; 14

Editions Didier Millet (publisher's collection) 68; 73 (top); 74 (top); 75 (top); 95 (top); 100 (box left); 212 (bottom); 216

Education Environment blog (education.environnement.ecoles.over-blog.com) 26

Encore! 213 (bottom)

ESSEC-Asia Pacific 217 (ESSEC)

Etoile FC 220

Roland Fauconnier (private collection) Cover (pic 11; 21); 8–9; 85 (top; bottom)

French Chamber of Commerce in Singapore 190 (bottom); 191 (top; bottom)

French Embassy 95 (bottom); 180 (top; bottom); 205; 212 (top)

Françoise Frontisi-Ducroux (private collection) Cover (pic 17); 136; 138

Grenoble Graduate School of Business 217 (Grenoble)

Hulton Archives/Getty 148

Imperial War Museum 158

Indosiam 15 (top; centre); 16 (bottom); 17 (top); 81

INSEAD 217 (INSEAD)

International SOS Cover (pic 16; 19); 197

Library of Congress, US 104 (bottom)

Lycée français de Singapour 206

Florence Malraux (private collection) Cover (pic 24; 25); 124

McMaster University of Canada 114

MEP Singapore Archives Cover (pic 9; 12; 20; 22; 23; 33; 34); 15 (bottom); 44 (top; bottom); 48 (bottom); 51; 54; 56 (top; bottom); 60; 99 (bottom); 105 (top; bottom); 106 (top); 109 (top); 111; 121; 131 (top; bottom); 132 (top; bottom); 134 (bottom); 154; 156; 157; 166 (top); 168; 187 (centre; bottom)

Michelin/SMPT Cover (pic 35); 99 (top); 176 (bottom); 215

Martine Mondié 104 (top)

Musée Clemenceau collection 122

National Archives of Singapore 21; 70 (top); 112 (bottom); 123; 149; 172 (top)

National Museum of Singapore Cover (pic 1); Back cover; 4; 11; 18; 20 (top; bottom); 22 (top); 23 (top; bottom); 30; 32; 33 (top; bottom); 34; 35 (top; centre; bottom); 37; 38 (top; bottom); 45; 58; 61; 62; 64 (bottom); 70 (bottom); 73 (centre; bottom); 78; 79; 93; 116; 153; 160

New Concorde 177

NGM Publishers 140 (all)

Paul Swaen Old Maps 16 (top)

M. Pillay 150 (bottom)

Maxime Pilon (private collection) 103 (top); 134 (top)

Denise Plancon (private collection) 203 (top); 204 (top)

Private lender, courtesy of National Maritime Museum, Greenwich, UK 43

Radio France International 210 (centre)

Raffles Hotel collection 84 (top)

Republic of Singapore Navy Cover (pic 8); 214

Roger Viollet/Getty 159

Royal Malaysian Police Museum 137

SDV Logistics 195 (top; centre)

Société Générale 204 (bottom)

Singapore Press Holdings 169 (top); 175; 178 (bottom); 181; 182 (bottom); 184 (bottom); 200 (bottom)

St Joseph's Institution Cover (pic 7; 10); 46; 47; 48 (top); 50; 52; 53; 107 (top)

STMicroelectronics 194 (bottom)

Thales 194 (top)

The French Alumni 201

Time and Life Pictures/Getty Cover (pic 30); 141; 174 (top)

TV5Monde 210 (bottom)

Voilah! 213 (top)

Wee Chwee Heng, Kampulan Akitekt Cover (pic 15); 219 (top left; right)

Danièle Weiler (private collection) Cover (pic 5); 49; 86; 94; 102; 103 (bottom); 106 (bottom); 107 (bottom); 110 (bottom); 110 (top); 118 (top; bottom); 150 (top)

Wiki Commons Cover (pic 26); 12; 13 (top); 20 (bottom); 25; 28; 36; 69; 80 (top left); 100 (box centre; right); 145

Jules Verne Club (www.jules-verne-club.de) 80 (bottom)

William Cho/Getty 172 (bottom)

INDEX

This index is compiled on a word-by-word rather than on a letter-by-letter basis, e.g., South Pole precedes Southampton. Principal locations for entries are denoted in **bold**. Locations for illustrative matter are denoted in *italics*.

A

B

C

D

FRONT COVER

1 View of the Protestant Church, 1837, by Barthélemy Lauvergne. **2** Duvaucel's gecko. **3** Air France B777 aeroplane. **4** Rooster from the gate of A. Clouët and Co. Ltd. **5** Marne Road signage. **6** St Joseph's Institution, c. 1930. **7** Bishop Jean Baptiste Boucho. **8** The Republic of Singapore Navy frigate RSS *Formidable*, a transfer of technology by the French company DCNS. **9** Bishop Esprit Marie Joseph Florens. **10** Father Jean-Marie Beurel. **11** Henri Fauconnier. **12** Father Charles-Bénédicte Nain. **13** Brochure of the *French Fortnight* held from 18 to 30 September 1967. **14** Logo of A. Clouët and Co. Ltd. **15** Lycée Français de Singapour. **16** Dr Pascal Rey-Herme, co-founder of International SOS. **17** Joseph Ducroux. **18** Alfred Clouët, founder of Ayam Brand sardines. **19** Arnaud Vaissié, co-founder of International SOS. **20** Mother Mathilde. **21** Marie Fauconnier. **22** Georges Clemenceau. **23** Father Emile Mariette. **24** Clara Malraux. **25** André Malraux. **26** Victor Segalen. **27** Jacky Deromedi. **28** Adolphe Combanaire. **29** MRT train built by Alstom. **30** Pierre Boulle. **31** *La Gazette Française*, the magazine of the French Association of Singapore. **32** *Lien*, the magazine of the Alliance Française of Singapore. **33** Bishop Laurent Marie Joseph Imbert. **34** Bishop Adrien Devals. **35** Bibendum, the Michelin Man.

Also published by Editions Didier Millet:

Rimbaud in Java: The Lost Voyage
My Journey from Paris to Java (Honoré de Balzac)
Singapore: A Pictorial History 1819–2000
Singapore: A Biography
Singapore Biodiversity